A STAR,
IS A STAR, IS A STAR!

Books by Christopher P. Andersen

THE NAME GAME

A STAR, IS A STAR, IS A STAR!

A STAR, IS A STAR, IS A STAR!

The Lives and Loves of

by

DOUBLEDAY & COMPANY, INC.

IS A STAR!

Susan Hayward

Christopher P. Andersen

GARDEN CITY, NEW YORK 1980

ISBN: 0-385-15598-0
Library of Congress Catalog Card Number 80-908

PRINTED IN THE UNITED STATES OF AMERICA
FIRST EDITION

For Valerie, another gutsy lady
and for The Kid

Acknowledgments

Millions counted themselves Susan Hayward fans, but precious few ever knew her. I visited her homes in California, Georgia and Florida, sat for hours in darkened projection rooms watching nearly every foot of film she ever shot, visited her Brooklyn birthplace, walked the halls of the schools she attended and the garden of the little church she and Eaton Chalkley built near Atlanta—all in search of Susan.

I am particularly grateful to a number of people who were close to Susan for their cooperation: Susan's brother Walter Marrener; Bob and Martin Emslie, who were there at her birth and continued to be her friends throughout her life; to school chum Sister Miriam J. Rooney; to her physician Lee Siegel; to her maid and companion Curly Crowder; to Father Michael Regan, pastor of the church Susan built in Carrollton; to her longtime astrologer and adviser, Carroll Righter, and to Ron Nelson, who shared the last nine years of Susan's life.

My thanks also to Susan's favorite director and close friend Daniel Mann, to Charlton Heston, Kirk Douglas, Gregory Peck, Paulette Goddard, the late John Wayne,

Robert Wise, Mr. and Mrs. Henry Hathaway, Robert Stevens, Harold Clurman, Roland Winters, Martin Gabel and the people of Fort Lauderdale and of Carrollton, Georgia.

For their help, I also thank the staffs of the Academy of Motion Picture Arts and Sciences and the Lincoln Center Library and Museum of Performing Arts; the Miami *Herald;* the Miami *News;* the Fort Lauderdale *News*; the Atlanta *Constitution;* Pictorial Parade; Wide World Photos; Movie Star News; the Memory Shop; Doug McClelland; Lou Valentino; the New York Public Library; Don Rosen and Films Inc., and Cathy Bakos.

The author is also indebted to Doubleday Associate Publisher Stewart Richardson and to associate editor Blair Brown for their encouragement, enthusiasm, judgment and superlative professionalism. My appreciation also goes to Alex Gotfryd for his fine jacket design.

As always, my parents Jeanette (an inveterate film buff) and Edward Andersen and my sister Valerie Kay were an invaluable source of advice and support. Yet no one is more deserving of my gratitude than my wife (and crack proofreader) Valerie, who shared the experience of researching and writing Susan's story and who cried at the end.

Contents

ALONE

Her life was the ultimate tearjerker

Introduction

She had whatever it is that makes cookies tough. She was both vixen and victim, a self-described "Brooklyn broad" who felt the pain more deeply and fought it more fiercely than any of her contemporaries. At the height of a dazzling career that spanned four decades and sixty-five films, Susan Hayward was not only the top female box office draw in the world (the No. 1 male star at the time was John Wayne), but also the top money-maker for *two* studios: MGM and Twentieth Century-Fox. At one point, fully one-quarter of Fox's production budget—over $12.5 million in pre-inflation money—was riding on Hayward. She was nominated for the Academy Award as Best Actress of the Year no less than five times, and finally won for her nerve-shattering portrayal of the wrongly executed Barbara Graham in *I Want to Live!* "In motion pictures," Oscar-winning director Robert Wise once observed, "Susan Hayward is as important a figure as Sarah Bernhardt was to the stage."

Like Katharine Hepburn, Bette Davis, Joan Crawford and Barbara Stanwyck, Susan was an early feminist symbol —a no-nonsense woman who invariably proved more than a match for any man. Unlike theirs, her willfulness was not at the expense of a single ounce of femininity. During the 1950s, voluptuous, flame-haired Susan was a glamorous, full-blown sex symbol whose only real competition as a celluloid siren was a fast-rising blond phenomenon called Marilyn Monroe. Hayward was, quite simply, an utterly unique blend of intelligence, vulnerability, sexuality and guts. That's what the people came to see, and they came by the millions—clutching Kleenexes—for nearly forty years.

Off screen as well as on, Susan Hayward's life was one of soaring triumph and soul-searing tragedy. The many conflicting elements in her complex personality enabled her to carve a special niche for herself in our collective psyche. Susan was a many-hued portrait, not a caricature or a cartoon. She mirrored the light and the dark sides of the human character with a special vibrancy, but did not neglect the many shades of gray.

Susan was, when in character, invariably hard-boiled *and* soft-shelled—from the tragic boozers in *Smash-Up*, *My Foolish Heart* and *I'll Cry Tomorrow* to the crippled singer Jane Froman in *With a Song in My Heart*, to the misunderstood "fallen women" of *David and Bathsheba*, *The President's Lady*, *I Want to Live!* and *Back Street*.

In her own life, she was the kid from the Brooklyn tenements who wound up sleeping on satin sheets but never stopped hoarding wrapping paper. She could be cold and aloof, but was infallibly loyal to the few close friends she had. She insisted on sheltering her homelife from publicity, yet starred in one of the messiest divorce cases in Hollywood history. She prided herself on her carefully cultivated sense of decorum, but was charged with assault when she attacked a starlet who caught her in bed with their mutual boyfriend. An absentee movie star mother,

Susan fought ferociously for custody of her twin sons, then shipped them off to a strict military academy. She tried to kill herself at the height of her career, and when it was all but over made medical history desperately trying to stay alive.

Not everyone who knew Susan Hayward loved her; indeed, some bitterly resented her. Yet, in the end, no one could deny her talent, or her courage. She planted her tiny, stiletto-heeled feet firmly on Hollywood soil and dared all comers to knock the chip off her bare shoulder. In the process, she became more than just a household name. She became a legend.

Aloof. Shy. Obstinate. Brilliant. Spiteful. Vulnerable. Hard. Temperamental. Driven. Cold. Passionate. Loyal. Tough. Sad. To her friends, she was "Irish," "Hooligan" or simply "Red." All these words described Susan, but none so adequately as "star."

Christopher P. Andersen

New York City

"She has real fire inside."
—Walter Wanger

"Hollywood abandoned Susan, but she clawed her way to the top."
—Hedda Hopper

"Susan has the soul of a ballet dancer, and the appetite of a ditchdigger. She's a hellcat."
—Jess Barker

EDYTHE

I

Flashback

If Susan was a symbol of woman both tough and tormented on screen, these were qualities she came by naturally. Her paternal grandmother, Kate Harrington, was a sensitive yet fiercely independent Irishwoman whose desire to act on stage incensed her County Cork tribe. Cinnamon-haired, buxom Katie lived out her fantasy—if only for a time—acting with a small repertory company in the tiny, stone-walled theaters of such Irish towns as Killarney, Waterford and Limerick. Then, one night she awakened with a start from a dream that would alter the course of her life: Kate Harrington saw the round, delicately handsome face and slight build of the person she was destined to marry. Several months later, she met the man who fit the image—a French Huguenot named Joseph Marrener—and promptly abandoned her dreams of becoming another Mrs. Campbell to become Mrs. Marrener and forge a new life with her young husband in America.

Their son—Susan's father—inherited Kate's flair for showmanship. Walter Marrener was small, pale and nervous, with narrow shoulders and darting gray-green eyes. But his unimpressive appearance did not stop him from donning a carny barker's uniform of straw hat and red-and-white striped coat and luring suckers into the sideshow at

Coney Island's Dreamland. Off season, he made ends meet by manning the ticket window at the Academy of Music on Manhattan's bustling 14th Street. But like his mother Kate, Walter would give up these tenuous links with show business to conform to the more prosaic obligations of a spouse.

Ellen was not yet out of her teens when Walter met and married her. The daughter of Swedish immigrants, she was also quite small—barely 5 feet 1 inch—but her angular features and assertive, no-nonsense nature gave her a curious physical advantage over those with whom she came in contact. It was Ellen who would come to dominate life in the Marrener household, for she also brought with her an element that had heretofore been lacking in the family: unfettered ambition.

Walter never returned to Coney Island; instead, he took a steady job with the City of New York as a subway guard and sometime dispatcher for the IRT. The Marreners moved into a third floor apartment in a decaying tenement house on Brooklyn's Church Avenue near 35th Street and began raising a family of their own. Their first child, Florence, was to become her mother's daughter—volatile, aggressive, at times overwhelming. Eighteen months later, Walter Jr. was born. A premature baby, Wally suffered as an infant from an abdominal obstruction that made it virtually impossible to retain food. At two he weighed only seven pounds, and by the time he was three he had been so weakened by the malady that he had to wear heavy leg braces. When it was time for Wally to get a new pair, his mother scooped him up in her arms and carried him to a streetcar for the journey downtown.

On one such Dickensian trip, a woman sitting in the seat opposite them watched sympathetically. She finally turned to Ellen Marrener and said, "You look troubled." The comment from a total stranger might otherwise have upset the cool, composed Mrs. Marrener. But for some unexplicable reason she felt compelled to pour her heart out to this particular person. The woman listened patiently, then, before getting off at her stop, told Ellen to take the braces off. "He'll be all right," she said. No explanation was offered, and Ellen required none. Instead of going on to the clinic, Ellen took Wally straight home and did as the woman had instructed. Miraculously, he was able to take a few hesitant steps without the steel supports; within a month Wally was running with the other children. Repeatedly told this story by her mother, Wally's little sister Edythe—who would change her name to Susan Hayward for the purpose of storming Hollywood—saw the episode as nothing less than proof of the value of prophecies and omens. "Do you see now," she would say to anyone who questioned her devout belief in astrology, "why we have always felt that for us omens were right?"

Indeed, moments after Edythe was born in the front room of the Marreners' four-room Church Avenue flat the morning of June 30, 1918, her portly godmother Lena Emslie followed Scottish tradition and pressed a shiny dime into the infant's clenched fist. Edythe wouldn't let it go. But Edythe, five years Wally's junior, would have to reach adulthood before that sign of impending wealth came to pass. Until then, life for the Marreners would be not unlike the struggle of the Nolan family in Betty Smith's *A Tree Grows in Brooklyn.* "In fact," Susan would reminisce, "we *were* the Nolans, and I was the dreamy Francie Nolan who, like the lone tree outside her fire escape window, Francie's adored, n'er-do-well father promised, couldn't be stopped from 'bustin' right up through the cement and growin'!' "

Edythe's father certainly fit the bill. Dominated by Ellen—their bitter arguments shook the century-old structure to its brick foundation and were anxiously overheard by all the inhabitants of the tenement—he retreated to the rooftops to fly the kites he had fashioned out of scraps of wood, wrapping paper and rags. Aloft, they were magical, billowing airships of every conceivable design, from proud American eagles to bumptious double box kites to the familiar trapezoids that dipped, swooped and soared high above the sooty city blight. Marrener enlisted the help of neighborhood kids like Lena Emslie's son Martin, who eagerly clambered up the fire escape to help launch another beauty skyward. "E," as only her father called Edythe, crouched in awed silence as Marrener sailed as many as seventeen at a single time. The most spectacular, she and Martin agreed, was an enormous Old Glory that Marrener sent aloft each Fourth of July. More than just the kites made Marrener one of the most popular parents in the neighborhood; every kid within a mile radius knew that whenever a kite string broke, they could collect a $1 reward from Marrener by retrieving one of his babies.

Walter saw in his youngest the promise of Katie Harrington. "Ever since I was a little girl," Susan later recalled, "I have always believed what my father told me. 'E,' he would say, 'as long as you believe, an angel sits on your shoulder and protects you.' As I grew older, that angel became less real, more a symbol of God, of a beneficent power, whatever you want to call it. As long as I believed in it, no problem seemed too big for me to meet, no day seemed without hope. Only when I forgot to believe, when I failed to trust, did I despair and permit problems of career, of maintaining a home for my two children, of personal frustrations to overcome me. My father taught me from childhood to fight for whatever I believed in. He was always saying, 'You must be like a rubber ball. The harder they hit, the higher you'll bounce. That is, if you're a good ball to start with. And if you're not, you might as well give up anyway.' "

Edythe learned fast. Once, on an impulse, she borrowed a bicycle belonging to one of the boys in the neighborhood without his permission. She was gone only a few minutes, just around the block, but he was waiting for her at the curb. "It's a beautiful bike," she smiled, slowing up in front of him. Before she could get off, he pushed her into the gutter. As soon as she got back on her feet, he punched her in the nose, climbed aboard and sped off. Edythe ran the two blocks, sniffling every step of the way. She expected sympathy from her father, but he was indignant. "Next time," he ordered, "you stay there and hit him back."

For every ounce of grit that Walter contributed to Edythe's makeup, Ellen added an equal measure of ambition. Mother looked down her aquiline nose at the other inhabitants of her drab world, giving everyone who knew her the uneasy feeling that to her they mattered little or not at all. "It was she who believed I could do anything I set my mind to," Susan wrote to a friend. "It was she, too, who always fought our inclinations as youngsters to say, 'I can't do this, or I can't do that,' by telling us not to say we can't do a thing, because of course we could do anything anyone else could."

Ellen emphasized almost daily, in fact, that it was "as easy to marry a rich man as it is a poor one"—an observation that both girls were readily willing to accept, and with good reason. Growing up poor in Brooklyn during the Depression left an indelible mark on each member of the Marrener clan. Ellen kept the four cramped rooms they inhabited immaculate, and there were grudging signs of affluence: a polished cherrywood upright piano heaped with silver-framed family photographs, for example, on which little Edythe would practice *The Spinning Song* and later *The Minute Waltz*. With the exceptions of these few genteel touches on which Ellen insisted, the Marreners usually went wanting. Florence, her mother's unabashed favorite, was given priority, managing to stay well attired even when the rest of the family looked like refugees who had just passed through Ellis Island. Edythe wore the same gray linen dress day in and day out; since there was no money for the cleaners, spilled cocoa was a minor tragedy —it meant that Edythe would wear that brown stain like a badge of her poverty for months. Once she had worn holes in her shoes, Edythe could not consider buying a new pair. Instead, she ripped up cereal boxes and stuffed the cardboard into them.

An icebox seldom remained for more than a month before it was repossessed, and it seemed that no sooner did they bring home a new stove than three burly, humorless men would come take it back again, leaving Ellen to settle on a secondhand model for three dollars. Life on the installment plan probably had its greatest impact on the youngest member of the family. Even as the world's highest-salaried movie star, she proudly boasted that she would "never go one penny into debt."

The good memories, however, remained. For all their scraping, the Marreners allowed Edythe the privilege of picking out her own birthday cake at Ebinger's bakery every year, regardless of the staggeringly high sixty cent price. Edythe, the tagalong who always came under the protective wing of big brother Wally, played with the other neighborhood children on the polluted Gowanus Canal, where there hung in the air a pungent odor of gasoline fumes and decaying fish. The games they played—not the calendar—demarked the seasons. There was the bottletop season, where commerce in caps of all varieties flourished, and during the baseball-card season the shrewdest traders could wrangle a rare Babe Ruth for only three Lou Gehrigs. The "immy" season was for shooting cat-eyes and pearlies (in Brooklyn "immies" was the generic term for marbles) and the steal-the-ice-from-the-iceman season gave some youngsters their first relatively harmless taste of larceny. The summer months comprised the punchball season, when fists replaced bats.

Of course, Edythe's father reigned supreme during the kite-flying season of early spring, but her favorite time was the selling-old-newspapers-to-the-junkman season. Requiring considerably more finesse than stealing from the iceman, this pastime involved slipping as many flat rocks as possible between the layers of yellowing newspapers to make them weigh more, and thereby fetch a higher price from the hapless junk dealer. Rarely did the junkman, a heavyset Irishman, fail to catch on. In truth, he enjoyed chasing brats out of his yard as much as they delighted in trying to outfox him.

The adults got their revenge in other ways at other times. During the Thanksgiving season, when Edythe and her friends would dress up in tattered clothes—something they always seemed to have plenty of—and sing beneath tenement windows for pennies, some sadistic grown-ups would heat the pennies on a stove before tossing them down. When the waifs ran to pick up their reward after a chorus of "Over the River and Through the Woods," they would—much to the delight of their tormentors—burn their fingertips.

Pain and tenacity to overcome it were, from the very beginning, essential elements in the forging of Edythe's personality. One day in 1924, while chasing a paper parachute down busy Snyder Avenue, the tousled tomboy of six ignored the grown-ups shouting from their stoops for her to get back on the sidewalk. Just as she caught up to the elusive toy, Edythe looked up into the teethlike grille of a Chevrolet coupe. It was too late for the driver to avoid the child. Edythe merely stood, frozen with fear as the car struck. She flew, almost as if in slow motion, ten feet in the air and fell to the pavement with a hideous thud. All who saw it feared she was dead.

Within moments, Ellen broke the circle of stunned onlookers to see the crumpled, unconscious body. Edythe looked like a discarded rag doll; both legs had been shattered and her right hip was severely dislocated. The distraught driver, pleading over and over again that there had been no way to avoid hitting her, frantically motioned to people in the crowd to help get Edythe into his car for the drive to Kings County Hospital. Ellen would have none of it. "You're not taking her anywhere," she snapped, cradling her daughter in her arms. "I'll take care of her." The neighbors, some in the street, others standing on stoops or hanging out of their windows, watched silently as the iron-willed Mrs. Marrener carried Edythe home and upstairs to the children's bedroom. She showed not a trace of emotion.

At home, an elaborate, Rube Goldberg system of pulleys was gerryrigged to suspend Edythe's broken legs. She remained there seven months, and for two years following that Ellen or Wally pulled her in a small wooden cart to P.S. 181, where she hobbled about on crutches. Unable to afford the kind of medical care that would have assured a full recovery, Ellen nevertheless took Edythe to the local free clinic every week to monitor her progress. The bones never would knit together perfectly, but there was good fortune even in that. Not only did the injury leave Edythe with the defiantly sexy hip-swiveling walk that was to become one of Susan Hayward's screen trademarks, but three decades later she called on the experience—as she would so many personal tragedies—to portray singer Jane Froman, crippled by a plane crash, in *With a Song in My Heart*. That role would bring her the third of five Oscar nominations.

Even as a youngster, Edythe displayed a star quality that

meant she would never be popular with her peers. What further aggravated those who came in contact with her was Edythe's penchant for returning a friendly wave or smile with an icy stare. Few were aware that the stuck-up little would-be actress was so nearsighted she couldn't see anything or anyone more than a few feet away without thick glasses—and Edythe was far too vain to be seen wearing those in public.

Edythe seemed oblivious to it all. At twelve, she broke new ground by taking over Wally's paper route when he became ill—thus becoming the first newsgirl for the Brooklyn *Eagle.* The newsboys were not pleased at this invasion of a male bastion. They responded by tying tin cans and garbage to her borrowed (this time with permission) bicycle. No matter. The gutsy kid saw to it that every one of her papers got delivered—and earlier than those carried by her male counterparts.

At about the same time, the Marreners stepped up to a larger apartment on Brooklyn's Bedford Avenue. ("The place looked like a mansion to me," she later recalled), but there was still very little money to go around. Whatever she could scrape together, Edythe plunked down at such movie palaces as the Glenwood, Fabian's Fox or the RKO Kenmore to see her favorite Bette Davis or Lew Ayres picture. The film she loved most presaged her taste in roles: the schmaltzy *Break of Hearts* with Charles Boyer and Katharine Hepburn. Edythe was not always relegated to the role of spectator; when the Fox featured its famous pre-movie magic act, she often bounded onstage to volunteer as the magician's pull-a-rabbit-out-of-a-hat assistant. During New York's sweltering, humid summers, however, even Boyer and Hepburn took a back seat to the public swimming pool, where Edythe used the dime she otherwise would have spent on a movie ticket to rent a bathing suit and plunge into the Pernod green, over-chlorinated water for relief. "The suit was always gray and never fit," she remembered, "but I always felt like a bathing beauty."

Just as Edythe was about to graduate from P.S. 181 and enter Girls' Commercial High, she came down with scarlet fever. The ominous quarantine sign on her door kept out her first boyfriend, dark-haired Eddie Dixon, but not Carmine Catusco, the delivery boy for Stokes, the butcher. Carmine's scruffy good looks fascinated Edythe and every other girl in the neighborhood. He came and talked with her for hours, and though it was Deacon Titus of the Baptist Church at Nostrand and Lenox Road who brought her jigsaw puzzles and hard candy, it was the delivery boy from the butcher shop whose kindness and selflessness she would recount well after she escaped from the slums.

At Girls' Commercial High, Edythe further honed her acting talents, and in the process further alienated her classmates. She failed to make Arista, the school honor society (though the 1935 school yearbook mistakenly lists her as a member), and wept out her disappointment on the plump bosom of her drama teacher, Dorothy Yawger. She would never quite get over it. When asked during her triumphant return to the school if she ever made Arista, she said, "No, the girls didn't want me." Although she was an art major, Edythe pursued her training as an actress with characteristic single-mindedness, cannily passing up romantic leads in school productions for meatier parts that would equip her for the vixen roles on which she would eventually launch her screen career. "Edythe always chose the part no one else would take," Yawger remembered. "Usually it was the unpleasant role—like a toothless old woman—any part with dramatic possibilities. She did them all well." Classmate Mary Rooney, now a Carmelite nun in upstate New York, was one of the five hundred students who were crammed into the school auditorium on an October afternoon for a routine assembly when a hush fell over the crowd as the aloof, unpopular Edythe stood up to recite Edgar Allan Poe's *The Bells*. Whatever their feelings about Edythe the schoolmate, they were spellbound by the actress. She finished to her first standing ovation. Edythe was sixteen.

It was during this period that Edythe decided to try her wings as an actress outside the confines of school. Through Wally and old family friend Bob Emslie, both members of the Mason's Order of DeMolay (Flatbush Chapter), she began acting in DeMolay theatrical productions held at the Midwood Masonic Temple on Kings Highway. Her smallish and somewhat incongruous part as Lady Beauchamp in the comedy *So This Is London*, performed at the Temple on Friday, March 16, 1934, marked her first mention in a newspaper. Her old employer the *Eagle* printed the following item:

> "So This Is London, a comedy in three acts, was produced last night by the Flatbush Chapter Order of DeMolay, at its eighth annual show and dance in the Midwood Masonic Temple, Kings Highway and 32nd St.
>
> Members of the chapter took the male roles in the performance. Friends portrayed the women characters. Frank Steinfelt was coach of the show. In the cast were:
>
> Walter Bowers
> Edith Swanberg
> Grace Whitehead
> Stephen Perry
> Florence Mulligan
> Frank Steinfelt
> Robert K. Mirrieless, Jr.
> Edith Marrenner [sic]
> Milton T. Way
> Robert Stephan

Despite the fact that both her first and last name were misspelled, Edythe returned a year later to portray Faith Crombie in Noel Coward's *I'll Leave It to You*. This time, they got the spellings right.

Still, it would be some years before Edythe actually

picked up a paycheck for uttering a line of dialogue. With the exception of that paper route, the first money she earned was for her painting. The art classes at Girls' Commercial held a competition, and Edythe decided to try an unusual study of marine life. She concentrated on jellyfish, first making small cutouts in white paper and pasting them on top of the canvas, then splattering paint on them. When the paint dried, she peeled off the cutouts; what remained were white jellyfish suspended in the sea. The results were striking, Edythe thought, but as she leaned back to admire her masterpiece another student playfully splashed the painting with water from his freshly cleaned paintbrush. The jellyfish were ruined, but rather than pull out of the contest, Edythe found a way to salvage her efforts. She sat down and carefully embellished the watermarks. The resulting "abstract" fetched first prize—seventy-five dollars. Check in hand, Edythe grabbed her pal Martha Little by the arm, marched down to Macy's and plunked the money down on a pale yellow, broad-brimmed hat.

Even before graduation in June of 1935, Edythe had decided what she would do with her life. The caption beneath Edythe's yearbook photograph came to sum up not only her career, but her tumultuous private life:

> Marrener, Edyth [sic]
> 2568 Bedford Ave.
> MOST DRAMATIC

Working in a handkerchief factory was not exactly the kind of career that Edythe had in mind, even though she managed to advance to head designer before her boss decided her approach was too unconventional and fired her. It gave her the opportunity to pound Manhattan pavement full-time in search of an acting job. All the physical ingredients were there. Her mother had endowed her with an hourglass figure and the delicate look of Limoges porcelain; from her father she got that striking copper hair, flashing eyes that changed from peridot to amber with her moods and enough pouty lip to help her switch from sultry to surly with ease.

Experience, however, is what she lacked, and Edythe found it impossible to get beyond the "stuck-up" receptionists once they got a look at her torn camel's hair coat, homemade beanie and unadorned, almost adolescent face. So while she attended the Feagan Drama School on a one-year scholarship, Edythe concentrated instead on landing a modeling job. Often heading out from Brooklyn for Madison Avenue with just enough money for a return subway token, she would always find enough time after making the rounds to rendezvous with Martha Little at the President Cafeteria on Lexington Avenue. Afterward, they window-shopped and talked endlessly about their futures and the seemingly unattainable dream of going home to Brooklyn in a taxi rather than via the smelly subway.

Edythe was made all the more miserable by her own sister's success. Shunning Feagan and any dramatic training as a waste of time, Florence had struck out on her own and within a week landed in the chorus of Ned Wayburn's *Scandals*. Soon thereafter, she even wangled a bit part for herself in the hit Broadway musical *New Moon*. Facially, the resemblance among all the Marrener children was strong, though not the eyes; where "E's" were changeable amber, Wally and Florence looked at the world through eyes of pale blue. Strangely enough, they would come to resemble one another even more as the years wore on. In her early twenties, however, Florence was slightly taller than Edythe, with long, silky legs and a showgirl look that more closely fit the Ziegfeld Era ideal of beauty. Florence was not the type to tread softly on her sister's feelings, and liberally lorded it over the family's aspiring actress. It was all Ellen could do to prevent bloodshed within the family.

Edythe sought solace of sorts in a brief romance with one of her fellow students at Feagan. David was lanky, sloe-eyed and soulful—a Flatbush Henry Fonda—and he shared her aspirations. If they didn't actually declare their intentions of becoming another Lunt and Fontanne, that vision was never far from their minds. On a crisp November morning in 1935, Edythe gobbled down her customary breakfast of cold cereal and coffee, and as she had done every morning for the past few months, bounded out the front door in search of work. At least that was the way it looked to the rest of the Marrener household. No notice was taken of the scuffed, dark brown valise discreetly tucked under her ten-dollar camel's hair coat, or of the over-earnest manner in which Edythe announced that she'd be back in plenty of time for dinner. It was only six blocks to the subway station; in order not to attract undue attention, she resisted the urge to run. A rush-hour crowd of Manhattan-bound commuters already crammed the station, but Edythe instantly spotted broad-shouldered David over the heads of the mob. She thought he looked exceptionally handsome in his crisp blue suit with the fashionably baggy, cuffed trousers and wide lapels. He reached deep into his right pocket and pulled out two copper ten cent tokens.

"Our passport to freedom," he beamed, slipping one of the tokens into the slot and grandly motioning Edythe through the turnstile.

"It's going to take a lot more than two subway tokens if we're going to get married," Edythe cracked, "especially since I'm going to give up my scholarship at Feagan." Her comment seemed to genuinely take David by surprise.

As soon as they arrived at bustling Times Square, David cabled his father in Philadelphia for money. The Western Union clerk peered up at the eager couple from beneath a green plastic visor. "Typecasting," Edythe mumbled to

David, suppressing a giggle. It would take at least a day for the money order to arrive, the clerk told them. Edythe was crestfallen, and miffed that David had not thought of this sooner. For this one night, he deposited her at the YWCA and went to stay with friends.

Edythe was to meet him the next morning in the lobby of the Y. When she did, she was taken aback to see that he was not alone. A larger, solid-looking man in his early fifties hulked beside him. The stranger introduced himself as David's father.

"Do you love this girl?" he asked his son.

There was an interminable silence before David answered.

"Well . . ." he murmured, staring sheepishly at his size 14 saddle loafers.

"What about the scholarship?" his father demanded.

"Scholarship?" asked Edythe. "What scholarship?"

"My son has applied for a scholarship at Feagan Drama School, young lady. He told me a scholarship has opened up at the school and now he thinks there's a good chance he can get it. As I'm sure you know, David is a very talented young actor."

"I'll say," she marveled, fixing a shriveling stare at her conniving lover. David dared not look up. Edythe picked up her suitcase and marched up to David until they were toe-to-toe. "Killing's too good for you," she smirked. "I'm gonna get you where you live. Sir," Edythe said, turning to David's father before she headed out the door, "your precious son can kiss my ass and his precious scholarship good-bye."

Edythe returned to her scholarship at Feagan—David wisely dropped out—and, armed with her folio and scrapbook, renewed her assault on every photographer, agent, artist and fashion director in New York. She was as scared as the other fresh-faced novices, but swept into every studio as if she owned the place. She was a standout, but that wasn't enough in a profession where confidence and the clamor for attention is standard. In despair, Edythe finally told her mother she was ready to quit. "When the secretaries in those theatrical agencies ask me what experience I've had," she complained, "I don't have to answer. All I have to do is look at my cheap coat, the beanie I've made myself and this face without any makeup. I'll never get past the receptionist!" Ellen listened patiently, then calmly convinced her to keep on trying—just for one more day.

Edythe made the trip to midtown as she always made it, aboard the noisy IRT. She carried her coat over one arm, her homemade beanie protruding from the pocket. Checking out her reflection in a flower store window one last time, she sucked in a deep breath and breezed through the revolving door into the oak-paneled offices of the Walter Thornton Agency.

"A redhead!" the receptionist screamed, hopping to her feet. "Come on in, we just got a call for a girl with red hair." Over the next six months, Edythe rose to become one of the Thornton Agency's top money-makers—the girl seen opening refrigerator doors, smoking sexily (she was now gradually developing a fondness for unfiltered Chesterfields), chewing peppermints, brushing her teeth, showing off her Camay complexion. She was saucy enough for the splashy, four-color magazine ads that often required a low-cut evening gown and a come-hither gaze. She was wholesome enough to model Rubbermaid kitchen gloves and housewifely chenille bathrobes for mail order catalogues. Her fee: five dollars an hour—top dollar at the time.

There could have been no better training for love scenes. "I had a new man in every ad," she would say years later, "and we kissed harder and longer for those stills than we were ever permitted to do in a movie. That was my education. I kissed more guys and never saw them again. I remember some of those poses got my back out of whack a few times, once so severely that the doctor's bills were bigger than my modeling fees." None of her male models would ever make it in Hollywood. "I guess," she smiled, "I must have ruined them."

After a time, one modeling assignment blurred into another; Edythe no longer thrilled seeing her face on the side of a passing bus or staring down from a billboard. But her earnings were enough to finance the family's move across the trolley tracks from Bedford Avenue and Avenue D to Ditmas and East 21st Street. The Marreners' new address was a far cry from the old walk-up tenement on Church Avenue—a spacious six-room flat with parquet floors, French doors and louvered windows looking out over an elm-lined boulevard. Trees! Even in this more middle-class part of the borough, Edythe stood out. There were other stylishly dressed, attractive girls, but she always carried a hatbox—a symbol of her profession. No one enjoyed being the neighborhood mystery woman more than "the girl with the hatbox."

Edythe remained with Thornton, a wiry, dapper man then in his mid-forties, for a year and a half. Their relationship was destined to end in a bitter legal tangle, but during the time she was in his employ, Thornton was impressed with what he perceived to be Edythe's underlying shyness. At a Halloween party he threw for his stable of models, Thornton noticed that his prize find stood alone, sipping a martini and speaking to no one. Thornton's wife Dolly, taking pity on this unlikely wallflower, urged her husband to intervene. "Go ahead and dance with her," she said, nudging the reluctant Thornton. "No one's asked her to dance." He did, but once the music stopped Edythe faded back into the woodwork. In truth, Edythe froze in a roomful of strangers; she was not a party girl and, as the reigning queen of Fox twenty-five years later, shunned Hollywood's premiere-and-private-screening circuit. Even as a sixteen-year-old model, she was not unaware of her icy public persona, and at times seemed to cultivate it.

She also displayed a not inconsiderable flair for self-dramatization in a letter she wrote to Thornton in answer to his request for some biographical information: "The first indication I had that red hair was different was when Charlie screamed 'You old readhead, you.' I had knocked Charlie's toy wagon to kingdom come and this was his way of getting even. 'Redhead!' But it didn't stop there. It kept getting worse as I grew older. 'Carrot-top, brick-top, ginger-head.' I learned very young to develop a counterattack vicious enough to take the wind out of their sails and that, Mr. Thornton, is how we redheaded women get to be looked upon as temperamental, quick-tempered and the like. It's merely a defense mechanism that develops in our youth." Further on in the letter, she talked about colors and clothes: "In beige, I feel like a very good little girl; butter wouldn't melt in my mouth. I've worn a beige hat and coat a great deal lately, and I'm tired of being an angel."

For all her avid introspection, Edythe was not perceived by all to be a shrinking violet. "The first time I saw her," remembered commercial artist Jon Whitcomb, "Susan had a kind of self-confidence that made you remember her. Long before such catchphrases as 'positive thinking' came into vogue, she was using it to propel herself to fame."

SUSAN

"She's cold as a polar bear's foot."
—Susan's first agent

"Susan had brass knuckles on her tongue.
She went through life with her fists up."
—a friend

II

She Liked the Orange Trees

David O. Selznick had spent nearly three years and over $50,000 looking for an actress to play Scarlett O'Hara, yet Atlanta was to burn on schedule this chilly December night with the role still vacant. Almost from the time he bought the rights to the film *Gone With the Wind* from Margaret Mitchell, there had been seemingly insurmountable problems. The script, which had been worked on by every Hollywood writer from F. Scott Fitzgerald to Oliver H. P. Garrett to Sidney Howard, was being written and revised right up until the final day of shooting.

Selznick's personal choice for the role of Rhett Butler was Gary Cooper, but he was soon persuaded that Clark Gable would provide the raw magnetism (not to mention box office megatonage) needed for the part. Leslie Howard, originally approached by Selznick to portray aristocratic, melancholy Ashley Wilkes, turned it down at first. Ray Milland, Melvyn Douglas and Shepperd Strudwick (who had recently decided in the interest of self-preservation to discard his real name—James Stewart) were all weighed as possibilities before Howard finally relented. Joan Fontaine, Frances Dee, Andrea Leeds and Anne Shirley (who had been billed in movies for years as Dawn O'Day) were all considered before Fontaine's sister Olivia De Havilland was finally cast as Melanie.

Scarlett remained the essential role to be filled, however, and Selznick, a towering, brooding bear of a man who glowered at the world through thick-rimmed glasses, became obsessed with the challenge. He had already established himself as an independent to be reckoned with by producing two blockbusters—*A Star Is Born* and *The Prisoner of Zenda*—in a single year. Later triumphs would include *Rebecca, The Third Man, Duel in the Sun,* and *All's Quiet on the Western Front*—not to mention *Tender Is the Night,* which starred Selznick's second wife, Jennifer Jones.

But at 36, he knew that *Gone With the Wind* offered a true grasp at immortality. So did the hundreds of young actresses who streamed to Los Angeles hoping to land what was being billed as the greatest role in the greatest movie of all time. A score were being seriously considered. At that point, George Cukor was to direct, and he personally supervised every screen test—right down to the make-up, costume fittings and lessons in Southern diction. No one was better qualified to take on the monumental task. Cukor had directed Florence Eldridge in *The Great Gatsby,* Ethel Barrymore in *The Constant Wife,* Laurette Taylor in *Her Cardboard Lover* and *The Furies,* Dorothy Gish in *Young Love* and Bette Davis in *Broadway.* If that weren't enough to establish him as the greatest living director of women in films, there was *The Royal Family, A Bill of Divorcement* (Katharine Hepburn's first hit), *Dinner at Eight, Little Women* and Garbo's *Camille.*

For the role of Scarlett, Cukor had already considered

Paulette Goddard (who seemed to have the role sewn up at this early stage), Norma Shearer, Lana Turner, Miriam Hopkins, Joan Fontaine, Loretta Young, Jean Arthur, Joan Crawford, Kate Hepburn, Lucille Ball, Joan Bennett, Bette Davis and Tallulah Bankhead by the time he spotted the October 30, 1937 issue of *The Saturday Evening Post.* A sweater-clad teenager with knowing eyes and a lush mane that tumbled over her shoulders beckoned Cukor to the newsstand. He nodded to himself as he paid the man behind the counter ten cents for two copies, then leafed through one as he squeezed the other under his left arm. Edythe had been selected by photographer Ivan Dmitri to illustrate Thornton's first-person piece on the modeling business, aptly titled *The Merchant of Venus.* The day the issue appeared, Dmitri received a call from Cukor in Los Angeles. The director, whose name was already a household word, wanted the telephone number of "that girl." Well aware of the search that had been going on for the perfect Scarlett (as was most of the nation), Dmitri fumbled frantically for his notebook and blurted out the number. He knew she wouldn't mind; from the moment she set foot in his domain, Dmitri recognized the Brooklyn-born ambition ready to break through the porcelain-perfect surface.

That afternoon, not more than three hours after Cukor's initial call, Dmitri picked up his phone. "Ivan, I'm in the movies!" screamed Edythe at the other end. But when he congratulated her, she snapped back, "Well, it's about time! I've been studying dramatics for months now!" Not that she was letting on to Cukor's minions how eager she was to join the caravan to Hollywood. Ellen advised that a certain amount of reticence on Edythe's part would make her all the more desirable. Edythe's father, on the other hand, was concerned that such a move was premature.

"You'll be a great actress," he told his daughter, holding her hand in his. "There's no doubt of that, E. But you're not ready now. I hope you don't get the part. It won't be good for you." He was promptly overruled by Ellen. After all, it was a once-in-a-lifetime opportunity not only for Edythe, but for Florence as well. It took no amount of coaxing to get Florence to give up her brief career in the chorus so that she could chaperone her little sister to Hollywood.

Before his Scarlett hopeful departed, Thornton asked Edythe if she wouldn't place her signature on a little contract giving him 10 per cent of all her future earnings. Anxious to leave, she willingly signed the document, along with a publicity photograph thanking him for "whatever success I may be fortunate enough to gain." Two years later, when she managed to win a smallish part in a film, he reminded her of the contract and demanded his one-tenth share, which he accurately estimated would equal at least $100,000 in the long run. Despite his claims, Thornton wound up winning nothing but the enmity of his one-time protégée, whose last words on the subject were characteristically blunt. "He," she told a New York *Post* reporter, "is a nasty man." Still, on the day Thornton and his wife saw her off for Hollywood at Penn Station, there was not a hint of the animosity to come. Politely, Edythe asked Mrs. Thornton if she could kiss her husband good-bye before boarding the Century Limited. It was the first display of affection Thornton had ever seen from Edythe, and the last.

The Hollywood that awaited Edythe and Florence as their train pulled into the train station that November afternoon was more than just the capital of the film industry. It was, in 1937, the Rome of a new religion, and the procession of the faithful through box office turnstiles each year amounted to twice the world's population. If the movie houses themselves were gilt-encrusted cathedrals where anyone might come to worship, then the studios were the inner recesses of the Vatican, strictly for the anointed. There were many priests and priestesses—Joan Crawford, Clark Gable, Bette Davis, to name a few—but the real power was concentrated in the hands of just five studio bosses. Louis B. Mayer reigned supreme at MGM, Jack Warner at Warner Brothers, B. P. Schulberg at Paramount, Darryl F. Zanuck at Twentieth Century-Fox and the tyrannical Harry Cohn at Columbia. These men, along with talented independent producers like Walt Disney, the malapropian Sam ("Include me out") Goldwyn and and David O. Selznick, decreed what the moviegoing public would see—and, more importantly to Edythe, *who* they would see. Before an actor or actress was unleashed on the silver screen, these moguls made all the alterations they deemed necessary. Noses were bobbed, teeth straightened, hair colored and bodies reshaped. Nowhere on earth was a name considered more important; practically no actor or actress reached stardom under the one he or she was given at birth. Hence Frederick Austerlitz (better known as Fred Astaire) danced his way to stardom with a succession of comely partners, from Virginia McMath (a.k.a. Ginger Rogers). Margarita Cansino (Rita Hayworth) and Tula Finklea (billed in several films as Lilly Norwood before hitting it big as Cyd Charisse). Joe Yule, Jr., and Frances Gumm were America's sweethearts: fans worshipped them as Mickey Rooney and Judy Garland.

Edythe knew this as she set foot on the platform, breathing in the not-yet-polluted, warm California air and scanning the horizon for the white, wooden HOLLYWOOD sign that had beckoned thousands to Lotusland. In Edythe's case there was a major difference, or so she thought as she walked briskly to the waiting studio limousines. They had come to her, not vice versa. There had been tests earlier in New York—in black-and-white and color—and the powers that be had obviously wanted to see more. As Florence chatted animatedly with the Bronx-born driver, Edythe stared silently at the passing pink stucco structures, turning her father's words over again and again in her mind. Was she ready for this? Could a kid from Brooklyn play the belle of Tara? She had hastily read the book on the train, and clutched a dog-eared copy as the Cadillac pulled into the circular drive of their hotel.

Edythe would not have noticed if it were the Taj Mahal; she was far too busy trying to figure out how she could possibly pull off a convincing Scarlett O'Hara. Edythe had been given the same twenty pages of dialogue for the three test scenes that Goddard, Bennett, Arthur, Turner and a latecomer to the race named Vivien Leigh were to read. Florence fed her the lines efficiently enough, but she was still having trouble with the accent. Edythe had already spent an afternoon with Susan Myrick, the film's expert on Southern speech and manners and the woman who was to work with all the actors on acquiring just the right sound. Yet on the eve of her test, Edythe felt more insecure than ever.

At least she looked more the part than any of the early contenders. By far the youngest candidate, she swept onto the set in a flowered muslin gown tightly cinched to give her at least the appearance of having Scarlett's fabled 17-inch waist—"the smallest in three counties." The fact that it was still warm from the previous Scarlett made her slightly uneasy, but Edythe was ecstatic to learn that Cukor, a nervous, nearsighted little man (he would eventually be replaced as director by Victor Fleming) had finally decided not to worry about Southern accents in the tests. She stood awkwardly in the center of the sound stage at first, confused by the welter of wires and cables. Where was she supposed to go? What was she supposed to do? Edythe did not let the panic that gripped her register on that face. Suddenly, she felt a tap on her shoulder. "The camera," smiled Cukor, "is over there." Edythe quickly recouped. The scene played with Mammy lacing up her corset was hilarious, yet it was evident that the newcomer was perhaps a bit too enthusiastic. The Brooklyn spunk that had carried her this far now eclipsed the vulnerable, neurotic qualities necessary for the role. Cukor winced but said nothing.

Scene Two. Leslie Howard's stand-in as Ashley Wilkes for this and several of the other tests is Alan Marshal, who good-naturedly waited in the wings, arms folded, as the hyperkinetic Cukor prepped each Scarlett. This scene, the most important in determining who gets the role, comes early in the film. Scarlett lures the unsuspecting Ashley into the darkened library at Twelve Oaks to profess her love for him, only to be rebuffed by Wilkes in favor of his true love, Melanie.

"Isn't it enough that you've collected every man's heart today?" Marshal recited woodenly. "Do you want to make it unanimous? Well, you've always had my heart, you know. You cut your teeth on it."

"Ashley, Ashley, tell me—you must. Oh, don't tease me now. Have I your heart? Oh, my dear, I love you, I tell you, I love you and I know you must care for me because . . . Ashley, do you care? You do, don't you?" Outraged by his indifference, Scarlett momentarily unleashes her fury, slapping the aristocratic Wilkes square in the face. The slap is convincing, but that's all.

"Cut," screamed Cukor, unamused as Edythe dissolves with laughter. "No! No! No! Not that way! I want you to read it this way." Cukor adjusted his glasses and began reading the lines.

Edythe was no longer laughing. "Look," she interrupted, "who's reading this, you or me?" A hush fell over the set, but to everyone's dismay Cukor merely settled back in his canvas chair and signaled for the cameras to roll again. This time the scene went far more as Cukor wanted it, though it still lacked the underlying neurotic quality Scarlett demanded. "Look," he repeated in a kindly voice, taking her aside, "you must learn to project more." Edythe looked at him blankly. "Project? What does 'project' mean?" The third, less demanding test scene was also played between Scarlett and Ashley toward the end of the picture. Despite her brief confrontation with Cukor, Edythe was confident as she changed back into her street clothes and headed for her hotel that she still had at least a fighting chance for the part. After all, wasn't a hot-tempered viper what they were after?

The business of waiting for word from the front office began, and over the next three weeks tensions between the two sisters mounted. With an assist from Selznick's publicity machine, both were encouraged to take part in the Hollywood social whirl, and they willingly obliged. Edythe and Florence were supplied with suitable escorts—rising young actors who might also benefit from being noticed at the Macambo or the Coconut Grove—but Edythe's status as a Scarlett contender (albeit a dark horse) made her a prize commodity on the party circuit.

Back home, Walter Marrener's always precarious health took a turn for the worse. At the time of Edythe's test, he was bedridden with uremic poisoning. Still, Ellen fretted most about her daughters. There was no explicit reference to the tensions that were developing between the sisters, but their mother could read between the lines. Family

Susan Hayward as Lillian Roth in *I'll Cry Tomorrow.* CREDIT: PICTORIAL PARADE

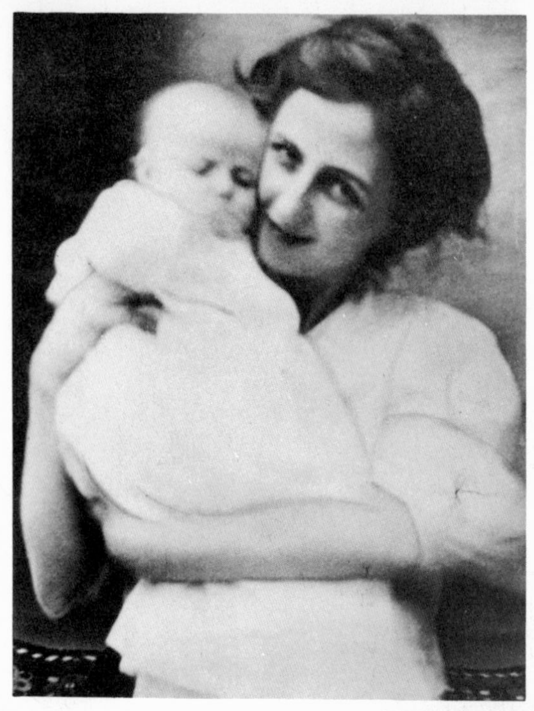

Ellen Marrener and four-month Edythe. CREDIT: PICTORIAL PARADE

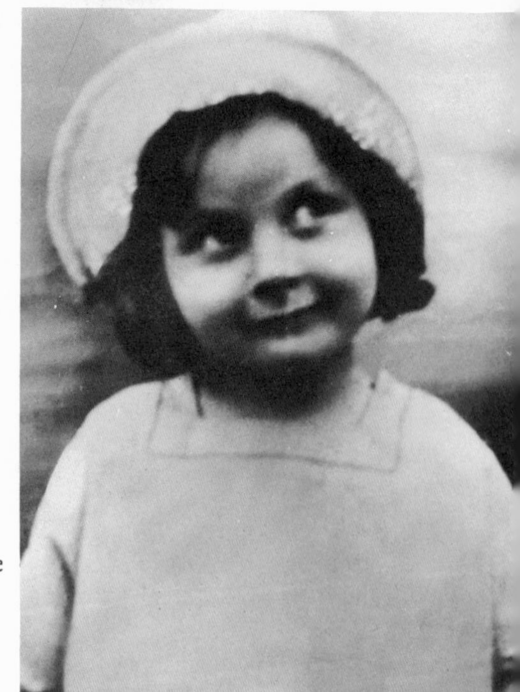

Preschooler Edythe mugs for the camera.

As a nine-year-old bathing beauty at Coney Island.

Marrenner, Edyth
2568 Bedford Avenue

Dramatic Club—V. O. A
Honors in Math., Science
Art
Arista

One of our prize actresse

Edythe's misspelled name in the Girls Commercial High yearbook, 1935. She was also mistakenly identified as a member of Arista, the scholastic society.
CREDIT: PICTORIAL PARADE

The girl in the 1936 Noxzema ad.

TRY THIS C
for V

• Feet tired and
home a jar of N
soothing, medic
restful and ref
won't stain sto

Greaseless, Stainless and Oh, So Soothing

Chief Lifeguard McMonigle of Coney Island, like so many other experts, selects Noxzema as first aid for sunburn.

• What a grand and glorious feeling when you apply soothing, cooling Noxzema to fiery, painful sunburn! No wonder this snow-white medicated cream is the nation's favorite sunburn treatment, used in first-aid hospitals at America's biggest beaches. Greaseless, too, won't stain clothes. Get a jar today. 35¢, 50¢ and Hospital Size. At drug and syndicate stores.

Cheesecake stills for Warner's

CREDIT: MOVIE STAR NEWS

CREDIT: MOVIE STAR NEWS

CREDIT: MOVIE STAR NEWS

Susan Hayward takes aim with five other Warner's contract players, including Janet Shaw (second from left), Carole Landis (second from right) and at far right, Peggy Moran.

Susan's legs stood up well to those of Ellen Drew and future pin-up queen Betty Grable.

Susan Hayward in the mid-1940s.

Susan at twenty—sweet and sultry. CREDIT: MOVIE STAR NEWS

friend Martin Emslie was heading for California on business, so, Ellen reasoned, why not ask him to check up on the girls. "I'm afraid," she admitted to Martin, "that they're going to kill each other." Martin arrived in Los Angeles in early December and was greeted by the Marrener girls at the train station. During his three-day stay, Martin was treated to an insider's view of the starlet's life during the 1930s. Each morning, the girls came back from a night of partying with a different man—and each morning Martin, who had a room down the corridor from theirs, was awakened by the sound of laughter while Edythe and Florence fumbled for their keys. Their behavior dumbfounded Martin, who, as Ellen's chosen representative of the family, piously threatened to inform Selznick of their carousing. "The man has spent his money to bring you out here," preached Emslie. "You have got to behave properly or I'm going to tell him what you're up to. It's a disgrace." Chastened, Edythe and Florence listened politely, agreed to mend their ways—and did just as they pleased as soon as their meddlesome family friend left.

Since they seldom got home before dawn, the girls were fast asleep when the telegram from home arrived at 8 A.M. It was all Edythe could do to stumble to the door. Father was dead. He was fifty-eight years old. Florence, awakened by her sister's sobs, took the crumpled yellow message from her hand and read it. Ellen went on to say that it was pointless for them to return to New York for the funeral. They could not afford it, and now that Walter was gone they would have a hard enough time squeaking by on his meager death benefits. Walter Marrener's remains were cremated, and his ashes interred at Brooklyn's Cyprus Cemetery. There were only three mourners at the service—Martin Emslie, Marrener's surrogate son from the kite-flying days, Wally, Jr. (now contributing to the family coffers by giving skating lessons at the Rockefeller Center rink) and Ellen. After more than thirty years of marriage Ellen was unemotional, almost matter-of-fact during her husband's final rites. They lasted less than three minutes.

One week after receiving news of her father's death, Edythe was summoned to David Selznick's office. Whether or not she thought she had the part of Scarlett or any other role in the film, the kid from Brooklyn strode down the hall leading to the producer's inner sanctum with the same confidence that bowled them over on Madison Avenue. The great man himself was taken aback by Edythe as she reached across the massive carved mahogany desk to shake his hand. Edythe had already developed the knack of tilting her head slightly downward, then staring up at her prey with a soul-searing intensity. For a fleeting moment, Selznick saw the tantalizing fire-and-ice quality that had leaped out at Cukor from the cover of *The Saturday Evening Post*. A far cry from Norman Rockwell. Clearing his throat, Selznick said what he had originally intended to say. "We've studied your tests," he sighed, leaning back in his high-backed leather chair. "You need more experience. You'd better go back to Brooklyn and get some in stock."

Edythe sat motionless, looking straight at the great man. A slight, noncommital smile curled the edges of her mouth. "No, Mr. Selznick," she smiled. "I think I'll stay. I like the orange trees."

Selznick was now incensed. "Then turn in your return tickets to New York at the front office," he barked.

"Can't," she said as she walked out the door, turning to fix him with her leveling gaze. "I've already cashed them in to live on. Bye."

III

No Turning Back

Even in 1937, the holiday season in California was surreal; palm trees were strung with brightly colored lights and garlands of plastic holly arched over Wilshire Boulevard. The black-topped streets shimmered like mercury in the 90-degree heat, and by noon Salvation Army Santas had the choice of either doffing their beards and red suits or passing out on the sidewalk. For Edythe and Florence, like so many of the Depression poor who had grown up shoveling snow and, in some cases scavenging for coal to fuel the furnace, balmy L.A. was nothing short of paradise.

Without Edythe's living allowance from Selznick, the Marrener sisters soon found themselves evicted from their $150-a-month apartment and were forced to find less costly lodgings elsewhere. They wired their well-to-do lawyer-aunt for money, and once they got it, moved into a seedy, neo-Moorish bungalow court on the outskirts of Beverly Hills. Their two-bedroom unit, though run-down and in sorry need of a paint job, was roomy enough for an extra occupant or two, so the girls sent for Ellen and Wally. Over the next few weeks, life at Casa Marrener was meager at best. Wally, at 5 feet 4 inches an aspiring jockey, looked for work as a stable hand at local racetracks. Meanwhile,

Edythe and Florence made the rounds of agents and studios to no avail. Her sense of survival unimpaired, Edythe would don her uniform of cashmere turtleneck, black skirt and high heeled pumps, and strike out the door each morning at nine. Her jaw was square-set and her slightly haughty expression revealed nothing of the desperation within.

One childhood item that Edythe had longed for but never discovered beneath the family Christmas tree was her own bicycle, and at nineteen she was no closer to affording one than when she was ten. But she had the fifty cents to rent one, and this Saturday she decided to treat herself to a two-wheeled tour of L.A. Pedaling a cobalt blue Schwinn down Elm, she crossed over onto Sunset and toward the pink stucco spires of the Beverly Hills Hotel. The thick atmosphere was heavy with the smell of magnolias and money. To the left, narrow streets with the names of trees and flowers like Birch, Maple and Oak crawled up toward Bel Air and the canyons beyond. On the right, broader avenues lined with forty-foot palms flowed to the desolate plain that was downtown Los Angeles.

Nowhere on earth was there such a hodgepodge of high-class architecture: tile-roofed haciendas squatted next to Tudor mansions, pillared antebellums stood alongside sleek, sprawling split-levels and clapboard Victorians. Then as now, most of these homes were owned by wealthy physicians, real estate wheeler-dealers and businessmen. It was just as true that none of them mattered to the thousands who wandered, neatly folded movie star maps in hand, looking for the temples where their celluloid gods dwelled.

They were all there—Gable and Lombard, Greer Garson, Henry Fonda, Jimmy Stewart, Spencer Tracy, Garbo and Cary Grant—all within a five-mile radius. Mary Pickford still held court at Pickfair, though now with consort

Buddy Rogers and not Douglas Fairbanks. Yet the real Queen of the Box Office was a young actress who got to bed by 9 P.M.—Shirley Temple. She would be succeeded the following year by an only slightly less callow actor named Mickey Rooney. He too would spend three years on top, catering to the small-town Andy Hardy fantasies of a Depression-weary generation. Box Office Attraction No. 6, Robert Taylor, looked out his bedroom window this morning to see Edythe fly by on her bike. For a moment he wondered if he hadn't seen the comely little redhead in the tight sweater and wool skirt on the lot at Metro. Edythe did not see Taylor watching her. Ever vain, she had taken off her glasses and slipped them into her skirt pocket. No matter that she could barely see past the handlebars—no one would see her wearing those ugly glasses in public.

Benny Medford sat in the living room of his comparatively modest cottage, scanning *Variety* and sipping a gin and tonic. He had already been an agent for a decade, and though he had unearthed a few talents who looked promising enough, he had yet to discover the star who could establish him as a force to be reckoned with. Benny was one of the smaller cogs in the Hollywood machine, and looked the part. His bulbous brown shoes were perpetually scuffed, though more often than not their dull appearance derived from the ashes that fell from cigarettes he smoked furiously throughout the day. Squinting through the blue cloud of cigarette smoke that enveloped him in his living room, Medford was reading about plans to film Daphne du Maurier's *Rebecca* when he heard the crash. Leaping to his feet, he knocked over his drink, cursing as he stumbled to the front picture window. He did not have to look far. There, sprawled out on the lawn just a few feet from him, was Edythe. The front wheel of her overturned bike was still spinning.

"Damn, damn, damn!" she said, struggling to her feet. Edythe calmly adjusted her skirt, which had been all but wrapped around her neck in the collision with Medford's rose bushes, walked slowly up to the two-wheeled casualty, took her glasses out of a case in her pocket and gave the bike a swift kick.

Medford could not suppress his laughter, and Edythe spun around in stunned surprise, her eyes flashing. Then she, too, dissolved in hysterics. Was she all right? Yes, just mad as hell. Did she want to come in and wash the grass stains off her hands? Inside, Edythe noticed *Variety* crumpled on the floor, and mentioned that she, too, was in show business. "In pictures?" "No, but I'd like to be." Medford sensed at once the spark that had been missing in the other aspiring actresses—that incandescence that both shines through and illuminates a character on screen.

"Do you have an agent?" Medford asked casually.

"No," Edythe answered, tossing back her luxurious red hair. "Got any ideas?"

"Have you done anything yet?"

"I've acted since I was a child, got plenty of experience on the stage back in New York. I've studied with the finest drama coaches and . . ."

"You can forget all that stage acting stuff here," he declared, erasing what she had said with a wave of his fingers. "What works on stage doesn't work in the movies. Have you done anything in pictures, anything on film?"

"David Selznick brought me out here to try for the role of Scarlett O'Hara. I did a screen test."

"Cukor direct it?"

"Yes."

The next day, Medford, the tin canister containing Edythe's five-minute Scarlett test tucked tightly under his arm, walked into the office of Warner talent executive

Max Arnow. After screening the clip, Arnow leaned forward in his chair, made a triangle with his hands and nodded. Medford leaned forward.

"Well, Max?"

"Terrible. Awful. A rotten Scarlett O'Hara. I can see why Selznick canned her." Arnow paused, perhaps enjoying the fact that his friend was squirming in the next chair. "But there's something there—an intangible quality worth developing. I think we can make something out of her." Benny rushed to the phone with the news. Warners wanted her to sign up for six months as one of its $100-a-week contract players.

The first item on the agenda was to change her name. Edythe was far too sedate for the screen image they had in mind. Edythe herself suggested the name of her grandmother, Katie Harrington, but Arnow felt it smacked of burlesque; so the brainstorming began. Another up-and-coming actress from Brooklyn, Margarita Cansino, had been doing rather well under the name Rita Hayworth. Hayworth, Haywood . . . Arnow tossed it about in his mind. He had been working a lot lately with superagent Leland Hayward, and liked the sound of the name. Medford agreed. From his private garden of favorite names, Medford plucked Susan, and Susan Hayward was born.

When Lucille Le Sueur was told that she would hence be known to the public as Joan Crawford, she screamed, "I hate it! Sounds like 'crayfish.'" But Edythe viewed her name change with equanimity. It was, after all, a necessary step toward stardom. And that's what she was there for.

Arnow promptly enrolled his new protégée in the Warner drama school, where she joined other promising contract players like Ronald Reagan, Carole Landis, Penny Singleton and Jane Wyman under the tutelage of studio coach Frank Beckwith. A nervous man with sunken eyes and a habit of frantically jingling change in his pocket when scenes weren't going quite right, Beckwith was instantly impressed by Susan Hayward, née Edythe Marrener. She was easily the most beautiful of his new charges, and the most intelligent. There was an icy self-assurance and that aggressively sexy walk, but Beckwith quickly determined that she lacked vulnerability. "This new girl doesn't quite have the heart," Beckwith reported to Arnow. "She has a wonderful mind, but we've got to give her the heart." To do that, Beckwith concentrated on Susan, giving her the heaviest dramatic scenes during the daily classes. "It took months," Arnow would later claim, "to teach her how to cry."

While Beckwith groomed her for greater things, Susan's main contribution to Warner's at first consisted of posing for cheesecake starlet stills—on a broomstick and wearing a black bathing suit as "Miss Halloween," brandishing an ax as the kind of "Miss Thanksgiving" a Pilgrim surely never saw, and with a gargantuan and decidedly phallic firecracker as—surprise—"Miss Fourth of July." The photographer told her to relax, but Susan, so anxious to please, threw herself into each and every role. "What are you doing?" cracked a press agent as he watched one of these sessions. "You look like you're up for an Oscar already."

Hayward finally made her debut on the big screen in December of 1937, whirling and high-kicking with two hundred other girls in the broadcast finale of Busby Berkeley's *Hollywood Hotel*, starring Dick Powell. A typical Berkeley extravaganza, *Hollywood Hotel* would have meant nothing to Susan's career had it not marked the first time her path crossed with that of the powerful Louella Parsons, whose network radio show inspired the movie and who played herself in the film.

Parsons, writing for the powerful Hearst chain, was a

woman to be feared and courted. She was, in fact, the first syndicated Hollywood columnist, and had been unearthing the private lives of silent stars like Francis X. Bushman, Gloria Swanson and John Gilbert when Susan was still a toddler back in Brooklyn. By 1937 she had been in the business over a dozen years and a serious challenge from a crazy-hatted newcomer named Hedda Hopper was still more than a year away.

Louella's monopoly seemed secure for now, and as Queen of Gossip she had the power to hype or shatter a career on which millions of studio dollars were banked. Recalls Joan Fontaine in her autobiography, *No Bed of Roses:* "Flowers, cases of champagne, assorted lavish gifts arrived at the door of her house on Maple Drive whenever a birthday, anniversary or Christmas came around. Her secretary would alert the studio publicity departments and the publicity-aware producers. A skillful line in Miss Parsons' column in the Los Angeles *Examiner* would remind the ambitious actor." One Christmas, Louella went the rounds of all the studios in her chauffeur-driven station wagon. Dropping into each publicity department in turn and imbibing a cup of cheer at the office parties, Louella would wait until her car was loaded with presents. Next studio, another libation, another armload of loot. The chauffeur was also celebrating the Yule season, and as Louella emerged from the last stop, now leaning heavily on the arm of the tipsy driver, they found that the station wagon had been rifled. Thousands of dollars worth of perfume, wine, silver frames, alligator handbags and monogrammed lingerie had been spirited away. The morning after Christmas, Miss Parsons' secretary dutifully telephoned all the studios. The station wagon would be calling at the studio gate again. The Queen expected it to be refilled with duplicate gifts. It was.

Such was the power of Parsons, who with one small item in one of her columns could destroy marriages, drive down the stock of entire studios, make or break careers. Susan was soon to learn the latter firsthand. Parsons spotted Susan in the chorus of *Hollywood Hotel* and instantly took a motherly interest in her. *Hotel* spawned the idea for a nine-week national tour of the road show, in which Parsons would showcase the talents of Warner's young stars. There were four or five 45-minute shows a day, each consisting of a series of comedy sketches, dramatic selections and variety acts built around a format in which Parsons played herself and the actors tried to impress her and win a plug in her column. Hayward joined such promising up-and-comers as Reagan, Wyman, Arleen Whelan, Joy Hodges and June Preisser aboard the airliner which carried "Louella Parsons and Her Flying Stars" from city to city.

Hayward greeted the news from Medford that she had been handpicked by Louella herself with typical enthusiasm and determination. The first stop was San Francisco, and everyone involved in the project was edgy—except the star. Even if the show folded after a week, Louella had been guaranteed $3,300 a week for nine weeks. The other dozen or so performers were to divide $4,000 among them only for as long as the "Louella and Her Flying Stars" survived on the circuit. Susan watched backstage as Louella checked her notes, adjusted her girdle and waddled to the massive wooden desk in the middle of the stage. Susan marveled at her latest mentor's girth, and yet how spindly her legs appeared. Seated, Louella was given a once-over by the hairdresser as she continued to study her lines. Louella's powdery cheeks and warm eyes often made her look more like someone's kind-hearted grandmother than the merciless wielder of the most vicious pen in Hollywood. But now, oblivious to everything but the performance she was soon to give, her features hardened.

By the time Hayward was ready to make her entrance, it was clear from the response Reagan, Wyman and the others had received that the public was more than ready for this new blend of Hollywood and vaudeville. The high point was yet to come. The other performers had decided to make little of their entrances; they simply floated onstage. Susan knew how she wanted to introduce herself to the audience, and though dubious at first, Parsons yielded. With Louella sitting in the shadows behind her desk, Susan marched out in a clingy blue velvet dress and straight up to the footlights. Hands planted firmly on her hips, she thrust her chin toward the audience and hollered, "Anyone here from Brooklyn?" Wherever they were playing and whatever the makeup of the crowd, this single question was guaranteed to bring the house down.

During her skits Susan was no less memorable, and the fact that she was clearly the favorite of every male in the audience did little to win the friendship of other women on the tour who had toiled much longer in the Hollywood vineyards. To Joy Hodges, Susan seemed too direct, too humorless—a definite loner. No one could quite bring themselves to ask Susan to join them for dinner, and though she struck up instant friendships with doormen, waiters and stagehands in every city they visited, she was uncomfortable around her fellow professionals. Susan's icy persona rankled the others, none of whom realized that it was she who feared them—not the other way around. Even Reagan, who had dated Susan once at the behest of Warner's publicity department, was now keeping his distance—though that may have had as much to do with the fact that he was rapidly falling in love with future wife Wyman.

Left to her own devices, the Lone Wolf of the tour preferred to stay in her hotel room reading, rather than join the rest of the cast on the town. The exception was New

York, and only then because she delighted in seeing family and old friends. Early in the tour, however, she decided to accept the dinner invitation of a Chicago businessman who had seen the show and admired her work. They managed to work in more than one evening together, and soon Susan, hungry for human contact, was smitten. Every night after that she dropped everything to call him from wherever they happened to be playing.

Meantime, Louella and her protégés were packing them in everywhere. SRO crowds jammed every theater from Detroit's Orpheum to the Seattle Grand to see the show, and it was decided to do a full five shows daily. Inevitably, tensions mounted. Wyman, aware that Hayward had seen Reagan occasionally back in Hollywood, had taken an instant dislike to her imagined rival. She was particularly incensed by the one comedy scene which Susan and Reagan shared. With the spotlight shining down on the two of them, Susan stabbed Ronnie, and every time he stood up, she clobbered him. The audience shrieked—and Reagan strained to keep a straight face himself. Susan, ever the pro, played it absolutely straight—much to the astonishment of her more seasoned colleagues. Wyman seethed in the wings. From where she stood, Reagan's fiancé was convinced that Susan was looking right at her when she clobbered Ronnie, and it was obvious that she wasn't pulling her punches. Furious, Wyman complained to Parsons, who in turn asked Hayward to be a little more careful. Susan seemed at first on the verge of tears when confronted by the boss, but that soon turned to Irish anger.

"I'm not hurting Ronnie on purpose, Miss Parsons. It's all Miss Wyman's fault. She stands there in the wings like a statue, watching me all the time. It makes me so nervous I don't know what I'm doing."

"Too bad about her," Wyman snapped when Parsons

relayed the countercharge. "If I don't stand and watch she'll knock Ronnie out. She hits him too hard! She just slaps him that hard because she thinks it makes me mad."

That Christmas, Parsons and Co. were performing in Montreal. A heavy snow had blanketed the city, and Miss Parsons was giving a cast party in her suite at the Windsor—undoubtedly in anticipation of the kind of tribute her chauffeur was busy collecting on her behalf back in Hollywood. A Christmas tree, thrown up hours before by the compliant hotel management, glowed in the center of the room. To the side, a table was heaped with gaily wrapped gifts—mostly from one trouper to the other, but some mailed from friends and relatives scattered about the country. Reagan admired the navy blue sweater Wyman had given him. Preisser splashed on some of the cologne sent by her sister Cherry. Parsons was in her accustomed position, holding court in an overstuffed chair. Everyone sipped the hotel's eggnog, liberally laced by the hostess with brandy and rum. Susan, alone on the couch, was surprised when someone plucked a package from the table and handed it to her.

"Looks like it's from your Chicago friend," smiled Joy Hodges. Susan, beaming, methodically unwrapped the white cardboard box, folded the paper neatly and put it to one side with the ribbons and bows she had collected; long after she was a household name Susan would still be saving Christmas wrapping paper. She held it up to her ear, shook it and smiled when the others laughed at her nonplussed expression. Opening it up, she pulled out a toy telephone—her love's not-so-gentle hint that she needn't waste her money or her time. For that moment, even Wyman pitied the girl from Flatbush. Three weeks later, Susan would learn with the rest of the country that Vivien Leigh had been chosen to play Scarlett O'Hara.

Humiliated and alone, Susan ran to the theater where they were playing and walked out onto the still, darkened stage. Three stagehands knelt in a corner, working on a piece of scenery. They were oblivious to the lonely girl nearby. A single lightbulb dangled from the ceiling, casting strange shadows into the wings.

Susan was walking slowly across the stage when one of the three workmen stood up. "Hey Jim," he called to one of the men standing stage right. "Is Walter Marrener around? Send him over, will ya?"

Unbelieving, Susan walked over to the workman, her head cocked. "Tell me," she asked incredulously, "is there really someone here named Marrener?"

"Why, yes, miss," he replied, turning to point at a rugged young man emerging from the shadows, hammer in hand. "Here he comes now. Do you know him?"

"Walter Marrener was my father's name," Susan said, shaking her head in disbelief. "He was French-Huguenot, a subway trainman in Brooklyn. My name is Edythe Marrener—my real name, that is. They call me Susan Hayward."

The young stranger shrugged. "It's a small world. And who's to say your father and I were not related. I'm French-Huguenot, too, and it's not too common a name, Marrener. So maybe we had a mutual relative, way back in the past. I'd be happy to think so."

The girl inside Susan Hayward who still answered to the name Edythe suddenly felt the touch of her father's hand on her shoulder. Coming now, when she was plunged into the depths of despair, this sudden appearance of a man called Walter Marrener had to be more than just a coincidence. "God bless you," Edythe said to the stagehand. "God bless you, Walter Marrener, for what this has done for me."

Decades later, Susan Hayward the star would remember

this as one of "the most unforgettable moments in my life. I was lost and miserable, then all at once, hearing my father's name called out on that strange and blackened stage, I felt that I had been given a sign."

As she walked away from the laborer who bore her father's name and whom she would never see again, Susan whispered to herself, "Someone, Edythe, is caring for you."

Once the exhausting tour was over, Susan returned to more parts in the pictures. Before her twentieth birthday, she uttered a few lines at the beginning of a 1938 suspense film called *The Amazing Dr. Clitterhouse,* in which Edward G. Robinson portrayed a respected Park Avenue physician who decides that the only way to study the psychology and physiology of criminals is to become one. The villain of the improbable piece is a youthful-looking Humphrey Bogart. He winds up being killed by the good doctor when he threatens to blow Robinson's cover. Blond wiseacre Claire Trevor, playing the fence-with-the-heart-of-gold, falls for Clitterhouse just in time to save him from the gallows. The verdict: Not guilty by reason of insanity.

The general attitude toward this movie was reflected in the fact that Bogart regularly referred to it as *The Amazing Dr. Clitoris.* Hayward was grateful for the chance. The part of a telephone operator in Bette Davis's *The Sisters* was of even shorter duration. However, Susan did get to meet male lead Errol Flynn and Davis, with whom she would experience a professional rivalry on the set of *Where Love Has Gone* a quarter of a century later. There was also a small part in an 18-minute short, *Campus Cinderella,* focusing the talents of Warner starlet Penny Singleton. Years later, Singleton would settle for the title role in the commercially successful but otherwise thoroughly unmemorable *Blondie* film series.

Susan tried not to let on to her mother, brother and

sister, but she fretted that Warner's, like Selznick, did not know how to capitalize on her unique dramatic talents. "Anyone here from Brooklyn?" may have been a show-stopper on the vaudeville circuit, but as Medford had repeatedly warned her, success on the stage before a live audience did not necessarily spell success before the cameras. Not that studio chief Jack Warner was all that interested in giving her a chance. "One actor on his ass," he would proudly proclaim, "is worth two on their feet." And that's the way he kept them.

History repeated itself for Susan in the spring of 1938. Once again, she found herself at the mercy of Selznick. This time, the search was on not for a Scarlett, but for the right actress to tackle the coveted role of "I" de Winter in the movie adaptation of Daphne du Maurier's *Rebecca*. Once again, every eligible actress in Hollywood was tested, including Leigh, Loretta Young, Anne Baxter, Lana Turner, Geraldine Fitzgerald, Virginia Mayo and Joan Fontaine, the eventual winner. Selznick either had forgotten their little disagreement or was more magnanimous than she had realized, for Susan was called to the set to be directed in the test by John Cromwell. She had not delivered more than three lines when Cromwell loudly ordered the cameras to stop, snorted in disgust and stamped off the set, leaving Susan standing there alone while the crew squirmed in embarrassment. Medford rushed up to comfort her. "Don't let it get to you, honey," he said. "There's a lot of politics in this business, and when you're a star that guy will be a bum on the streets."

"I know he will," Susan said without a flicker. A week later, Cromwell was replaced as *Rebecca*'s director by Alfred Hitchcock.

Not long after her second Selznick fiasco, Susan was at last called by Warner's to play a part that lasted more than ninety seconds. *Girls on Probation* was the title of the film intended as a vehicle for Bette Davis's protégée Jane Bryan. "You get to play a real bitchy girl," Arnow told Susan, handing her the dog-eared script. "I think it'll be great for you."

Susan spotted the problem as soon as she got to the third page: The character she was to portray was a socialite. Susan knew her thick Brooklyn accent was no more suited to that than it was to Scarlett or "I" de Winter. So Susan decided to mask her faulty diction with an extra dose of vitriol. If she was villainous enough, Susan reasoned, perhaps no one would notice that she sounded more like a Dead End Kid than a debutante. Bryan, cast as a poor young woman working for a dry cleaning firm, borrows an evening dress from a fellow worker to wear—Cinderella style—to a black-tie dinner party. The dress, unbeknownst to our heroine, belongs to snooty Susan, who promptly has the innocent working girl fired and tossed in the slammer. It was the only role of any size or substance that Warner's had come up with for her to date. Susan was given fifth billing. As for the ploy to disguise her distinctive Flatbush cadence, it didn't work. After that point, Medford later recalled, "Nobody at Warner's would go for her. Her option was dropped."

Susan hit the streets again in search of work. During lunchtime, when the agents and producers and flacks congregated at Schwabb's or the Brown Derby for lunch, she headed for the supermarkets. She was not interested in buying anything; Susan scoured each store for free samples of breakfast cereals on which the Marreners would survive. On the not-so-rare occasions when either Susan or Florence was asked out, the family would dine on scraps of steak and salad triumphantly carried home from Ciro's or Romanoff's in a doggie bag elegantly inscribed with the restaurant's initials.

Amazingly, the Marreners managed to get by on this diet of shredded wheat and leftovers while Susan weighed her situation. No longer willing to forgo a part like Scarlett or I de Winter merely because she lacked that indefinable something called class, Susan sat through *The Prisoner of Zenda* one hundred times, studying Ronald Colman's diction and inflections. Slouched on an aisle seat in the sixth row at the Pantages, she began mumbling the lines as they were spoken on screen—much to the consternation of those sitting several rows behind her. At least a dozen times during the five showings she sat through each day, some matron in a flowered hat or a middle-aged man munching buttered popcorn turned to "sshhh" her. In the evenings, she mimicked Colman hours on end before the mirror in her bedroom.

Susan felt she was ready by the time she paid a call on Artie Jacobsen, an old friend from the Selznick days who happened to have just been made talent head at Paramount. She was ostensibly there for a loan, but bluff, no-nonsense Jacobsen quickly arranged an audition. Susan had prepared a reading of *Alter Ego*, a five-minute Arch Oboler radio sketch that she felt would best exhibit her dramatic range—particularly since she played all the parts. Medford, Jacobsen and two other Paramount casting executives sat in stunned silence as she ran through the piece without a hitch. Medford was the most dumbfounded of all—gone was any trace of Avenue D, supplanted by a finishing school polish. The three men huddled. Two wanted to sign her immediately to a stock $75-a-week contract. Mysteriously, Jacobsen held out. First, he wanted to hear her sing. Sing? Susan shrugged, promised they would be sorely disappointed, and gamely belted out a chorus of *The Man I Love*, a cappella.

As soon as she was finished, Susan doubled over. "I told

you fellas not to expect much," she laughed. The three huddled again, and this time the verdict was unanimous: Susan Hayward would get a starting salary of $250 weekly —"$75 for your talent," quipped Jacobsen, "and an extra $175 for your nerve."

Susan was fortunate to make her Paramount debut in one of the classic motion pictures of all time—the 1939 remake of *Beau Geste.* This time, she was more than equipped to render a convincing portrayal of Isobel Rivers, pretty ward of the Geste boys' adoptive aunt Lady Brandon. Cast as the childhood playmate of Gary Cooper, Ray Milland and Robert Preston (all of whom would costar with her in several more movies), Susan "waved good-bye to the boys at the beginning and hello to them at the end." The main object of her affections was Milland, who carried her cameo with him as he left to join his brothers in the Foreign Legion.

The day she arrived on the set of *Beau Geste* to film her first scenes, however, Susan was far too intent on walking away with the movie to allow herself to be shaken by a first meeting with Cooper, already one of the top three or four cinematic heroes of the day. She attacked each line of dialogue with such ferocity that director William Wellman, known throughout the trade as a man's director, moaned to his cameraman, "Good God, they've sprung a redhead Bette Davis on me." Most of Susan's scenes wound up on the cutting floor, but what remained—less than five minutes on screen—was sufficient to make her the new sensation on the lot. The Paramount machine instantly seized on the opportunity to promote her by circulating the rumors (totally unfounded) that the studio was going to change her name to Mary and crediting Wellman with her discovery.

If Warner's handling of her career was disappointing,

Paramount's approach utterly mystified Susan. After the triumph of *Beau Geste*, she was inexplicably cast in a string of B movies. In the first, *Our Leading Citizen*, she played the naïve daughter of a small-town lawyer battling communists, corruption, ambitious labor leaders and greedy capitalists—all at once. *Citizen* was simplistic and not particularly entertaining, and Susan joined other members of the cast in wondering why it was being made at all. The next "B" proved even more embarrassing for all involved. Bigmouths Joe E. Brown and Martha Raye cavorted as campus cut-ups, and Hayward played a red-hot faculty member ("I teach romance") known as "the firecracker" to the football team because she took it upon herself to tutor after-dark classes in necking on the campus grounds.

Why, Susan demanded, was she being handed such trash? Jacobsen conceded that *Our Leading Citizen* and *$1,000 a Touchdown* were not the best Paramount had to offer a talent of her caliber. Indeed, she had been picked to star in a number of the studio's major dramatic releases. What happened? In every case the leading lady, aware of her scene-stealing in *Beau Geste* and even those exciting Hayward scenes that had to be cut from the final version, vetoed Hayward as a possible threat. Until a star could be found who was secure enough to let fiery Susan appear on the same screen with her, Hayward would have to earn her pay dressing up Paramount's lesser offerings.

The fault, Susan determined, was clearly hers. She was the green kid; they knew what they were doing. If she was too threatening to directors and leading ladies alike, then she would make the necessary alterations to her personality. The new Susan Hayward was born at a cocktail party thrown by the studio for all Paramount's young hopefuls at the palatial Bel Air home of studio chief B. P. Schulberg. Clad in an off-the-shoulder gown of billowing pink organza, Susan made her entrance on the arm of a darkly handsome contract player who four years later would give it all up to go into real estate. She was uncertain of herself in the studio limousine coming over, and it was no help at all when a smiley Claudette Colbert stepped up to introduce herself to the trembling starlet. Working with greats like Cooper and Cukor was one thing, but Susan put socializing in a different category. Where was the character to hide behind, the accent to affect? *The Prisoner of Zenda* notwithstanding, surely these people could not be fooled by her airs.

As the evening wore on, however, Susan began to realize that *this* was the character to hide behind—not the girl from Flatbush, but the synthetic siren with the Park Avenue patina. It worked on Marlene Dietrich, who spent most of her time in animated conversation with Cary Grant. And on Paulette Goddard. Goddard was not only a guest, but the main topic of hushed gossip during the evening. Was she or was she not married to Charlie Chaplin, everyone wondered. The moviegoing public was sensitive to such unorthodox arrangements, and by now it was well known throughout the industry that this lack of clarification delayed Goddard's signing as Scarlett in *Gone With the Wind* several months and eventually cost her the role. Susan left the party at 11:45 P.M., blissfully unaware that the scandals surrounding her personal life—someday splashed across the front page of every tabloid in America —were to make Goddard's troubles pale in comparison.

The haughtier attitude that Hayward consciously adopted over the next few months only seemed to aggravate tensions on the set. Where once she was regarded by many as simply willful—insisting on playing scenes her way, refusing to cut her hair (something for which she would later be put on suspension), refusing to mingle with the cast or crew between takes—she now appeared impatiently arrogant. Of this bewildering period, she later wrote to a friend, "All my life I've been terribly frightened of people. At the studio it was the casting director, the cameraman, reporters and publicists who asked endless questions. I thought everyone was so brilliant and I felt so inadequate. Then at this party, all those famous stars seemed so poised, so sure of themselves. Or so I thought. That's when I got the idea that I should try and be like them.

"People around the studio had told me that I should change, that my attitude was wrong. So suddenly, overnight, I stopped being myself and tried to copy everyone else. As a result I got so mixed up and was more confused than ever. Some people did try to straighten me out, but their approach was wrong. A word of encouragement produced a glow inside, like good, fine wine. But mostly I was criticized. I guess it never occurred to anyone to find out why I behaved the way I did." Her solution? "The only way I knew how to protect myself was to try and scare people before they scared me. Other girls were going right to the top, while I got the parts no one else wanted."

At home, Ellen reassured her younger daughter that Paramount was bound to catch on soon. The resistance would subside, she promised, as soon as the bosses at the studio realized they could not hold back a major talent to protect the fragile egos of a few over-the-hill leading ladies. Meanwhile, Susan was making a good salary. "Yes, Mother," she sighed, shaking her head in disgust, "but I feel like a fraud for accepting it."

Susan continued her protracted war with the studio, and it can be said in part that she was given second billing to Albert Dekker in a first-rate thriller merely to get her off some very important backs. *Among the Living* starred veteran character actor Dekker as twin brothers—one an eminently sane business executive, the other a deranged killer who strangles his keeper and then terrorizes the small Southern town where his brother has revived the local steel mill. Susan was cast as the mercenary Millie Perkins, daughter of the maniac's frumpy landlady. While *Among the Living* was strictly a "B" and would not get the publicity push or the distribution necessary to make it a commercial hit, it proved beyond a doubt that Hayward could carry what the Los Angeles *Herald-Tribune* called a "superior psychological melodrama—head and shoulders above most of the filler shows ground out by Hollywood." "Susan Hayward," the *Herald-Tribune* added, "is especially good."

Millie Perkins, as Hayward portrayed her, is deliciously amoral. Promptly seducing the affection-starved boarder, she soaks him for as much as she can, then—unaware that he is the killer—enlists his help in bagging the fiend and pocketing the $5,000 reward. She comes perilously close to joining Dekker's growing list of victims when her screams attract the local townsfolk, all armed to the teeth and ready to lynch him on the spot. Whipped into frenzy by the incorrigible Millie, the mob winds up plugging Dekker as he tries to hide in a cemetery. He is found dead, sprawled at the base of his mother's tombstone.

Among the Living was regarded by Dekker as his best effort in a career that spanned three decades and reached its nadir when he was cast as *Dr. Cyclops*. In a parting shot at the scandalmongers who helped make Hollywood the world's most neurotic town, Dekker was found dead in his bedroom in 1968, hanging from a beam in women's black silk underwear, his worst notices scrawled all over his body in crimson lipstick.

Not altogether surprisingly, *Among* left Susan even more depressed. Her performance was by any standard superb, yet regardless of the critical accolades Paramount seemed no more willing than ever to assign her a starring role in a major picture. The problem of jealous grand dames remained. As Susan simmered, even the usually mild-mannered Medford began shouting at Artie Jacobsen over the telephone. There was a temporary solution, but would Susan buy it? Agents worked on a 10 per cent commission, supposedly molding and guiding the careers of a few clients, but producers and studios had an ingenious way of getting an even larger chunk of the actor's remaining salary. A Selznick or a Harry Cohn would give his contract players a percentage of the salary gotten for them on a loan-out to other studios and pocket the difference. Susan was under an exclusive seven-year contract to Paramount, and a refusal by her to do any of the mediocre scripts she was handed would result in an instant suspension. Jacobsen and Medford needn't have worried. Susan jumped at their suggestion: that she be loaned out to Republic Pictures for a Judy Canova comedy, *Sis Hopkins*.

Under the stewardship of pennypinching Herbert J. Yates, Republic had deservedly gained a reputation for cranking out low-budget films, generally short on style and substance and long on action. *Sis Hopkins*, however, was intended by Yates not only to launch the movie career of hillbilly comic Canova, but also to mark the studio's first full-fledged attempt at producing a musical comedy. Yates plunked down $50,000 for the rights to film Rose Melville's Broadway hit, and two bright young tunesmiths, composer Jule Styne and lyricist Frank Loesser, were hired to write some new songs for the movie. Styne would go on to write *Funny Lady* and *Sweet Charity*; Loesser would be best known for *Guys and Dolls*. For *Sis Hopkins* they came up with a couple of forgettable ditties, including something called *Look at You Look at Me*, notable only because it marked the first time Hayward got to sing on screen. Many of those who had worked with her felt Susan was perfectly cast as the snooty daughter of a plumbing tycoon, wickedly set on undermining her kindly-but-dumb country cousin Canova.

Susan may have been the heavy in *Sis Hopkins,* but she was a lovable heavy, nonetheless. She worried aloud that she would be typed as a "doll-faced ingenue" unless her next role seemed genuinely sinister. Enter Gregory Ratoff, another of Susan's godfathers back at Warner's. Having just directed newcomer Ingrid Bergman in her first American film, *Intermezzo,* Ratoff was now casting for his next Bergman movie, based on Charles Bonner's novel, *Legacy.* Ratoff was himself the personification of the European producer-director in Hollywood—a gruff Viennese barking orders between puffs on an obscene cigar. His expensive suits fit as well as could be expected, and his shoes glowed with a patina—a halo, really—that, no matter how much Kiwi or spit they used, none of the men around him could reproduce. Ratoff himself was an actor. As the leering producer Max Fabian in *All About Eve,* he was the brunt of a classic exchange between newcomer Marilyn Monroe and a sardonic George Sanders. "Why," she asks Sanders, "do they all look like scared rabbits?" "Because," he replied, "they usually are." *Legacy* (which would eventually be retitled *Adam Had Four Sons*) was the story of a self-sacrificing Swedish governess (Bergman) holding a motherless family of four boys together at the turn of the century. While Bergman grew only faintly more gray, the four rambunctious lads (portrayed by child actors Billy Ray, Steven Muller, Bobby Walberg and Wallace Chadwell) grew into adulthood (Richard Denning, Johnny Downs, Robert Shaw and Charles Lind). Bergman manages to overcome the predictable array of problems until she is faced with Hester Stoddard, the libidinous, conniving wife of the hopelesssly naïve Downs. Nymphomaniacal and utterly remorseless, Hester is the very personification of evil—so much so that the name itself was to become synonymous with such qualities.

Susan lusted after the role of Hester. To be sure, the possibilities were intriguing, but could she convince Ratoff that she was right for the part? She made her usual entrance into his office at Columbia, breezing past stunned receptionists and secretaries like a red tornado and planting herself on one of the two chairs that faced his desk. Ratoff looked like a mischievous little boy behind the broad expanse, his pudgy face mirrored in the desktop. His reaction to Susan's suggestion that she be cast as Hester was predictable.

"Absurd," he laughed. "Dis is a part for a voman of de vorld. Vich you, my dear, sveet Susan, are definitely not!"

No amount of cajoling or persuading would get him to change his mind, he insisted. But as Susan left his office an hour later, she was far from ready to concede defeat. Susan was a close friend of Ratoff's wife, the Russian stage actress Eugenie Leontovich, and she sensed correctly that in Leontovich she had an ally. Over the next several days, Mrs. Ratoff, who herself had played more than one villainess on the screen, slowly wore down her husband's resistance to casting anyone but an experienced "bad woman" like Joan Crawford or Barbara Stanwyck as Hester. Once that conversion had been accomplished, she slyly dropped the name of Susan. When the call finally came from Ratoff, Susan did not even feign surprise.

"I'm glad to see you finally came to your senses, Gregory," she smirked. "I've already learned my lines. When do we start shooting?"

Once the actual filming began, Susan discovered that

Ratoff was as lovably irascible a director as he was a friend. At one point, when Susan had difficulty during a scene in which she squares off with Bergman, Ratoff exploded. "Susan," he roared in desperation, "you are se most steenking actress I've ever seen!"

Rather than being shriveled by his criticism, as she had so often been with other directors, Susan was never hurt by Ratoff's tongue-in-cheek tantrums. More often than not, they would cause her to double over with laughter. Susan also discovered that beneath the gruff exterior was a sensitive artist capable of challenging and inspiring his actors without intimidating them. Once Susan, Bergman or any of the other actors got it right, Ratoff would not hesitate to bound to his feet shouting, "Ah, you are marvelous—vunderful!"

Third-billed Susan found her nemesis in *Adam* equally pleasant and rewarding to work with. Bergman, whom Susan came to regard as her favorite actress, saw the potential in the hard-working Hayward and went out of her way to help Susan create a memorably rotten-to-the-core character. "Some actors and actresses are like blank walls," Susan would recall of the experience years later, "so unresponsive you can't do your best. Ingrid is just the opposite—she worked as hard for my close-ups as for her own."

The person who most excited Susan, however, was not Bergman or Ratoff, but Hester herself, who was always in action, usually moving forward, constantly revealing her aggressive, destructive personality. It was a profoundly physical role in that sense; Hester may be as well remembered for her cocky, thumbs-in-the-belt-loops stance as for her lines of dialogue.

Ratoff and Bergman notwithstanding, this is also the way Hayward is best remembered by the cast and crew of *Adam*. She repeatedly castigated Downs for interfering with her close-ups, and on more than one occasion laced into an actor she accused of intentionally stepping on her lines. Once the cameras stopped rolling, Susan retreated to her trailer or headed home to Mama, Wally and Florence. Again, her reluctance to socialize with her colleagues was viewed as further proof of Susan's now-fabled arrogance. Ambitious. Unscrupulous. Selfish. All were words used to describe Hester Stoddard—and Susan Hayward.

Susan walked away with *Adam Had Four Sons*, much to the delight of Ratoff (after whom she would name one of her twin sons years later) and the utter chagrin of most of her co-workers on the picture. So convincing was her portrayal of the sinister Hester, in fact, that the character's name became synonymous with adultery to an entire generation of wartime moviegoers. For the first time, not only audiences but critics took notice. The New York *Times* all but overlooked Bergman in praise for Susan, as did *Variety* and the Los Angeles *Times*. Ellen now assured her daughter that Paramount could no longer overlook its most promising young star. She was wrong.

Even as weekend crowds lined up to see *Adam* at Radio City Music Hall—possibly the raciest film ever shown until then at the family-oriented movie palace—Susan received her marching orders to hit the Paramount promotional circuit like any other contract player. By way of rubbing salt into an open wound, the studio often dispatched Susan to make appearances on behalf of other people's pictures while her own career languished. She dutifully obeyed, but not without insisting that her sister go along to protect her from the armies of stage-door Johnnys who bombarded every starlet on the road with flowers, candy and calls. As a chaperone, the comparatively libertine Florence was hardly ideal—though she eagerly took on the job of luring the pestering male groupies away from Susan.

For a brief time, Paramount acceded to Columbia's request that Susan journey to New York to promote *Adam*, and it was always Florence who accompanied her. The tour marked Susan's first taste of star perks—a flower-filled Louis XIV suite at the Waldorf-Astoria decorated in subtle shades of blue and green, a chauffeur-driven Fleetwood limousine with a bar and teak writing desk in the back, her own hairdresser, a gaggle of publicists. Proclaimed "the redheaded pride of Gowanus" by *Daily Mirror* film critic Lee Mortimer, Susan gloried in the attention. Reporters flocked to interview the local-girl-made-good, photographers snapped her window shopping on Fifth Avenue, and for the first time she found herself signing autographs. At 4 P.M. on the first full day of activities, three dozen people jammed into Susan's Waldorf suite to watch fashion illustrator Russell Patterson compare Susan's legs to those of four girls in the chorus of Broadway's *Pal Joey* and proclaim her "President of the Perfect Legs Institution."

That evening, Susan headed out on the town with several of Columbia's New York-based corporate executives, a few of the studio's key Wall Street money men and their bejeweled wives. The play—a musical—was followed by a late supper at Sardi's and drinks at Sherman Billingsley's Stork Club. Susan invited her newfound friends back to the hotel for a nightcap, but when she opened the door she was taken aback to see Florence with a dozen old pals from Brooklyn. None of them were feeling any pain.

"How can you do this to me?" Susan demanded. Friends on both sides winced. "What are you doing here? How can I entertain *my* friends if you have the place filled up with yours? This is supposed to be a business trip for *me!*"

Everyone straggled out in embarrassment, and when it

came time for Susan to return to Hollywood she went without Florence. "I didn't want to stay behind," Florence later recalled of the incident. "I wanted to be back in California with my family. I have to have family around, otherwise I fall apart. Maybe that's the thing in me that's so weak. I'm not strong and self-sufficient like Susan. I need someone around to want and love me."

On that score, at least, Florence was right: sniveling was not for Susan. Once back in Hollywood, she grew increasingly restless as she watched choice parts go to other actresses. As she had with Ratoff, Susan directly approached the directors of several upcoming projects and asked for a part. At about the same time as *Adam Had Four Sons*, she spotted another juicy dramatic role as Olivia De Havilland's nemesis in 1941's *Hold Back the Dawn*. Paulette Goddard wound up with the part Susan wanted, and De Havilland was nominated as Best Actress for her efforts. (Olivia's little sister Joan Fontaine won, however, for *Suspicion*.) Three years later, Susan made a lunge for the lead in *The Snake Pit*, and this time it was De Havilland who edged her out.

Susan had reached the end of her rope by the time she was summoned along with the other pretty young starlets to decorate a national sales meeting of Paramount executives, distributors and theater owners. A dozen studio cars made the rounds of Los Angeles and environs, picking up Paramount lovelies and depositing them at the Ambassador Hotel, where they were to be introduced to the throng from the stage.

Paramount's top executives sat on folding chairs stage left and took turns at the microphone while each smiling girl mumbled something, curtsied prettily and scuttled off the stage. Susan had something different in mind. Introduced by William Le Baron, head of production, she marched center stage, planted her feet firmly in front of the footlights and said, "Wouldn't you fellows like to see me in pictures?"

Until now, they had paid little attention to what was being said. There was a smattering of applause.

"I'm the girl they send on the sleeper jumps. Several of you asked why I'm not in more Paramount pictures, and I must admit I have never heard a more interesting question."

The clapping grew louder and stronger now.

"Well, Mr. Le Baron, why *aren't* I in more pictures?"

The roof fell in with a roar of applause, and the stunned executives on the stage exchanged looks of consternation. Gutsy Susan had taken the ultimate risk by openly challenging her bosses. There was no turning back.

IV

Ready When You Are, C.B.

Hollywood was abuzz with rumors about her impending demise, but defiant Susan caught the eye of Paramount's most important director. Cecil B. De Mille had been a national institution practically since he and Sam Goldwyn made the first full-length film—*The Squaw Man*—in 1913. De Mille was still fourteen years away from his greatest epic—the 1956 remake of his 1923 biblical blockbuster *The Ten Commandments*—yet he was already the undisputed King of the Epics. *Reap the Wild Wind* was to be De Mille's seagoing answer to *Gone With the Wind*. The lead of Loxie Claiborne, feisty owner of a Key West salvage outfit in the 1880s, had already gone to Paulette Goddard—no longer a casting problem, as she had been back during the search for Scarlett O'Hara, now that she was quite unmistakably divorced from Charlie Chaplin. Loxie's chief competitors in the salvage game are the unscrupulous Raymond Massey and his younger brother, played by a callow Robert Preston. They always manage to be at the site of a wreck to claim salvage rights first—probably because they make a practice of paying off crew members to scuttle the ships for them. A thirty-ish John Wayne, in the first of his three films with Susan, portrays a young sea captain unfairly robbed of his command who seeks revenge on one of his superiors (a misleadingly effete Ray Milland) by conspiring to sink the flagship of the merchant fleet, the steam-powered Southern Cross.

If Paramount was not exactly sure of how to handle Hayward, De Mille had no difficulty seeing her as Druscilla Alston, Loxie's sweet but willful cousin. Hopelessly smitten with Preston in the film, she ignores all the warnings of friends and relatives to stay away from him. Without his knowledge she stows away in the hold of the Southern Cross—only to drown when Wayne, according to plan, rams the ship into a reef. Susan's first death scene is a classic. Gaily rummaging through a trunk filled with silks bound from Charleston to Boston, she's trying on the teal blue scarf Preston has given her when the Southern Cross smacks into the barrier and begins to sink. She is, unbeknownst to all, sealed in this watery tomb. It is not until the climax of the film, when a suitably contrite Wayne dives down to examine the wreckage and returns with Druscilla's scarf that her tragic fate becomes clear to the rest.

For Susan, *Reap the Wild Wind* was more than just a terrific part in a De Mille blockbuster; it was her chance, as she put it, to "show that son of a bitch Selznick once and for all that I'm a damn good actress." She met with De Mille in his memento-filled office at the studio and was impressed with how much he differed from Cukor, Gregory Ratoff, William Wellman and the other directors she had worked with so far. Unencumbered by any of the nervous tics that beset the others, he was a large, soft-spoken man with courtly manners and a surprisingly gentle handshake. He asked her to read a few lines of dialogue—the

Southern accent that had vexed her during the Scarlett tests three years before was no problem now—and hired her on the spot.

Susan found that the De Mille behind the desk and the De Mille behind the camera were two radically different men. On the set, he wore jodhpurs and nervously slapped his knee-high boots with a riding crop. He barked orders like a tank commander and demanded total, blind and instant obedience from cast and crew.

In Susan he had met his match. She appeared on the set for the first day's shooting outfitted in a ball gown of pastel pinks, blues and greens. Before the cameras rolled, Susan turned to the director. "Excuse me, Mr. De Mille, but do you think that . . ."

"Young lady," came the reply, "I hired you for this film because I want an actress who can think for herself."

"But, Mr. De Mille, this scene . . ."

"*Do* that and you will take a load of worry off my mind and add countless years to your own career."

Susan spun around on her heels and, without attempting to utter another word in defiance of the Great One, walked off the set. "The director kept riding me," she would recall of the incident many years later. "One day he got particularly nasty and I blew. I then bearded production chief Buddy De Sylva in his den and said, "I won't go back on that set until that man apologizes."

De Sylva called the director to his office—and he apologized. Susan had won. If she felt she needed the director's guidance for a particular scene, she did not hesitate to demand it of C.B. By the time *Reap the Wild Wind* was completed, it was De Mille—not Susan—who had thoroughly capitulated. "You are a very talented young lady," he told her the last day of filming. "And that talent will undoubtedly carry you to stardom. But if I never make another picture with you, my dear, it will be too soon."

After *Reap the Wild Wind,* Susan quietly jettisoned her agent Benny Medford and replaced him with Ned Marin. Unlike Walter Thornton, Medford took it graciously. Susan's career was gaining momentum, and she now required someone better equipped than he to fight her inevitable battles with the studios. Almost forty years later, Medford bore her no malice, freely conceding that she was one of the greatest actresses ever to light up the screen. Susan, he tried to explain dispassionately, was simply "cold as a polar bear's foot."

The switch in agents meant more—if not progressively more rewarding—work. In her first starring role, Susan again played with Paulette Goddard. This time they competed for the attentions of Fred MacMurray in George Marshall's woodsy saga *The Forest Rangers.* As overall-clad Montana ("Tana") Mason, owner of an Oregon logging mill, Susan had counted on marrying Ranger Fred until Goddard, a Manhattan socialite, bagged him literally overnight. Tana spent most of the movie trying to sabotage their marriage, at one point pushing their car off a mountain road so that she and the newlyweds spent their honeymoon shivering on a mountaintop.

The Forest Rangers gave wider exposure to Susan's not inconsiderable talents as a comedienne. Her next film, *I Married a Witch,* was also a comedy, but most of the laughs went to costars Veronica Lake and Fredric March. In this takeoff on *The House of the Seven Gables,* March was a New England gubernatorial candidate who is tormented by a witch his Puritan ancestors had burned at the stake three centuries before. Veronica Lake, as the vengeful sorceress, does everything she can to ensure that March's bride-to-be, Susan, is transformed into a first-rate shrew—a mate to make him desperately miserable for the remainder of his days. Inevitably, Lake falls in love with March and breaks the centuries-old curse that all the men in his family will have unhappy marriages. Meantime, Susan was called upon to be the very embodiment of earthly witchery.

Like all other Hollywood stars, Susan was expected during this period to make her contribution to the war effort. That same year, she played the homespun girl next door in a fifteen-minute variety short called *A Letter from Bataan*, and hammed it up in an all-star extravaganza, *Star Spangled Rhythm*.

Directed by George Marshall, *Star Spangled Rhythm* was built around the story of a Paramount switchboard operator (Betty Hutton) and guard Victor Moore as they try to convince Moore's sailor son that Dad heads the mighty studio. Hayward's contribution consisted of a blackout concerning the rubber shortage. Storming about in a barely-there negligee, she berates sugar daddy Ernest Truex for failing to give her romantic presents. The gift she most wants: a genuine, scarcer-than-hens'-teeth rubber girdle.

Even before *Star Spangled Rhythm*'s release, Susan was loaned out to Republic for *Hit Parade of 1943*, reissued some years later as *Change of Heart* after its Academy Award-nominated Harold Adamson-Jule Styne tune. This time she was a naïve songwriter who visits her cousin in New York (wiseacre Eve Arden) and winds up ghosting for handsome-but-rotten John Carroll. Hayward found her swarthy, mustachioed costar a perfectly compatible leading man off-camera as well as on. Carroll, soon to hold a commission as an Army captain, had just divorced actress Steffi Duna. The studios were delighted when Carroll and Hayward began dining at Chasen's and Romanoff's, and so was Susan. Ellen Marrener, still living with her daughters at their slightly seedy bungalow court flat, saw Carroll as the next Clark Gable and urged Susan to snare him. Carroll did not agree until he was overseas; then he wrote to tell her to have an engagement ring made.

Susan's mother had never had a diamond engagement ring, so Susan did not hesitate to pick out a brilliant-cut two-carat whopper. When Carroll got the bill, he hit the ceiling and wrote back to let his fiancée know that the purchase was out of the question. Her reply was blunt: The engagement was off; she had already paid for the ring herself. For several years, she continued to wear the bauble as a good-luck charm.

Susan was loaned out again, this time to United Artists to make another bit of wartime fluff—Edward H. Griffith's *Young and Willing*—before being offered her first really meaty dramatic role in *Adam Had Four Sons*. Based on the 1941 play be Francis Swann, entitled *Out of the Frying Pan*; *Young and Willing* was about four young actresses sharing a Greenwich Village apartment. Susan had subdued her Brooklynese to such an extent that she could convincingly portray the scrappy, Iowa-born "Queen of Corn" who operates a switchboard by day and auditions for plays at night.

Now rid of dashing Captain Carroll, Susan could concentrate on making her next project—also on loan to United Artists—count. Producer Samuel Bronston had undertaken the film biography of Jack London, and Paramount production chief Buddy De Sylva agreed that Susan was ripe for the role of London's understanding wife Charmian Kittredge. The choice had the blessing of the real Charmian, who was acting as an adviser on the Alfred Santell-directed picture. What excited Susan almost as much as the story was the actor being sought by the studio to play the lead—John Garfield.

Already the tough-guy heartthrob of millions, Garfield was also the first in a new crop of iconoclastic leading men. Susan saw in the Brooklyn Boy her male counterpart. However, Garfield's box office value was fully appreciated by Warner's, which had him under contract and now refused to share him with any other studio.

The decision not to let United Artists have temporary use of Garfield's talents spelled disaster for *Jack London*. Instead of Garfield, Santell settled for Michael O'Shea, a New York actor who, unlike Susan, had not managed to shake his thick New York patois. Susan succeeded in capturing the quiet inner strength of the beautiful Charmian, but it was not enough to bail out O'Shea. *Jack London* deservedly sank into oblivion—and with it Susan's hopes for getting her own career as a serious actress under full sail.

The dimly lit, smoky Hollywood Canteen was set up by Bette Davis as a haven for soldiers and sailors passing through Los Angeles on their way to the war in the Pacific or stationed at Army and Navy bases nearby. Here bit players and top-billed stars alike were expected to do their patriotic duty by serving coffee and doughnuts to the G.I.s and occasionally taking to the dance floor with them. One evening, a swabbie was jitterbugging with a glamorous lady several inches taller than he. "Say, you look just like Joan Crawford," he said, his feet little more than a blur. "Whatever happened to her?"

"I *am* Joan Crawford," the dignified lady replied.

"Yeah?" the sailor said, spinning her around again. "So whatever happened to ya?"

For Susan, the Canteen was more than an obligation—it was a haven from the phony Hollywood social scene where she knew she would never fit. The servicemen she met were her kind of people, and unlike many of the glacial glamour queens named Dietrich, Crawford, Stanwyck and Fontaine, Hayward had a robust, all-woman approachability that made her a star attraction where stars were in plentiful supply.

As with the other personalities on hand, Susan was introduced to the crowd at one point in the evening by the Canteen's delicately handsome emcee, Jess Barker. The first evening Susan made her appearance, he watched as she whipped out her glasses, put them on, gauged the distance to the stage and the number of steps it would take to get her there, then jammed the glasses back in her purse. He had heard much about the boisterous Susan Hayward, but here was a touch of vulnerability he had not expected.

Once she was introduced, however, there was no doubt as to who was in complete charge. Susan's rousing "Anyone here from Brooklyn?" line still ensured her the biggest ovation of the evening—barring Hedy Lamarr's occasional dispensation of kisses to swooning servicemen bound for the front.

Hayward had read as much about Barker as he had about her. He was depicted in the columns as something of a womanizer, and Susan was not anxious to be added to the long list of starlets he had been dating. He made it his business to change that. South Carolina-born Barker had wanted to be a professional baseball player, but his Ashley Wilkes good looks and a marginal acting ability landed him on the Great White Way supporting the likes of Ina Claire, Tallulah Bankhead and Lenore Ulric. A screen test directed by Susan's old pal Gregory Ratoff was sufficient to land Barker a contract with Columbia—particularly in view of the war drain on male talent being felt at the studio; Barker, because of a rapid heartbeat, was classified 4-F. Under the guidance of canny Harry Cohn, Barker's career was carefully mapped out. By putting him in a series of B— pictures and light comedies, they would slowly build Barker a loyal bobby-soxer following. This grand strategy had already lifted the pretty-faced likes of Tyrone Power and Van Johnson to stardom. Barker had already appeared in such forgettable flicks as *Good Luck, Mr. Yates, Government Girl, Cover Girl, Jam Session* and *She's a Soldier, Too* by the time he met Susan at the Hollywood Canteen.

Barker's first overtures to her were instantly rebuffed. Once he finally did get Susan to go out with him, she kept at arm's length. The first time Barker tried to kiss her, his efforts were rewarded with a stinging slap across the kisser. It was an unmistakable sign of things to come.

From the outset, Ellen Marrener disapproved of Jess Barker. He was, she warned her daughter, weak, soft and probably a gold digger. Her career would soar, Mama predicted, while his would flounder. Florence sided with Susan. Barker was handsome enough for little Susan, she shrugged. Susan could not ask for—or expect—much more. Wally, who had worked as a trainer at Santa Anita and other Southern California tracks before enlisting as a private in the Army, was sullen on the subject. He and Barker detested one another from the outset. Jess himself wasn't all that interested in marriage. He feared that wedlock would cost him his bobby-soxer fans. Nor did he welcome the added financial burden of a wife and children.

"Don't worry, Bub," Susan joked. "You'll never have to worry about supporting me. I can take care of myself, thank you."

Ellen wanted to make sure that her daughter meant it. If she was insisting on marrying Barker, Susan's mother counseled, then at least make him sign a premarital agreement that would separate his earnings from hers. Coming three decades before Jacqueline and Aristotle Onassis's prenuptial pact, the contract drawn up by Susan's lawyers was precedent-setting.

Jess had now softened his stand; he was now not so certain that his marriage would antagonize his young followers. But would he agree to the document carefully separating his income from Susan's? Since neither seemed in imminent danger of becoming a millionaire, he shrugged it off. While making preparations for the brief civil ceremony that would make them man and wife, Barker signed an official-looking piece of paper without reading it.

Although the studio would normally have passed judgment on the plans of one of its contract players, Paramount production chief Buddy De Sylva did not value Susan Hayward highly enough to care. New York-born De Sylva initially made his mark as a ukulele-strumming songwriter (*California, Here I Come*; *April Showers*; and—ironically—*If You Knew Susie*). In 1921 he founded Capitol Records and by the late 1930s he had ridden the wave of movie musicals to Hollywood. By 1940, De Sylva was executive vice-president in charge of production for Paramount, and as such wielded as much power as any Louis B. Mayer, Harry Cohn or David O. Selznick.

An arrogant, street-wise product of Tin Pan Alley, he saw too much of Susan in himself to be overly fond of her. So it came as quite a surprise when, shortly before she traipsed to the altar with Barker, she was summoned by De Sylva and informed that she would be loaned out to an independent producer to star in the topflight melodrama *Dark Waters*. She signed on the dotted line and was told the production would begin in two weeks.

Susan dashed home to Mama and Florence with the news. "This is it!" she excitedly proclaimed to Ellen that night, "All I needed was one good role. I'll show 'em now." She glared out the dirty window of their shabby bungalow. She touched the worn couch with the broken spring, and frowned at the splintering chairs that were forever causing runs in her precious nylons.

"We'll get out of this dump just as soon as this picture is previewed," Susan declared. "I promise."

Two days later, Susan stepped into the Paramount commissary for a cup of coffee and glanced through the trades. The article on the front page of *Variety* began, "Merle Oberon was signed yesterday to star in *Dark Waters*." Susan rushed to De Sylva's office, but his secretary said he would see her later. "It's unethical," she screamed. "It's illegal!"

"I'm sorry, Miss Hayward. Mr. De Sylva is not available right now. If you'd like to make an appointment . . ."

"Make an appointment? Don't worry, I'll be back this afternoon, and the almighty Mr. De Sylva had better be here to explain this!"

By the time she returned to De Sylva's office, Susan had gotten the news from the studio grapevine that The Man wanted to teach her some sort of lesson. She had been rude and uncooperative to directors and fellow actors, it was rumored—so much so that the rest of the leading ladies on the lot still refused to work with her. This might, De Sylva reasoned, constitute a much-needed lesson in humility.

When she finally got to see him, Susan, dressed in a bright yellow shirtwaist and nervously twisting the "lucky" ring she originally intended to be a gift from John Carroll, pleaded with De Sylva to change his mind. "I'm only a kid who wants a break," she sobbed. "Won't the studio back me up in this deal?"

De Sylva shook his head. "You must learn to cooperate," he said, his voice devoid of any emotion. "Maybe this will teach you."

"But I never meant to be rude or snippy," she assured him, pulling a pair of glasses from her purse. "See—I'm just nearsighted. People think I'm snubbing them when I just can't see them! Please don't do this cruel thing to me!"

De Sylva was unmoved. "You're young, Susan," he said, smiling. "There'll be other chances. And now, if you please, that's all."

That night at the Marreners' seedy apartment, Susan did the one thing she had not done since she arrived in Hollywood—she broke down and cried.

Tears soon yielded to hate. "One of these days, I'll hurt that man the way he's hurt me," she vowed.

Susan's mother listened patiently, knitting needles laying like crossed swords on the arm of her red tufted chair. "Your father and I didn't agree on very much, dear," she said softly. "But he always said the harder you're hit the higher you'll bounce. Remember, after your accident, when the doctors said you'd never walk again? This man De Sylva is doing you a favor. Now you'll be a top star—not because somebody handed it to you, but because you did it all by yourself. You'll be on top when he is on the bottom."

Ellen was right, but it would take several years before it became clear just how accurate her prediction was.

When she wasn't dating Barker at Perino's or Chasen's, Susan reserved two nights a week for home, washing her hair in the bathroom basin, putting on her favorite pink pajamas and settling in the living room to read best sellers, sketch, paint or play her secondhand organ. Food was her reigning passion. After packing away a huge meal, Susan would frequently devour a pound of Sees chocolates—her favorite—then whip up a batch of homemade french fries before going to bed.

On the town, Susan usually wore a suit in one of four colors—beige, black, white or brown—and one of two hats, both black and dating from her Warner glamour girl period. As her days as a single woman drew to a close, Susan predicted to interviewer Eleanor Harris that she would settle in a ranch house, "with horses leaning in the windows, copper pans on the walls, comfortable chairs and a fireplace. Two children will go with the house, as well as a devoted husband and plenty of money."

Susan's dreams were all to be realized—but not before a decade of triumph, turmoil and tragedy.

JESS

"You're real small with your
shoes off."
—Robert Mitchum

"You're real small with your
shoes *on*."
—Susan Hayward

* * *

"I'd like it better if it
was *Bathsheba and David*."
—Susan

* * *

"Men! I'd like to fry 'em
all in deep fat."
—Susan

V

A Star Is Born

Susan Hayward married Jess Barker on the morning of July 23, 1944, in a brief double-ring ceremony at Los Angeles' St. Thomas Episcopal Church attended only by her nervous studio press agents, Henry Rogers and Jean Pettebone. They smiled for photographers at the Canteen, where they met, then headed for a six-day honeymoon in San Francisco. Susan then returned to the set of *The Fighting Seabees* and Jess finished up his tiny part as a stage door gigolo in Rita Hayworth's *Cover Girl.* For the moment, at least, neither was willing to give up their respective apartments; they spent most of their time in his, though on hot nights they slept in hers because it was cooler. Nor did Susan hesitate to flee home to Mother when the Barkers' frequent arguments got out of hand.

During their decade-long marriage, Susan starred in twenty-three feature films. Jess played minor parts in nineteen. On the day of her wedding, she received her customary $1,700 weekly paycheck from Paramount. He was between jobs. This *Star Is Born* role reversal did not sit well with Susan. Seven weeks after the wedding, a dozen guests at a Beverly Hills party were drawn to the window by a shouting match on the front lawn. Susan and Jess stood screaming insults at each other, unconcerned that they were now the main entertainment of the evening. When the dust had settled, Susan stormed home to Mother.

It might have been the final break, had Susan not learned two weeks later that she was pregnant. They reconciled warmly, and both seemed genuinely interested in making a go of their marriage and careers. Anticipating the responsibilities of fatherhood, Jess attacked his career with renewed zeal. He needled his agent to get him work, pressed at every opportunity to test for a part and even stayed home evenings answering his own fan mail. Nevertheless, Jess's original fears about the effects of marriage on his matinee idol image proved justified. Barely five months after the nuptials, just before Christmas, Jess was told by Harry Cohn that his contract with Columbia had been officially terminated.

Susan was predictably understanding—on the surface. "You're a damn good actor, Jess," she reassured him. "They'll be beating down your door with good parts now that you're free. Believe me, darling. I've been there—I know." They made love that night, then she reached over to set the alarm for her 6 A.M. call at the studio.

Although she gave no outward sign of it, Susan sensed a disturbing change in Jess's personality. After he received the news of her pregnancy, he had pursued his work with renewed vigor. Now that he had been dropped by Columbia, he seemed all too willing to accept defeat. She knew he was not a dynamic personality; it was Jess's quiet, Southern gentleman air of confidence that had attracted her to him. But she worried that her success would now undermine his already shaky sense of self-worth.

She had reason for concern. *And Now Tomorrow*, her last picture while under contract to Paramount, was also one of her most popular movies at the studio. A potboiler

Susan at twenty—sweet and sultry. CREDIT: MOVIE STAR NEWS

The pristine love interest in *Beau Geste*, with Robert Preston, Ray Milland, Heather Thatcher, J. Carrol Naish and Gary Cooper. CREDIT: MOVIE STAR NEWS

Leading on killer Albert Dekker in *Among the Living*.

As Johnny Downs's nympho wife, Susan was pitted against Ingrid Bergman in the critically acclaimed *Adam Had Four Sons*.

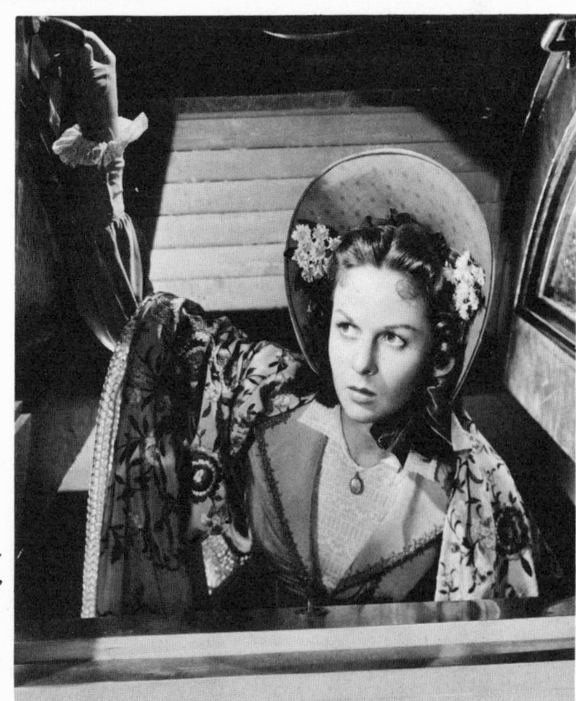

tragic stowaway in Cecil B. e Mille's seagoing GWTW, *ap the Wild Wind*.

Fredric March's vexatious but stunning bride in *I Married A Witch*. CREDIT: THE MEMORY SHOP, INC.

With John Wayne in one of their three films together, *The Fighting Seabees*. The Duke was her favorite screen lover. CREDIT: THE MEMORY SHOP, INC.

Mr. and Mrs. Jeff Barker.

Smash-up: The Story of a Woman. The 1947 Walter Wanger film marked a turning point in Susan Hayward's career. It was her first Oscar nomination.
CREDIT: THE MEMORY SHOP, INC.

Smash-up.

A sober Susan with Lee Bowman and Eddie Albert before she hits the bottle.

A dewy-eyed wartime good-bye for doomed lover Dana Andrews in *My Foolish Heart*.

Greg gets ready to hike the ball to Tim and Mom. CREDIT: PICTORIAL PARADE

based on the best-selling novel by Rachel Field, *And Now Tomorrow* marked Alan Ladd's return to the silver screen after a year-long hitch in the Army Air Force—a fact that ensured a wide audience. Once again the villain, a conniving Susan steals Barry Sullivan away from her deaf sister (Loretta Young). Eventually, Young regains her hearing and falls in love with the Polish doctor (Ladd) who brings this medical miracle about. Meantime, Susan has plenty of opportunities to vamp, scheme and blow cigarette smoke in her sister's face. Surprised by the strong reaction to Hayward's performance at preview showings, De Sylva began to have doubts about his treatment of her. Young was blasted by critics, as was the heretofore unassailable Ladd. Hayward emerged relatively unscathed.

Hayward's *Fighting Seabees* was a box office smash, giving her the widest visibility she had enjoyed since *Reap the Wild Wind.* As a hustling war correspondent for the "Trans-Pacific News Service," she jilts her Navy officer boyfriend (Barker look-alike Dennis O'Keefe) for rough-hewn Seabee "Wedge" Donovan (again, Duke Wayne) while covering the building of military installations on a Pacific Island. O'Keefe introduces the two, and it's hate at first sight. "Your friend," she tells O'Keefe after Wayne starts a fight, "is an ape with a hair-trigger temper." Later, she allows that "when he's nice, he's very very nice—and when he's not he's stinkin'." At one point, she confronts Wayne about his general orneriness: "Don't you have something under that tough hide of yours besides cylinders and carburetor?" It all leads to true love, of course, and Susan barely has time to confront the dilemma of being in love with both Wayne and O'Keefe before she is shot by a Japanese sniper while running across a beach. She recovers, though, just in time to see Wayne bite the dust defending the island. Directed by Edward Ludwig and boasting the biggest budget of any Republic picture to date, *The Fighting Seabees* showed Susan at her best—nervy, intelligent, passionate and beautiful—even though the picture was shot in black-and-white and she never got out of her drab war correspondent's uniform.

As rousing a bit of anti-Japanese propaganda as Hollywood ever produced, *The Fighting Seabees* was one of 1944's top grossers. More importantly for Susan, reviewers focused on her rather than on either of her male costars. "Susan and Seabees Glorified," blared the headline in the New York *Mirror*. "Full Steam A-Hayward!"

Before taking a year off to start her new family, Susan was again loaned out to United Artists—this time to tackle the demanding part of a New York society girl toying with the affections of a gritty ship's stoker (William Bendix) in Eugene O'Neill's complicated social commentary *The Hairy Ape*. For all its pretense, *The Hairy Ape* merely offered Susan yet another opportunity, as *Time* put it, to prove herself as "Hollywood's ablest bitch-player."

On February 19, 1945, Jess and Susan were watching a midnight motion picture when she began having labor pains. A bewildered Jess rushed Susan to St. John's Hospital in Santa Monica, where she gave birth prematurely to twin boys: Timothy (4 pounds, 12 ounces) and Gregory (named after old pal Gregory Ratoff) at 4 pounds 14 ounces. "I was ready for *one*," Susan told reporters the day after the delivery, "and now I'm going to have a terrible time getting enough diapers and quilted pads." The infants were placed by attending doctor Blake H. Watson in incubators, and remained there for a week before returning to the Barkers' new rented house in Bel Air with their proud parents. For the next four months Susan stayed home with Jess and tended the children. The difference was that she did it by choice, he did not. While Jess tested for parts that never came, the family lived off the money Susan had cagily set aside. It was not long before Susan convinced herself that she was being taken advantage of. Jess, she decided, was no different from that kid back in Brooklyn who was after her acting scholarship, or the man who jilted her in Canada or John Carroll. She wasted no time in confronting Jess with it.

Over the next year, the Barkers would be evicted from four different residences in the Los Angeles area. Their frequent shouting matches—punctuated by the occasional slamming of a door and crashing of crystal—were a major factor, but Susan managed to convince the press that the Barkers were being victimized by children-hating landlords and the postwar black market in housing. A November 2, 1946, article in the Los Angeles *Examiner* discussed the Barkers' plight under the headline SUSAN HAYWARD HOMELESS: BLASTS BLACK MARKET HOUSING. The photograph accompanying the story showed Jess and Susan perched atop suitcases with the twins as they were preparing to leave their rented home on Chevy Chase Drive in Beverly Hills—Eviction No. 2. As if to spotlight the difference in their acting talents, Jess is shown grinning incongruously while Susan has the heart-tugging, tearful look of a refugee clutching her homeless children. The L.A. *Examiner* went on:

> Screen Actress Susan Hayward, her husband, actor Jess Barker and their 20-month-old twins, Timothy and Gregory were on the move again—this time after their six months' tenure at 1712 Chevy Chase Drive, Beverly Hills, was up.
>
> "We're refugees from the black market," Miss Hayward said bitterly. "Every time we try to rent a place there's somebody's hand sticking under the table waiting for a sneak bonus, or else! And it's even worse

> when you want to buy a house. The prices don't just outrage you. They leave you limp."
>
> "We'd rather go live on some studio lot than be a party to such jet black dealings," Barker added.
>
> The film couple have no complaint against their landlord, Henry Barker (no relation). After they were forced out of a home in Bel Air, landlord Barker offered them his Beverly Hills home, but for six months only. Now he needed it himself.
>
> And they almost had another home yesterday morning. But it carried a "No Children" restriction. "I could have cried," the actress said. "You did," her husband announced.
>
> For the time being the family will live in one room at a Santa Monica hotel.
>
> Until, they said, "some reason returns to American life."

Their movable feast notwithstanding, Susan and Jess managed to convey to the Hollywood press an image of domestic tranquillity. No harridan in real life, Susan appeared a loving wife and mother, Jess the handsome head of a thriving young household. While still at the house in Bel Air, Susan kept up the charade.

When one reporter came to interview her, Susan pulled down a volume of Kipling from a shelf and opened to a dog-eared page. "Down to Gehenna, or up to the throne," she read aloud, "he travels fastest—who travels alone!" Susan closed the book and told the gullible interviewer, "The man who wrote those lines about traveling alone certainly wasn't talking about me!"

Jess, stoking the fireplace in their dark-paneled library, interrupted. "She wants you to ask about our twins. Ask her about the twins!"

"Jess will not bring up the subject of the twins," sighed Susan. "He doesn't even carry pictures of them in his wallet. But he does bring people to see them. Barkeepers and prizefighters, and bookies from the racetrack, and last Christmas he even brought a traffic cop."

"Somebody has to attend to the twins' double-billing," shrugged Jess. "That's where I come in."

The saccharine exchange continued. "The average wife," Susan explained to her wide-eyed guest, "can pour a leisurely cup of coffee for her husband and send him off to work with a mental picture of her gingham-clad prettiness as she waves good-bye. When I've poured Jess's second cup of coffee, I fly right into my own hat and coat—and follow him down the street!"

"The average husband," Jess added, "gets away with that old bromide, 'Don't bother your pretty head about business, dear; just leave it all to me!' I couldn't work that one with Susan; not after she's spent a dizzy day on the set, helping me watch things go wrong."

On the headboard of their double bed perched the two ceramic lovebirds that had topped their wedding cake. Symbolically, they would crumble to bits within two years and be relegated to a cardboard box in the bedroom closet. The Barkers were also eager to point out to practically anyone that they wore matching gold wedding rings, each inscribed with the other's name. In fact, the beaming couple eagerly pointed out, her first gift to him had been a pair of cuff links with his initials on one side and hers on the other. Jess's nicknames for Susan had obviously been carefully chosen and were used to exquisite effect as a public relations ploy. There was the pedestrian "Susie" (*never* Sue), "Pinky" (for her coloring) and "Francie" (after *A Tree Grows in Brooklyn*'s plucky heroine Francie Nolan). Susan had no nicknames for Jess.

The twins were also grist for the publicity mill. The "Barker Brothers," as Susan called them, began battling as soon as Greg realized that Tim was the first to walk. But it was blond-haired Tim who later proved himself the mischievous half of the Barker "double bill." To separate him from his more pacific redheaded brother, the Barkers put three playpens in the upstairs nursery—one for Tim, one for Greg and one in between.

In describing this idyllic family life, Susan even felt confident enough to joke about Jess's function as the family shopper. "He even gets butter," she condescended. "Of course, I'll admit my awe of him abated somewhat when I accidentally discovered he'd been giving the girls at the grocery counter an occasional bottle of Chanel No. 5!"

Behind the facade, the Barker household was turned upside down. Jess and Susan started out driving to work each morning in the same car—until it became painfully evident that it was only Susan who had somewhere to go. While Susan got up at dawn, Jess rolled over and went back to sleep—often not rising until noon. Susan's brother Wally, sister Florence and mother Ellen were all warned repeatedly not to disturb the slumbering Jess when they visited—an admonition that did not sit well with any of the Marrener clan. Wally would recall for decades the afternoon he called his younger sister and asked to borrow her spiffy white Cadillac convertible for a date. When he arrived to pick up the keys—they had been left for him atop the piano—only Jess and the boys were home. Barker told Wally that he could not use the car today because he would be using it. After an unpleasant exchange Wally simply reminded Jess that it was Susan's car to lend, grabbed the keys and drove off. Barker fumed.

None was more critical of Barker than Ellen, and they clashed violently and often. Susan shut her ears to her mother's constant plea that she leave Barker. What particularly irked Ellen, as it soon came to disturb Susan, was the simple fact that Jess did not seem to mind this emasculating relationship. They were wrong; Barker merely internalized his frustration. Jess did the family marketing, but it was Susan who picked up the tab. Bills arrived in his name, and were piled on the dining room table for Susan to pay. Whatever cash Jess needed also came from Susan. Eventually, Barker would swear in court that he found it "very embarrassing for bills to come into my house in my name and be paid by her." But for now—until he could get his career moving again—Jess was willing to take what Susan seemed willing to give.

Susan's contract with Paramount expired, like World War II, by 1945. No love was lost between the star and Buddy De Sylva, who placed her on probation more than once for refusing to cut her hair. De Sylva himself, however, was only weeks away from being fired as the studio's production chief. Unlike De Sylva, Susan was much in demand after leaving Paramount. Director Harold Clurman and RKO brought Susan to the screen in her first top-billed role (above *Watch on the Rhine* Oscar-winner Paul Lukas) in *Deadline at Dawn*. A mystery-melodrama scripted by Clifford Odets, *Deadline* had hard-boiled dance-hall girl Hayward helping a sailor (Bill Williams) who has just six hours to prove that he did not murder a certain female (Lola Lane). Lukas, portraying a grandfatherly cabbie, is eventually unveiled as the killer—but not before Susan delivered what the New York *Times*'s Bosley Crowther described as a "spirited" performance as a beguiling "night moth." Clurman was impressed by Hayward's consummate professionalism, and by her fire. When the censors objected to the low-cut dress she wore in *Deadline at Dawn*, she flashed, "We've got to have something for the folks in the balcony!" The cleavage remained. Most of the other major critics agreed with Crowther: *Deadline at Dawn* was a gritty, unrelenting look at the denizens of Manhattan's sordid side. Susan, one critic wrote many years later, was far and away the best thing in the movie—"pure Brooklyn and pure Hollywood."

Deadline presaged the dawn of a new era for Susan, but she was not inclined to hasten its arrival. She could afford to be choosey. The twins were occupation enough as she sat back and waited for the offers to pour in. Jess, meanwhile, saw a way out for himself. Independent producer Walter Wanger, now working for Universal, was out to top his 1939 classic *Stagecoach* with another Western by the same author. *Canyon Passage* was the splashy technicolor tale of frontier spitfire Lucy Overmire, torn between an unscrupulous banker and an idealistic young entrepreneur. Brian Donlevy was deemed suitably unctuous to play the part of the banker, and director Jacques Tourneur had corraled the likes of gravel-voiced Andy Devine and piano-plunkin' composer Hoagy Carmichael for character support. (Carmichael, in fact, would provide the most memorable moment in the picture by singing his own Oscar-nominated composition, *Ole Buttermilk Sky*.) The part of the idealistic young businessman had not yet been cast, however, and Jess was approached to test for the part.

Susan was elated. At last Jess had a job—well, at least a chance for one. Now they might be able to have something approaching a normal marriage, she thought—a marriage where the man was not cowed by his wife's success. When he received the *Canyon Passage* script, Jess was told in passing that the female lead was also vacant. It did not take long for him to realize that Susan was perfect for the role of Lucy Overmire. Susan was at first reluctant to read the script—after all, it was *his* opportunity—but after five straight hours of coaxing by Jess, she relented. A fine yarn, agreed—perfectly suited for Jess—but not for her. Susan resisted even more ferociously her husband's invitation to accompany him on his screen test for *Canyon Passage.* Once again, Jess prevailed. After Jess had been tested, director Tourneur asked if Susan, who was sitting on the sidelines, might like to do a test for the part of Lucy—as long as she was there. Susan demurred.

"Nope," she said, shaking her head. "Jess just asked me to come along and watch while he did his test. I'm just along for the ride."

Jess, confident that he had the male lead sewed up, saw no reason why his wife couldn't go through the motions. Susan, however, was incapable of doing anything but a consummately professional job. After a solid hour of cajoling, she caved in and did the test.

Two weeks had passed before the Barkers got the call at home. Wanger had decided on Dana Andrews for the male lead instead of Jess—and Susan to play opposite him! Susan had feared this might happen, and weighed the cost of accepting the offer against what devastating impact it might have on her already tumultuous marriage. It was while she was making this tough decision that Susan encountered a ghost from the past. The man who had only six years before tried to run her out of town—David O. Selznick—now wanted to see her about the possibility of inking a multi-picture contract. Susan savored the notion of serving the mogul a hefty slice of humble pie, and agreed to meet him at 1 P.M. sharp. Susan was there at 12:58.

It was 2:25 P.M. before Selznick's secretary walked into the beige-walled reception room to tell Hayward that the Boss was finally ready to see her. Keeping people waiting was a standard ploy of Selznick's. Susan took a final puff on a lipstick-stained Chesterfield, snubbed it out in an ashtray and drew herself up to her full 5 feet 3 inches. She walked into Selznick's office and, without bothering to sit, fixed him with a level gaze.

Selznick smiled insincerely and stood to shake her hand. "Sorry to keep you waiting . . ."

"I've been sitting out there for an hour and a half," she said curtly.

"Well, I said I was . . ."

"So if you want to see me, I'll be over at Universal making a movie for Walter Wanger. I can go in and see him and talk to him whenever I like." With that, she turned on her heels and walked toward the door.

"But I have a contract here for you to sign," said the newly chastened Selznick, pointing to a piece of legal-looking paper on his desk.

"You can take that paper," she said in her most aristocratic tone, "and stick it up your ass." Leaving a stunned Selznick behind, Susan headed straight for Universal and told Wanger she wanted to do *Canyon Passage*—regardless of the blow to Jess's pride and the consequences for their marriage. Before she left Wanger's office, he had signed her to a personal seven-year contract at $100,000 a year.

Walter Wanger and Susan hit it off instantly, though their background couldn't have been more dissimilar. White-maned, craggily handsome and with a Californian's weakness for loud clothing, he was born Walter Feuchtwanger in San Francisco, the son of a wealthy overalls manufacturer. After graduating from Dartmouth, he went to England for the purpose of enrolling in Oxford but wound up instead doing propaganda work for the Yanks during World War I. Impressed by the persuasive power of film, he took over motion picture production for Jesse Lasky's Famous Players Studio in 1919, and when Famous Players became Paramount he made Hollywood history by launching Rudolph Valentino in *The Sheik*.

Over the next four decades he jumped from Paramount to MGM to Columbia back to Paramount and on to United Artists and Universal. Along the way, he produced Garbo's *Queen Christina*, *Stagecoach*, the first technicolor Western (*Trail of the Lonesome Pine*) and Ingrid Bergman's *Indiscreet*. He had discovered Hedy Lamarr, and proved instrumental in the careers of Clara Bow, Claudette Colbert, Henry Fonda (whom he signed while the fresh-from-Omaha actor was taking a shower at his hotel), Charles Boyer, Madeleine Carroll, Miriam Hopkins, Kay Francis and the Marx Brothers. He would go on to produce such classics (of a sort) as *The Invasion of the Body Snatchers* and *Cleopatra* (originally intended by Wanger as a vehicle for Susan, not Elizabeth Taylor) and, of course, several of Susan's greatest films.

Once he laid eyes on Susan, Wanger was determined to harness the star power of this diminutive dynamo. Before he could do that in *Canyon Passage*, Wanger cannily realized the distraction of Jess's unemployment needed to be removed. The year before, Wanger had joined with his wife Joan Bennett and director Fritz Lang to form Diana Productions. The company's first production was to be *Scarlet Street*, starring Bennett and Edward G. Robinson. Wanger found a modest part in *Scarlet Street* for Jess, and Susan was relieved of her guilt feelings—for the moment at least.

Wanger was the first to realize that *Canyon Passage*, though a commercial and critical success, was not much of a challenge for his new star. So he searched for months to come up with the vehicle that would make proper use of Susan's talents. Wanger found it in *Smash-Up: The Story of a Woman*. Based on an original *New Yorker* magazine story by Frank Cavett and Algonquin Round Table wit Dorothy Parker, *Smash-Up* dealt with female alcoholism in much the same way *Lost Weekend*, starring Ray Milland in his Oscar-winning performance, had portrayed a male boozer only two years before. Hayward seemed almost assured of copping one the first time out as a nominee—she attacked the complex, sympathetic part of Angie Evans (the film's original title) as she had approached no other role in her career.

Angie is a successful nightclub singer who gives it all up to marry a heartthrobbing crooner (Lee Bowman) and in lonely desperation soon turns to the bottle. In the end, she comes perilously close to destroying herself and her family. There were many choice scenes to showcase Susan's penchant for gritty realism on the screen. In one episode, a soused Angie tries to get out of her dress and winds up stumbling around the bedroom with it stuck over her head. In another she sits numbly staring at her hands, wondering aloud why nobody takes her seriously anymore. The most shocking and memorable scene comes when Angie, drunk as usual, drops a cigarette and sets her house on fire—almost incinerating her small daughter in the process. Angie manages to rescue the little girl by fighting the flames with her own body, but the authorities take the child away from her anyway.

To prepare herself for her most difficult role to date, Susan immersed herself in the murky mental underworld of the alcoholic. She fast became an expert on the subject. More than any other actress, she would be linked in the minds of moviegoers with booze-bedeviled women; three of her five Academy Award nominations would be for just such gut-wrenching portrayals. The connection would eventually reach beyond Susan's screen image into her private life, but for now she was no more than a moderate social drinker.

Susan's first encounter with demon rum had occurred

when she was fourteen. "My father decided that I was beginning to ask too many questions about what went on in the Brooklyn saloons. So one day he came home from work on the IRT subway with a bottle of whiskey and made me sit down in the kitchen and drink it. Naturally, I got sick as you can get. Then he said, 'Now you know how it is.' "

Susan's research for *Smash-Up* included a trip to the L. A. County Library, a visit to a local stand-up-and-tell-all meeting of Alcoholics Anonymous, a personal study of drunks on both ends of the social scale and a drinking spree of her own. The results of the last experiment were predictably catastrophic: Susan spent an entire evening in the bathroom on her hands and knees.

Yet Susan knew from the outset that *Smash-Up* was more than a melodrama. It was a story with a valid social message. Once she began to seriously study the statistics, the actress was shocked to discover that, of the more than three million hardcore alcoholics in the country in 1947, at least one out of every six was a woman—and that proportion was growing steadily. "One of the reasons that I jumped at the chance to play the young wife in *Smash-Up*," she explained, "is that the movie deals with a serious social problem. More and more women were seeking careers, and the truth is that they can do almost anything as good as a man. But when these girls marry, some husbands treat them like they were something that came with the apartment. They shut the wives out of their own lives just like Lee Bowman does to me in the movie. Then they get enraged if the wife feels so insecure that she drinks. I've seen it happen to my own friends."

This "social problem" had hit a lot closer to home than that. Susan's sister, already married to the first of several husbands, was rumored to be having serious troubles of her own—troubles that would eventually leave her destitute. Susan looked elsewhere for her laboratory, however. With Jess along as guide and protector, Susan trolled sawdust-on-the-floor dives all over Los Angeles and environs. "It's a hard world," said Susan, "and a saloon is the best place to watch people trying to forget it. I borrowed a few mannerisms from a drunk little waitress I watched in one waterfront place. She was awfully cute and all the sailors kept bothering her, and she kept getting tighter and ignoring them. That's men again. They never let a woman forget she is a woman."

Smash-Up's Angie, however, was not at the lower end of the social scale. So by way of scrutinizing affluent alkies, Susan began accepting the cocktail party invitations she had for years rejected out of hand. The high rate of alcoholics among women in this sector of society was no more difficult to explain.

"Take that café society bunch in New York," Susan told Wanger. "The only way an intelligent woman can stand an evening with those phonies is to get stiff. They live in an unreal world that only alcohol can make sufferable." It was easy to see where Susan's sympathies lay. "In *Smash-Up* I have a rich husband who can give me everything I want and pay the doctor bills. But suppose I was the girl who sings in a honky-tonk? Who would pay her bills if drink got the best of her?"

From the time the shooting started on May 27 until it ended September 3, 1946, Susan worked eight hours a day, seven days a week. The experience was perhaps the most satisfying of her career. Production went smoothly, the actors were talented and cooperative, the crew professional. Most importantly, Susan for once had complete faith in her director, Stuart Heisler. The result was a portrait of alcohol-induced misery so convincing that Mrs.

Marty Mann, then head of the National Committee for Education against Alcoholism, exclaimed, "If I hadn't been informed differently, I'd swear Susan was an alcoholic."

Mrs. Mann was not the only one. "If they don't sober me up in my next movie," joked Susan, "I'll just have to paraphrase Thomas Wolfe and say, 'I can't go home again' —not to Brooklyn, anyway. Ever since I played that oversexed vamp in *Adam Had Four Sons*, my aunts have been uneasy about me." She also complained, tongue firmly planted in cheek, that she was never allowed to do a hangover scene where she could look "beautiful and realistic" like Ingrid Bergman. "Me, I just look realistic." When she returned from a day's shooting, Susan was greeted at the door by little Timothy. "Hello, stinker Mommie!" he lisped.

The reaction to Susan's performance in *Smash-Up* surprised even Susan. It was the turning point in her career—the first time she could feel she had actually been accepted by her peers. *Smash-Up* brought her the first of her Academy Award nominations, and though Susan was a long shot, this was one party she would not miss. She attended the presentation ceremonies on Jess's arm, and reacted with polite applause when it was announced from the podium that sentimental favorite Loretta Young had won the award for *The Farmer's Daughter*. It was enough to have been nominated, Susan thought—for now.

The feeling of goodwill and cooperation that prevailed on the set of *Smash-Up* was good for one more Susan Hayward picture. She was loaned to RKO for a suspense yarn entitled *They Won't Believe Me*, in which Robert Young is a rat accused—unjustly in this case—of murdering Hayward. Critics like James Agee praised Susan for "proficiently selling her special brand of sexiness," but the public wouldn't believe Young as a cold-blooded heel. Moviegoers stayed away in droves. It was another watershed for Susan. She announced that, from now on, she would pose for no more cheesecake stills to promote pictures.

Even before the disappointing box office receipts for *They Won't Believe Me* were in, Susan was in a lousy mood. She was filming *The Lost Moment* for Wanger, a moody psychological drama based on Henry James's novella *The Aspern Papers*. Hayward was cast as the schizophrenic Tina Bordereau, firm-handed mistress of a Venetian palazzo who at night becomes the lover of a long-dead poet—a lushly tressed apparition floating from candlelit room to candlelit room. Robert Cummings, an American publisher looking for the papers of the deceased poet, becomes a boarder at the Hayward house and eventually solves the puzzle of Susan's bizarre behavior.

No clash between actress and director would be bloodier than between Susan and her director on *The Lost Moment*, veteran stage actor Martin Gabel. Coming off several Broadway triumphs, the mellifluous-voiced bantam had taken on *Lost Moment* as his first directorial effort. Wanger gave Gabel free reign, and that meant license to use some of the theatrical devices he had found indispensable in the days before Lee Strasberg and Method. Susan was no stranger to such gimmicks. To work up the proper degree of rage for a particular scene, she would often retreat to her trailer or dressing room and pound on the door or stamp on the floor before emerging to go before the cameras in the required frame of mind.

Still, she had not bargained for Gabel. Appearing on the set in costume and ready for work—punctual as always—Susan greeted cast and crew as she had routinely done. Grips and costars alike merely ignored her. Putting on her glasses, she spotted cinematographer Hal Mohr chatting with a crew member and waved. She was certain he had seen her, but he turned away without a flicker of recognition. Even costar Agnes Moorehead, cast as Hayward's 105-year-old aunt, failed to return a nod. Susan, who still spent most breaks listening to records or reading in her dressing room, was not secure enough to handle this rejection. Why was she again being treated like a social pariah? Had she done something in her nearsighted haze to alienate everyone working on *The Lost Moment?* Gabel had said nothing. In fact, he seemed pleased with the way things were going. At home, Jess reassured her that there was nothing to it, adding that such rejection was all a figment of her overactive and paranoia-prone imagination.

Susan was not prepared to accept that explanation. After two weeks of shooting, she finally cornered a grip and demanded to know why she was being treated "like the Invisible Woman." Under Susan's hot glare, there was no way of evading the issue. A few yards away, Gabel was standing on the set, giving instructions to Moorehead. So as not to be overheard, the grip took Susan's arm and pulled her behind a boom. Gabel, he told her in hushed tones, had instructed that no one—not even members of the cast and crew—speak to her. Why? So she could maintain the mood necessary for a convincing portrayal of schizophrenia. Susan's nostrils flared. The grip watched as she walked briskly to the set, picked up a white ceramic lamp and crashed it over Gabel's head. A quarter of a century later, she told writer Don Lee Keith: "To this day I've never felt sorry. Well, it was a disastrous film. As miserable a failure as you've ever seen. Their name for it may have been *The Lost Moment*, but after I saw it I called it *The Lost Hour and a Half*." On October 16, 1947, she wrote Bob Emslie back in Brooklyn: "I don't particularly advise your patronage of *The Lost Moment*. But if you have nowhere else to sleep . . . Bad and utterly stupid direction that spoiled what might have been one of the most excellent pictures of its kind. I was miserable all thru [sic] it." But, she went on, "I think you will like a picture called *Tap Roots*, which is in technicolor and is the kind that you can take the kids to see."

If *The Lost Moment* was a complete fiasco, *Tap Roots* at the very least gave Susan the chance to create the role of a Scarlett type (in this case named Morna Dabney) in a sweeping civil war saga. That same year, Susan cut her hair short for the first time to star opposite Robert Montgomery in the backstage tale of an ambitious producer, *The Saxon Charm.*

The film, dealing with theatrical egos and the harsh realities of stardom, focused Susan's attention on her own problem. At her mother's urging, Susan demanded to know from Jess why he was not trying harder to find work. As always, these confrontations produced no light but intense heat. Without Jess's knowledge, on September 30, 1947, Susan asked her lawyers to file for divorce on her behalf. The news stunned the film world. Hadn't the Barkers been the happiest, tightest, most scandal-free couple in Hollywood? Insiders knew better. After being sent by the courts to a marriage counselor, however, Jess promised to try harder and Susan relented. She withdrew her divorce action on November 26—barely 51 days after she had mustered the strength to file it. It would be only a matter of time before Susan again took the initiative. On the road to solving her own domestic dilemma, she was once again detoured by her career.

Wanger had run into serious financial difficulties by the fall of 1947, and even before cameras started to roll on *Tulsa*, the last film Hayward was to do while under contract to Wanger, he was desperately searching for cash. Hayward was pressuring him to buy new properties for her, especially a script about a woman committed to an insane asylum, called *The Snake Pit.* Twentieth Century-Fox chief Darryl Zanuck decided that, instead, the part should go to Olivia De Havilland. No one could have done a better job with the role, but Zanuck was nonetheless eager to add the up-and-coming Hayward to his stable of sirens. Zanuck offered the beleaguered Wanger a way out: he could rid himself of his costliest asset ("If she'd had her way I would have owned more books than the New York Public Library," he once complained) and pocket $200,000 in the bargain—merely by selling the remainder of Susan's contract to Twentieth. Wanger reluctantly agreed, provided that Susan receive a salary commensurate with her box office potential—a then-staggering $200,000 per year.

Before she consented to the deal, Susan headed straight for the lavish Beverly Hills home of noted astrologer Carroll Righter. Since he had begun advising Marlene Dietrich in the mid-1930s, tall, aristocratic-looking Righter was undisputed star-reader of the stars. He was impressed by the volatile, vital Susan. Susan was, he determined after their first meeting, more emotional than the average Cancer—particularly now that there was a full moon. She knew she had to be exceptionally cautious at this crossroad. But Zanuck was clamoring for a decision. Should she go ahead and sign the seven-year contract or take a juicy part that was being dangled in front of her by another studio? Righter sat Susan down on the pale yellow settee in his living room and told her that her chart (for which he charged one hundred dollars) showed that she was now at a high point in her career, but that it would be followed by a dip. To sustain herself through that low period, she should sign the long-term contract. The optimum time for the signing: 3:23 A.M. Susan went home and set the alarm.

The contract and a ballpoint pen lay on the night table. When the buzzer went off, Susan got up, turned on the light, signed all six copies, switched off the light and went back to sleep.

That evening the Barkers celebrated at Perino's. Looking across the room, she spotted her old boss Buddy De Sylva. His face was creased with worry. "Maybe he's dreading what I've been waiting to hand him all these years," she said. "Pow—a sock right in the kisser."

De Sylva rose and approached Susan's table. "I heard about the contract," he said, smiling. "Congratulations. I told you there'd be other chances." Susan was surprised at her own reaction. She returned De Sylva's smile and extended her hand. "Mother said that the harder I'm hit, the higher I'll bounce." The next day, De Sylva was out at Paramount.

Righter had had another cogent observation to make, this one concerning her marriage to Jess. Since he was a Virgo, Righter warned, conflict was inevitable. Susan crossed her legs, smiled and changed the subject. She did not have to be warned of a brewing marital conflict: it was now well underway. Jess's career had ground to a standstill. He had taken over the running of the household and the raising of the children, aided by a nurse and then the housekeeper, Cleo. By default, Susan had now totally assumed the role of breadwinner. Both resented the situation, but neither did much to correct it. The first Christmas after Susan signed her contract with Twentieth, Jess found a check from Susan under the tree. He soon learned that she had also taken out a huge insurance policy on herself with him as the beneficiary. On the few occasions when she could bring herself to ask him to get a job, he merely smiled and said, "You knew I was an actor when you married me."

The damage to Jess's ego was irreversible now, and the only way that Susan and Jess could cope with the situation was to ease the pain with a Jack Daniel's or a rum and Coke. They never had less than two drinks in the evenings, and more often than not the tenuous emotional balance was disturbed. When the fireworks began exploding, Susan often fled from their expensive San Fernando Valley hacienda and sought sanctuary with friends. One of her publicists, Henry Rogers, became accustomed to hearing Susan rap on his door in the middle of the night. Jess was at it again, she informed them, and asked if she could spend the night on their living room couch. After one knock-down, drag-out fight she spent two weeks in the small flat of press agent Jean Pettebone. There she reveled in the simple domestic chores for which she had no time in her own home. Susan washed the dishes, made the beds, mopped the floors, cooked pot roast and sat on the edge of Jean Pettebone's bed pouring out her troubles. Pettebone wanted to know why Susan kept going back to Jess if he was such a rat.

"The answer is a question," Susan mused. "Have you ever been lonely?" Yet Susan and Jess were not about to give Hollywood the satisfaction of gloating over yet another broken marriage. She routinely praised his acting abilities as being far superior to hers, and often described him as "the most unforgettable man I ever met." Jess replied—strictly for the benefit of reporters—that "Susan has the soul of a ballet dancer and the appetite of a ditchdigger. She loses her temper, but never her figure. She saves wrapping paper, but sleeps between silk sheets. She's a real hellcat, in an adorable way."

On the road, Jess was on hand for every interview. More often than not, his role was that of Jewish Mother ("Eat your soup before it gets cold, dear"), but most reporters walked away feeling that was just the way he wanted it. The picture painted by Earl Wilson in his March 15, 1949, column was fairly typical in this regard. Wilson wrote,

> The idea was that Susan Hayward of Hollywood was going to buy some woolies—and I was going to help her shop.
>
> But Miss Hayward decided she couldn't keep warm enough in just woolies. She decided to buy a mink coat instead.
>
> "Why do you want to buy a mink coat, as though I didn't know?" I asked Miss H. as we started off for Maximilian's shop that has purveyed mink coats to Claudette Colbert, Mrs. Louis B. Mayer, et al.
>
> "Because I'm freezing in this town," shivered Susan.
>
> "But a Californian should be used to bitter cold," I cracked.
>
> "We're *not* used to it!" she insisted. Four of us—Susan, her husband, Jess Barker, a press agent and I—trooped into the fashionable shop and somebody managed to ask Susan, "What was the name?"
>
> She modestly said, "Hayward." Instantly we were given a small auditorium where Susan could look at these li'l old mink coats worth several thousand bucks.

After asking to see a variety of pelts and studying the skins herself, Hayward took the salesman into another room and plunked down $10,000 on an ankle-length Labrador mink coat. As they reached the street, Susan told Jess that she wanted to visit a dime store to make some purchases. "She said," wrote Wilson, "she had to start saving money right now."

As with these cozy anecdotes, the tale of the mink coat was gradually altered to fit the Barkers' image as the ideal show business family. Having put together enough money to furnish their living room, Susan told a *Photoplay* reporter, they were about to do just that when a San Francisco woman who had ordered a mink suddenly got cold feet. "Buy the coat," generous Jess supposedly said. "I like a nice bare living room where we can stick a projector and show pictures." In a more revealing aside, Susan conceded, "A cloth coat keeps you just as warm, but if you have to go to the hock shop, you get more for the mink. I've been there before. Who am I to say it can never happen again?"

The twins were trotted out at every opportunity before rotogravure photographers and inquisitive feature writers. Susan was seeing very little of them now, but enough to know that Tim was as rambunctious as his brother Greg was well behaved.

Susan was proud of being a strict disciplinarian—though she clearly would have blanched at the excesses of colleague Joan Crawford. Susan slammed into psychologists who cautioned against spanking. "I think boys need a good whack on the fanny every so often when they get out of hand," she declared. "It clears the air and does them good. It's a kind of protection against their own lack of self-control. I've observed kids who've never been spanked; to me they seem less secure. Somehow they get the idea that you don't care enough to exert yourself to whack them. Not that I advocate it as a regular thing," she explained. "But when the occasion calls for it, yes—if they're deliberately disobedient, if they endanger themselves by picking up a butcher knife or shooting out of the driveway on their bikes. You can always say it hurts me worse than it does you. Tim's answer to that one is, 'I'll bet it does . . .' Then he laughs. Even Greg is less upset by a spanking than a scolding."

These glimpses into life at Casa Barker also took note of

Susan's personal quirks. She suffered from acrophobia; more than once she froze with terror while climbing a ladder or reached for something to steady her while gazing out the fiftieth-floor window of a Manhattan skyscraper. And although she enjoyed flying, she and Jess were sufficiently fatalistic never to fly on the same plane for fear of leaving the children parentless in the event of a crash. Beyond her strict adherence to astrology, Susan was superstitious enough never to start a new movie unless Jess gave her a lucky red apple. And whenever she switched on the car radio while driving to work, Susan felt mysteriously compelled to let the song play on to the end—even if she detested it.

Susan maintained her arm's-length approach to the Beverly Hills social whirl. When one couple appeared at their door unannounced, Susan simply told them they were not welcome. On the rare occasions when the Barkers played host and hostess, dinner parties were small because the dining room could not easily accommodate more than two extra couples. Guests were forbidden to wear perfume at the table. "I suppose if I were a nice person I'd never mention it," she admitted. "But 'Indiscreet' with the roast ruins my appetite." Another house rule: dinners must be informal, and in every case attended by little Timothy and Greg. "Lots of adults don't care for dining with children," she explained. "To us, children *are* the home. We don't banish ours for the sake of company. Instead, we ask people who have children themselves and like them." Hence, whenever more formal entertaining was in order—and Susan made it crystal clear that she loathed giving and attending parties equally—Susan and Jess took their guests out to clubs like the Stork in New York and the Mocambo. On one typical evening they dined at the Stork, went with a friend to hear Erroll Garner, her favorite jazz pianist, then headed for El Morocco, where she polished off a plate of chop suey and most of Jess's steak before devouring their friend's sandwich. Both superb dancers, Jess and Susan took to the floor and soon she was carried away by the music. Accustomed to taking charge, she often forgot who was leading. "Would you care," Jess muttered, "to try this *solo?*" Susan, duly chastened, tried to control herself.

Every other aspect of Susan's personal life was carefully sanitized for public consumption. She was, millions of tabloid readers were accurately informed, lukewarm about television—though as an avid Dodger fan she was glued to the set during baseball season—and had a positive addiction for gloves in a rainbow of pastel shades. "I must have read somewhere," she cracked, "that you're not a lady unless you own twelve-button kidskins. My gloves are all short, so I guess I'm just half a lady." Her favorite color was yellow, but because Jess disliked it, around him she stuck to black, white or beige. The lady of the house liked to fish, collect semiprecious stones and help her sons glue together model airplanes. They practiced casting in the pool, and whenever a photographer was near ran hand-in-hand through fields of daisies. Susan preferred peonies to roses and gardenias to orchids, but she most loved tuberoses. As the years wore on she began expecting to find a gardenia under her pillow, placed there by Jess. She came to count on that personal touch, and eventually Jess was literally required to bring her flowers if he had any amorous intentions for the evening.

There were occasional flashes of reality. Old pal and mentor Louella Parsons, in an article proclaiming Susan one of "Hollywood's 10 Most Exciting Women," recalled their days together on the road. "Since those days," wrote Louella, "I watched this youngster with the burning ambition to get to the top as an actress zoom to fame. But I still find my Susie complex, elusive and unpredictable. She drives block-long Cadillac convertibles, yet refuses to put the top down. When I asked her why, she said, 'Oh, the wind blows my hair!' "

Considering her own meticulous p.r. campaign, Susan's next pet peeve seemed at the very least hypocritical. "Movie stars wearing gingham aprons and pretending to be busy in the kitchen look silly," she declared. "There have been too many chocolate cake and cornflakes stories about Hollywood and not enough star dust. Personally, I've had my fill of gingham. I'd rather buy a $400 gown and wear it on only one big, big occasion, then put it aside. And I'm not ashamed to say it's wonderful being a movie star, because where else can you have so much fun and get paid for it?"

This was Susan's no-nonsense glamour act for the press, and it certainly had more to do with her approach to life than the articles that stopped just short of crowning her Mother of the Year.

If Louella indulged her plucky protégée, Hedda was not so disposed. The two squared off one afternoon at Susan's. She showed up on Susan's doorstep wearing one of her elaborate trademark hats, and while ushering her guest into the living room, Hayward could not help thinking of the time Joseph Cotten got his revenge on the spiteful columnist by walking up to her at a celebrity-packed party and administering a swift kick in the rear. The target was so tempting . . . Hedda plopped down on the sofa, complimented Susan on the way she had decorated the room and pulled out her notebook.

"Well, my dear," Hedda purred, "what would you like to shout about today?"

Susan cocked her head. "Why should I tell you? You're supposed to have all the questions. That's your job."

"All right," Hopper shot back. "For a starter, whom or what do you hate most in Hollywood?"

"I love everybody." Susan smiled sweetly.

"You have lots of fights," Hedda reminded her. "Tell me about them."

"I deny that," Susan replied. "At least, none of them made much of a lasting impression on me."

"You used to fight with your husband, Jess Barker, didn't you?"

Susan did not even break stride. "Yes, I fought with him. But that's not commercial."

"What did you fight about?"

"We fought about everything," Susan shrugged. "About our gin rummy score. Don't all married people fight? Anyway, we don't fight anymore. I told you, I love everybody. Say, you're beginning to get me worried."

"You told me to ask the questions," Hedda coyly reminded her.

"Yes, I know. But you're acting like the district attorney."

"That's good. We'll title the interview 'The Trial of Susan Hayward.' "

Susan's patience was wearing thin. "I don't know about that," she replied.

"Now, Susan, you don't want to be pictured as a sweet, innocent and rather dull and colorless little character, do you?"

"No, I don't want that, but my husband doesn't want me to talk about our fights. He feels it's a dead issue."

"And does he run the family?"

"He certainly does."

Hedda saw an opening. "Does he run your career, too?"

"No, but he advises me."

"Do you and Jess have any two-career-in-one-family trouble?" Hedda sensed she was treading on dangerous ground, but went ahead anyway. "I know he's not quite as busy as you are . . ."

"That's ridiculous." Susan smiled. "There's never any argument about who's the greater actor. We each know that we are, and we're so sure of it we don't bother to discuss it."

Hedda was not entirely satisfied. "What do you think of him personally?"

"Love him."

"And what does he think of you?"

Susan pulled out the stops. "He thinks I'm the greatest actress and the most charming woman and the most wonderful mother in the world."

When it was all over, Susan had won an admirer. "There are few players," Hedda gushed in her column, "who take out more conscientious satisfaction from their jobs, who put in more hard work and thinking effort, and whose results show off increasingly better with each picture than Susan Hayward. That pretty little redhead is very definitely on my like-list."

The only true avenue of escape from bickering with Jess and fending off gossip-mongers was work. Susan's first project for Twentieth Century-Fox was a meaty role in *House of Strangers*, directed by Joseph Mankiewicz. Cast as a society girl, she falls in love with lawyer Richard Conte, the good apple among immigrant barber-turned-banker Edward G. Robinson's four sons. When Conte goes to jail for bribing a juror to save his father and his bank, she waits for him to complete his seven-year sentence. Robinson won a Cannes Film Festival Award as Best Actor, but was passed over by the Academy. The most exciting moments in the film, however, were provided by Conte and Susan. The raw sexual tension between the lushly beautiful Hayward and the square-jawed Conte was palpable to moviegoers, who made *House of Strangers* an international box office hit.

Making *House of Strangers* was not an altogether pleasant experience for Susan. "I remember once we were shooting some scenes in Central Park. When I'd see the crowds surge around me and hear the youngsters screaming, I would step out of the studio limousine, make a sweeping bow, then go in front of the camera with a big, warm glow inside of me. The crowds gave me something I had to have.

"But on another day, when we were shooting on upper Fifth Avenue, I felt terribly hurt because those sophisticated Gold Coasters were too bored to notice me. Even the damn pigeons at the fancy end of Central Park were aloof. I hated them."

Ever-conscious of her Brooklyn working-class roots, Susan resented all forms of pretentiousness. On a trip to New York, the Barkers attended a Broadway show and the next day over lunch at "21" told a local reporter exactly what she thought of stage actors. "I get so fed up hearing about the *great* talents on Broadway," Susan commented between sips of rum and Coke. She had gained five pounds —as she usually did between pictures—but her body-hugging black wool showed that she was still svelte. "I mean that wholeheartedly. Out here, everybody talks about movie work being a lark, that the real test is the theater. That's bull! The stage actor has weeks, months to create a part, set a mood, establish characterization."

The lecture continued. "Do you know what it's like in the movies? I arrive on the set by nine A.M. at the latest and get introduced to my leading man. At nine-fifteen I'm cued to make love to the guy, cry over him or laugh with him. And sister, you'd better be in the mood. That sort of thing is unheard of in the theater. For all our toil and trouble, we Hollywood people have to pay more taxes, too."

The waiter placed a bowl of soup before Susan, but she kept right on talking to the intimidated reporter. "Eat your minestrone, dear," Jess suggested sternly.

"See," said Susan, "he doesn't like to hear me speak this way about his beloved theater. But I can't help myself. Somebody's got to stick up for the movie actor. Maybe I'm a little jealous of the stage folk. Maybe I envy them because they have the time to achieve perfection in their roles. They're much, much happier . . .

"Who's kicking me?" Susan blurted in Jess's direction. He smiled nervously. "As I was saying," she continued, "the fellow on the stage is far happier than we are in the movies, and I'm speaking of actors who have genuine love of acting. Out of all the years I've been in Hollywood I can only recall two or three moments when I really experienced the feeling of perfection. Once it occurred in *Smash-Up*. And once you know that feeling, you constantly look for it. I'm sure the stage people achieve that sort of thing often."

"Yeah," Jess added, "when they're *working*. Did you know that something like ninety per cent of the Equity members are unemployed?"

"I know, I know," she replied. "For all our suffering in Hollywood, I guess it's worth it. We have a big house and a pool and a nice life." She turned to Jess, placed her hand on his and seemed intent on making what she was about to say appear heartfelt. The cameras were rolling. "We don't always agree, Jess and I," she beamed, "but we're very happy. It's a first marriage for both of us, probably our last, and I haven't met another man who is as funny as my husband. We live a suburban life. We both like good eating because we've both been hungry. And best of all, we have two wonderful sons. Darling, do you realize that in seven years our boys will be going to high school?"

"Sure," he nodded. "I always said you were an old bag."

Susan cleared her throat and laughed. It was a worthy performance for both of them.

If Jess was dependent on his wife in every other way, Susan did rely heavily on him for advice in choosing roles. Goldwyn-RKO wanted her to star in another "woman's picture"—*My Foolish Heart*, based on J. D. Salinger's *New Yorker* short story, *Uncle Wiggily in Connecticut*. The script, written by the twins who had collaborated on the screenplay for *Casablanca*—Julius and Philip Epstein—dealt brilliantly with a college coed whose World War II lover (played by Dana Andrews) is killed in an explosion and leaves her pregnant. She marries a major (Kent Smith), convinces him the child is his and then begins her downward spiral into booze, disillusionment and despair. Once again the neurotic, ever-tippling protagonist nearly destroys her own child (Gigi Perreau) in the process. This was only one of the many similarities between *My Foolish Heart* and *Smash-Up* that gave Susan pause. Would she be typecast as the chromium-plated, razor-tongued beauty whose private pain is so intense that it threatens herself and her loved ones with destruction? Would Hollywood come to think she was capable of playing nothing but drunks? Jess sat down at the kitchen table and convinced her to discard her apprehensions. If anything, *My Foolish Heart* was superior to *Smash-Up*—more complex and perhaps even more literate. And no one, he said, looking her straight in the eye, could tackle the role better than Susan. He was right.

There was another, more practical consideration when it came to filming, however. Leading man Dana Andrews was himself an alcoholic—a condition that would plague him until he finally kicked the sauce in the early 1970s. Like many other Hollywood drinkers, however, Andrews did not seem to bring his problem with him to the set. He was always on hand for the morning call, and the shooting went remarkably smoothly. Andrews was intrigued by his costar, and since he made no social demands on Susan (he hit the bottle alone as soon as the day's shooting was over), she found him a most agreeable sort. "She's a strong woman with a steel will," he told a friend after meeting Jess. "If she ever marries an equally strong man, it might prove interesting to watch."

The first major motion picture of the era to ride on the coattails of its enormously popular theme song, *My Foolish Heart* opened at Radio City Music Hall to ecstatic reviews. "In her best screen job to date," raved *Look*, "Susan Hayward makes the tragedy of a girl in wartime very real indeed." Leggy Betty Grable, reigning queen at Twentieth Century-Fox and the nation's top box office draw throughout the 1940s, read the notices with interest. *My Foolish Heart* landed Susan her second Oscar nomination, and again she lost—this time Olivia De Havilland received the award for *The Heiress*. Susan was not getting used to it.

VI

Smashup

The 1950s would be Susan's decade, and she knew it. It was a time of challenge for the film industry, as television began to make its first major inroads. Independent producers were accruing even more power, and the studios faced their first period of decline since the birth of the medium. Blondes still ruled at Twentieth—Grable, Celeste Holm and June Haver among them—though the studio also boasted the likes of breathtaking brunettes Gene Tierney, Linda Darnell (who had snatched the lead in *Forever Amber* out from under Susan's nose four years before), Jeanne Crain and Anne Baxter. The redheaded newcomer was destined to surpass them and every other actress in Hollywood, all within two years.

Susan honestly believed that redheads made better actresses. "Emotions of natural redheads are close to the surface," she explained. "Film acting requires a girl to produce any one of a dozen emotions before the cameras without preliminary buildup, so the redhead has an immediate advantage." She harkened back to her work on *Tulsa* for an illustration. "Suppose I'm sitting in a puddle of oil with my clothes smeared, my face dirty and my feelings somewhere between frustration and downright anger. This happened in *Tulsa.* We finish the day's work without completing the scene. So, the next morning at the unearthly hour of nine A.M., I am carefully smeared with oil again, exactly as I was the day before, placed in an identical puddle. The director says, 'Let's take it from such and such line.' I have to build up yesterday's emotion as quickly as you would turn on a faucet. In these days of increasing costs, a director will not wait all day for an actress to start emoting."

There was another, equally important factor in Hayward's appeal. With few exceptions, most forceful women on the screen were dynamic and independent at the expense of their femininity. Joan Crawford, Bette Davis, Katharine Hepburn and Barbara Stanwyck, for example, could never be described as sex symbols in the strictest sense. Susan was different. She was perhaps the first star ever to pull it off. She was full-breasted, softly enticing, and yet at her best was as powerful a feminist as any of the others. There was never a picture in which Susan was anything but All Woman. By 1952, Susan was the top-grossing talent for two studios—Twentieth and MGM—bringing in $12.5 million to Twentieth alone. She had already begun her reign as the nation's No. 1 female star—a bigger box office attraction even than Fox's other megawatt sex symbol, Marilyn Monroe.

Susan's triumphant decade began with *I'd Climb the Highest Mountain,* the story (originally intended for Jeanne Crain, who had to bow out because of pregnancy) of yet another sophisticated city woman who marries circuit-riding preacher William Lundigan and manages to carve out a life for herself and her husband in the Georgia hill country. Along the way, she suffers the obligatory miscarriage, battles a typhus epidemic and routes a wealthy widow (Lynn Bari) with designs on her husband. *I'd Climb the Highest Mountain* was a technicolor blockbuster for Twentieth, but Susan would never take her part in the picture all that seriously. When a reporter told her more than twenty years later that it was one of his favorite Hayward roles, she was utterly incredulous. "You gotta be kidding," she told him. "I never saw myself as much of a preacher's wife. I didn't like wearing all those pretty dresses or having to be so genteel." The movie, filmed on location in Georgia, was important to Susan for another reason. Still cool to Lundigan, Bari and her other costars, she took an instant liking to a local restaurateur who had a bit part in the film. Harvey Hester—dubbed "Uncle" Harvey by Susan—was gregarious, down-to-earth and perhaps a touch star-struck. Several years down the road, after much tragedy and heartache in Susan's life, he would play a pivotal part in setting it right.

The on-location stint in Georgia also provided Susan with her first glimpse of the South and its giving, warm-hearted people. It also gave her a brush with death. On one of the rare days when she was not needed on the set, Susan took off in her chauffeur-driven studio limousine on a local sightseeing tour. Climbing up onto a rock, she lost her footing while trying to take a snapshot of the 729-foot Amicalola Falls near Dawsonville in North Georgia. Her young chauffeur, William Gray, caught her just in time, and in the process almost went over the falls with her. It was only one example—albeit the most spectacular—of the locals' selflessness. Once back in Hollywood, however, a newspaper carried the story that she had detested the region and its population of rednecks. Susan, genuinely upset at the fabrication, called "Uncle" Harvey back in Georgia to assure him it was all lies. "Hell, Miss Hayward," he replied, "none of us down here believed that stuff in the papers." She was relieved, but at the same time infuriated that the press would try and create this image of her as a ruthless, ambitious harridan. It was an early volley in the war Susan waged with the press for most of her career—a test of nerves that very nearly destroyed her.

Rawhide offered Susan the kind of vital woman's role she was always avidly searching for. Paired for the first time with Tyrone Power, Susan settled easily into the role of Vinnie Holt, a riverboat singer taking her three-year-old niece to St. Louis after her parents were killed out West. Feisty, tough-talking Vinnie has the bad fortune of stopping at Power's stage station just before bandits led by Richard Carlson take the occupants hostage. It is assumed by the outlaws that Power, Hayward and little Judy Ann Dunn are a family, and they go along. The trio manages to survive the ordeal, and Susan administers the *coup de grace* to arch-villain Jack Elam by plugging him just as he is about to gun down Ty.

Henry Hathaway directed *Rawhide* (which had no relation to the hit of the same name that ran for five years on television), and soon formed his assessment of the willful Hayward. "Mr. H." had participated in her test of *Alter Ego* for Paramount years before, so he was not surprised to find her consummately professional, blissfully easy to direct. But she wore her Brooklyn-bred insecurity on her sleeve. Susan, Hathaway sensed instantly, was "very secretive, very alone." While other members of the cast socialized, she disappeared into the desert to search for arrowheads. "Susan was always on the defensive," Hathaway recalled. "When you dance with her," he added, echoing Jess's frequent complaint, "she leads."

One morning, the tall, stately Mr. H. sent his assistant director to Susan's trailer. He found her sitting with her feet up, reading a magazine. She was completely made up and ready to start work. The assistant director told her that she was wanted on the set. "Is it nine A.M. yet?" Surprised, the assistant director glanced at his watch. It was 8:26.

"I work," said Susan without looking up from her magazine, "from nine to six P.M."

At 9 A.M. sharp, Susan emerged from the trailer. Hathaway seethed, but chose not to make an issue of it. By the time 6 P.M. rolled around, Susan was ready to leave.

"This scene can be wrapped up in just 15 minutes," she was told.

Susan was unmoved, glacial.

"Look, I asked you to come on the set a little early this morning because that is when I like to photograph women; their faces are fresher, younger-looking then. Now that you're being so uncooperative, you're going to work every goddamn day and I'm going to shoot all your close-ups between five and six P.M.!"

"Mr. H.," Susan laughed, "I was *only* kidding." Whether she had been or not, Hathaway had won. For the rest of the picture, she consented to shoot early and leave late—but only fifteen minutes early and fifteen minutes late.

The morning Darryl Zanuck called to say that Gregory Peck and Susan were going to star in *David and Bathsheba*, her reaction was predictable. "I'd like it better if they called it *Bathsheba and David*." In reality, she got the shivers. All she could recall from her Sunday school days was that Bathsheba had taken a bath and rocked a kingdom. What she was surprised to discover was that the Book of Samuel dismissed her in a few lines. She had taken a bath all right—on a rooftop in full view of King David. All that the Bible described was Bathsheba's body, and then only to say that it "was very beautiful to look upon." Susan quickly called Zanuck back. "Don't I do anything except take a bath while Greg Peck looks on?" she asked.

Zanuck promised that she would be pleased with Philip Dunne's excellent script. Dunne, Susan learned, had decided that Bathsheba was one of ancient Israel's most cunning and important historical figures. She was, after all, clever enough to ensnare David, hold him and get their son Solomon crowned over the King's older sons. "She was a siren, all right," said Susan, "and not unlike some girls I've known in Brooklyn—and in Hollywood—and once I got acquainted with her I felt better. If she had lived in Brooklyn she would have acted the same way she did three thousand years ago. Her type is ageless."

As with her unintentional cliffhanging in North Georgia while making *I'd Climb the Highest Mountain*, Susan's life was once again threatened. On location outside Nogales, Arizona, director Henry King yelled "Cut" on a battle scene just as a small Beechcraft carrying a free-lance photographer swooped down over the set—which recreated ancient Jerusalem—to get a better shot. Susan and Peck, chatting as they headed back to their trailers, looked up at the sky when they heard the engines buzz. They were not the only ones irritated by the airborne intruder; a herd of dromedaries which had been imported for the day's shooting bolted from their handlers and stampeded straight for the cast and crew. Without a second to spare, Susan, Peck, Raymond Massey and King dove behind the gargantuan Technicolor cameras and out of harm's way.

Predictably, what most attracted the attention of the press was the bath scene. *Life* ran a full-color spread of Susan reenacting the scene behind translucent glass. On the set, she had had to play it before 82 crewmen, 39 photographers and a score of onlookers. It took two days of shooting before director King was satisfied. But costar Peck, with whom she would join forces the following year, did not see quite as much as the original David; throughout the bath sequence Susan wore her best 1951 strapless bathing suit. Critics were at best lukewarm about this latest epic (a group of San Francisco columnists went so far as to cite Susan's performance as the worst of 1951), but on the strength of story, director and stars, it became the year's *top*-grossing film. Susan was the first to recognize the film's shortcomings. "Some movies you make for art," she shrugged, "others for money. This year we're in business for money."

That line might have been uttered by the next character she was called upon to portray, model-turned-mogul Harriet Boyd in *I Can Get It for You Wholesale.* Fortunately, this saga of Seventh Avenue was tailored to her dramatic talents like one of her pastel kid gloves. A female Sammy Glick of the rag trade, Harriet is ruthless, ambitious and, once again, inadvertently destructive to the ones she loves most. Eventually she is tamed by Dan Dailey, but only after betraying family and friends and pushing them all to the brink of oblivion in the process. *I Can Get It for You Wholesale,* which as a hit Harold Rome musical a decade later would introduce the world to a brash newcomer named Barbra Streisand, was filmed almost entirely in Susan's hometown. Walking along Fifth, Madison and Park, Susan was haunted by the memory of countless rejections when she was a struggling young model. She had shown them all, she thought: every receptionist at every modeling agency who had turned her away without a second thought now knew her name. These feelings, dredged up from the not-so-distant past, contributed to her intense, searing portrayal of a woman gripped by the desire for money and fame—and revenge.

If Susan never forgot an enemy, neither could she be faulted for forgetting her friends. She was uncompromising in her loyalty to the handful of pals she had accumulated over the years. Quietly, almost secretly, she had the studio limousine drive her from her suite at the Waldorf-Astoria to Brooklyn, where she visited with chums from the old days. She also rendezvoused with some of them in Manhattan, where she lunched with girlhood friend Sarah Little—now an editor of *House Beautiful*—at the Plaza, and had cocktails with old DeMolay pal Bob Emslie and his wife. All marveled at Susan's good humor, and at Jess's attentiveness. He even went so far as to carry with him a book of her press clippings, which he whipped out and displayed at a moment's notice.

For her part, Susan, when asked to name her favorite actor, always straight-facedly answered, "Jess Barker." Her respect for his talent apparently was not sufficient for her to find him a job—though as the First Lady of Fox and No. 1 box office draw in the land, she clearly could have used her influence to obtain for him at the very least a supporting role in one of her films. Jess never mentioned this reluctance on her part. Having made it to the top of the Hollywood heap through sheer grit and talent, she simply could not bring herself to give another that boost up the ladder—the help that she never got.

If the Oscar was the ultimate proof Susan sought of her superstardom, then placing her handprints and footprints in the forecourt of Grauman's Chinese Theatre must have rated a close second. Three weeks before the premiere of *David and Bathsheba* at Grauman's, Susan was helped by owner Sid Grauman as she knelt before an applauding throng of admirers and committed her tiny handprints and spiked-heel prints to posterity next to the prints of Ava Gardner, Red Skelton, the Marx Brothers and—ironically enough—Betty Grable's leg. The ceremony did not end there. Partly because she was in reality a 24-carat film queen, Susan took a handful of gold dust and carefully sprinkled it over the prints. Hers remain the only prints at Grauman's (renamed Mann's in 1978) thus etched in gold.

If there was any doubt that her fame was global, it was dispelled by the report that, on the tiny South Pacific island of Kwajalien, Navy man Ralph Cipolado had polled the entire population of 197 and determined that Susan was their favorite star, followed closely by old David himself, Gregory Peck. So familiar was everyone with Susan, in fact, that on September 14, 1951, while on vacation at Campbell River in British Columbia, she could not cash a check because no one would believe she was the real McCoy. "Sure you're Susan Hayward," the teller said, smirking, "—and *I'm* Grace Kelly."

"Look," Susan replied with a sigh, "I admit I've put on a few pounds during this vacation, but I am who I say I am." Reaching deep into her purse, she pulled out an engraved silver cigarette case and handed it to the teller, who reluctantly cashed the check. Dated 1944, the cigarette case expressed thanks from the Canadian government for Susan's work on behalf of the country's World War II bond drive.

Howard Hughes wanted Susan for *Stella*, RKO's first real attempt at a moneymaking "woman's picture." After reading the script, Susan made one of the toughest decisions of her career. She could not honestly take on the project, she told Zanuck and Hughes. If it meant suspension, so be it. Susan did not star in *Stella* (Ann Sheridan was unfortunate enough to have agreed to do it), nor was she put on suspension.

While Hughes, now more intrigued than ever with this

headstrong beauty, instructed his minions at RKO to come up with a film more suitable for her, Zanuck was forced to decide between Jeanne Crain and Susan for the lead in *With a Song in My Heart*. Both women had begged Zanuck for the three-hankie biography of singer Jane Froman, whose career was almost destroyed when her right leg was nearly severed in a tragic 1943 plane crash. Froman's gallant battle against pain had grafted additional millions to her already sizable public following as a vocalist.

Zanuck did not take long to decide that Susan possessed the necessary stamina for the role, and Susan went into training for it like a prizefighter. She even went so far as to allow her hair to be cut for the role. Even though she was to lip-sync to Froman's voice, Susan took vocal lessons with World War I vaudeville trouper Elsie Janis, rehearsed eight hours a day at the studio and kept the Froman records playing constantly at home. Froman, perched atop a stool in the recording studio laying down the twenty-six-song soundtrack, had done several numbers when, in the middle of *I'll Walk Alone*, she noticed the small figure of Susan Hayward crouched in the corner studying her mannerisms intently. "I wanted Susan Hayward in the first place," Froman said after *With a Song in My Heart* was a certified smash critically and commercially. "Not only because we looked somewhat alike, but because her speaking voice had a throaty quality similar to mine, which would make believable my singing voice coming out of her mouth. I found her a remarkable person. I worked two months in advance to record twenty-six songs for *With a Song in My Heart*. Every day as I walked into the recording studio, there would be Susan sitting quietly in a corner watching me. It was uncanny!" When she saw the first rushes, Froman was astounded by Hayward's pantomime. "Did I move my arms that certain way?" the singer asked herself. She headed for a mirror, began singing and realized instantly that the Hayward imitation was incredibly accurate. "Susan looks like a singer," Froman marveled. "Every singer knows that when you breathe—it shows. She understands how to stand, to move, that gestures mean something. But," she hastened to add, "Susan didn't copy me slavishly, either. She had tricks of her own up her sleeve."

From the early scene when she explodes from a taxi and plows into a lady shopper on the way to an audition to the crash near Lisbon from which she emerged one of only fifteen survivors (out of the thirty-nine passengers) to her spectacular postwar comeback tour of one hundred concerts in seven countries, *With a Song in My Heart* was sheer Hayward.

There were plenty of other ingredients that helped make *With a Song in My Heart* a natural: gutsy pep talks from fellow Flatbusher Thelma Ritter (one of Susan's few friends off-screen as well as on), a bittersweet marriage to pianist-songwriter David Wayne doomed to failure by her superior talent, and a storybook marriage to the copilot of the downed plane (Rory Calhoun). The finale alone was worth the price of admission: on crutches and backed by a military chorus, Susan/Jane belted out a region-by-region back-home medley for the boys overseas. To the wild applause of the G.I.'s, she ran through every tune from "America the Beautiful" to "Give My Regards to Broadway," "Chicago," "California, Here I Come," "Carry Me Back to Old Virginie" and "Deep in the Heart of Texas." Susan knew from the outset it would be a rouser. After all, "Anyone here from Brooklyn?" had always worked remarkably well for her.

Froman's praise for Susan's acting was repeated in interview after interview, and she even wrote an "open letter" showering the actress with kudos that ran in the now-defunct *American Weekly*. Susan clearly felt it was she who was doing Froman a favor—the popularity of the film revived the singer's sagging career—so the best she could offer was a grudging respect. Hayward surprised most of her studio colleagues when she agreed to do a magazine cover with Froman, but clearly showed who was the true star by keeping Froman waiting for two hours while she primped for the photo session. When the magazine hit the stands, it was clear that Susan had cleverly manipulated the pose so that she dominated the cover.

Susan liked *With a Song in My Heart* so much that it was the first movie of hers Susan allowed her children to see. At seven, both were able to enjoy the songs and comprehend some of the plot, though Gregory kept nudging his mom and asking when the funny parts were coming up. The Academy apparently agreed that the film, which again placed in the top ten grossers for the year, merited its female star a third Oscar nomination as Best Actress. Susan, outfitted in green organza, drew the biggest ovation of the evening as she stepped out of her block-long studio limo and past the crowds that pressed against the barricades. Without her glasses, she could see none of the individual faces; the adoring throng was one vibrating blur.

Inside, her confidence of victory grew as Alfred Newman picked up the Award for his score of *With a Song in My Heart* (over *Singin' in the Rain*, among others). Thelma Ritter was up at bat next in the Best Supporting Actress category, but lost to Gloria Grahame in *The Bad and the Beautiful*. Gary Cooper deservedly got his second Oscar, for *High Noon*, and old friend De Mille walked away with Best Picture honors for *The Greatest Show on Earth*.

By the time the nominations for Best Actress were read, Susan had worked herself up into an internal frenzy. Yet

Shirley Booth had out-tear-jerked even Hayward in *Come Back, Little Sheba*. As Booth trotted toward the stage to accept the golden statuette, more than a few eyes were cast in Susan's direction to catch her reaction. To everyone's surprise, there was none. She smiled benignly, and even managed a semblance of enthusiasm in her applause. Still, a bitter resentment of the Hollywood establishment that had dealt her this third defeat brewed beneath the surface. Losing did not sit well with Susan. There were consolations, however. Susan was awarded *Photoplay*'s Gold Medal as "the nation's most-enjoyed actress of 1952," and was named the World's Favorite Actress by the Foreign Press Association.

Even before the release of *With a Song in My Heart*, Susan teamed up again for the film version of Ernest Hemingway's *The Snows of Kilimanjaro*. In 1927, the British banished the Masai tribe from its 8,000-feet high grazing lands to the 4,000-feet plateaus in the shadow of Mt. Kilimanjaro. The Masai chief and witch doctor promptly placed a curse on the land and a white rancher died in a plane crash. Then a countess who had settled there killed her lover. A series of shootings, knifings and scandals took place—enough to lend some credence to the "Masai Curse."

The Snows of Kilimanjaro, directed by *David and Bathsheba*'s Henry King, was cursed even before the principal photography began. Cinematographer Leon Shamroy sent Charles Clarke to shoot some street scenes in Cairo just as street fighting broke out between supporters of King Farouk and Gamal Abdel Nasser. Advised by American consular officials to leave at once for his own safety, Clarke flew to Nairobi, climbed into a jeep and headed into the bush in search of charging rhinos and hippopotamuses frolicking in a lake. The rhinos wound up very nearly tipping his jeep over, and Clarke came close to drowning when a hippo surfaced under his small boat.

Back in Hollywood, the Masai curse worked its black magic on the sound stage at Twentieth. Hildegarde Neff came down with the flu, forcing major revisions in the shooting schedule, and Gregory Peck injured his knee while carrying Ava Gardner from a battlefield. Ava got the most mileage out of *Snows*, though Hayward was perfect for the role of the "rich bitch" wife who redeems herself by nursing a critically injured Peck in a tent at the base of the mountain. Critics groaned, Hemingway himself claimed never to have seen it and labeled the work *The Snows of Zanuck*, but Peck and Hayward were still a dynamic duo at the box office.

Zanuck launched his twenty-sixth year as a producer by presenting a gift to Howard Hughes: Susan Hayward to star opposite up-and-comer Robert Mitchum in the rodeo opera *This Man Is Mine*. The Nicholas Ray film, retitled *The Lusty Men* just prior to its release, might just as well have been called *The Lusty Woman*. Desperately in love with Arthur Kennedy and yearning for the middle-class life of a rancher's wife, she sees that future threatened when rodeo bum Mitchum encourages cowhand Kennedy to go into broncobusting. Hayward snarls and spits for nearly two hours, but the high point of the movie comes when, after a barfly (Eleanor Todd) flirts with Kennedy, Susan unceremoniously drop-kicks her out the door.

The film was memorable for other reasons. It introduced two of the era's most combustible talents to one another. Faced with Susan's reputation for temperament, however, it was Mitchum who backed off. While every other actor and crew member was at the mercy of his practical jokes, Susan was carefully avoided. Perhaps because of this reticence on Mitchum's part, a chill developed between them that would continue through the making of their next film together the following year, *White Witch Doctor.*

Susan's intense loyalty to the precious few friends she did have was proven once again when, stepping off the set of *The Lusty Men,* she was informed by a reporter that her old mentor Walter Wanger had shot dark-haired agent Jennings Lang in a jealous rage over Joan Bennett. How did Susan feel about her old pal now? "Walter Wanger is a great man and a good friend. I owe everything to him."

The promotional tour for *With a Song in My Heart* offered a unique opportunity for Susan to return to her Brooklyn high school in triumph, and Susan seized it. Prospect Heights High School (Girls' Commercial High when Edythe Marrener was a student there) was turned topsy-turvy long before her black Cadillac limousine bore her to the school's main entrance. Girls hung out of windows, straining to catch a glimpse of the school's most celebrated alumna. When she finally arrived, two dozen student leaders formed an honor guard lining the path from the curb to the entrance. Susan, clad in a demure black wool suit, stole and velvet cloche, had been chain-smoking her Chesterfields in the car, confiding to Jess that she regarded this as one of the most significant events of her life. As they were suddenly engulfed by gawky, gawking young girls, she snubbed out her cigarette in the armrest ashtray. A burly cop bearing more than a passing resemblance to Wallace Beery escorted Susan past the admiring throng. Two older men stood nearby watching impatiently.

"Who in the hell is it?" one of them asked his companion.

"Oh," answered the other fellow once he got a glimpse of the star through the crowd, "it's just little Edythe Marrener."

Inside the auditorium, the students were cued to burst into song as soon as the doors swung open to reveal the guest of honor. When they did, five hundred students sang —what else?—*With a Song in My Heart*. As she neared the stage, the singing gave way to wild applause that drowned out the school band. Principal Edna Ficks introduced Susan as "our most distinguished graduate," and although Susan obviously relished the moment, she claimed to be so "overwhelmed by the reception that she found it difficult to speak." But she did, and the words were self-revealing: "As you go out into the world," Susan told the enraptured audience, "always keep your chin up and keep a happy heart. Young as you are, you have one. Try never to lose it."

Class President Mary Alice Badley then presented Susan with the key to the school. The auditorium was emptied, and a second shift of fifteen hundred girls filed in. Susan was introduced again, Mary Alice Badley again gave her the key to the school and this time Caroline Moody, president of the scholastic Arista society, presented a pin to Susan and asked her to wear it for old times' sake. The hurt of fifteen years before was still there. She reminded everyone that good grades weren't enough: one had to be elected to Arista. "The girls," she said sadly, "didn't want me." The third, last and youngest shift of fifteen hundred came in to *Pomp and Circumstance* and switched almost immediately to *With a Song in My Heart*.

During the entire affair, Jess sat quietly in the back, standing only when Susan introduced him to each group. Jess, having grown accustomed to the role of Mr. Hayward, seemed to be enjoying it almost as much as Susan. He stood on the sidelines as his wife presented Florence O'Grady with a polished apple, dropped in on an art class, signed the guest register at the library and sat at one of her

Bathsheba only had eyes for David (Gregory Peck). CREDIT: THE MEMORY SHOP, INC.

Sid Grauman lends a hand to Susan Hayward as she plants her prints—the only ones sprinkled with gold dust—in the forecourt of his Chinese Theater. CREDIT: THE MEMORY SHOP, INC.

Clawing her way through the Seventh Avenue jungle with George Sanders and Dan Dailey in *I Can Get It for You Wholesale*.

Belting out the title tune as Jane Froman in *With a Song in My Heart*.

The Homecoming: "Susan Hayward Day" at Brooklyn's Prospect Heights High School. CREDIT: THE MEMORY SHOP, INC.

Hemingway's *Snows of Kilimanjaro* brought Hayward and Peck together again. CREDIT: THE MEMORY SHOP, INC.

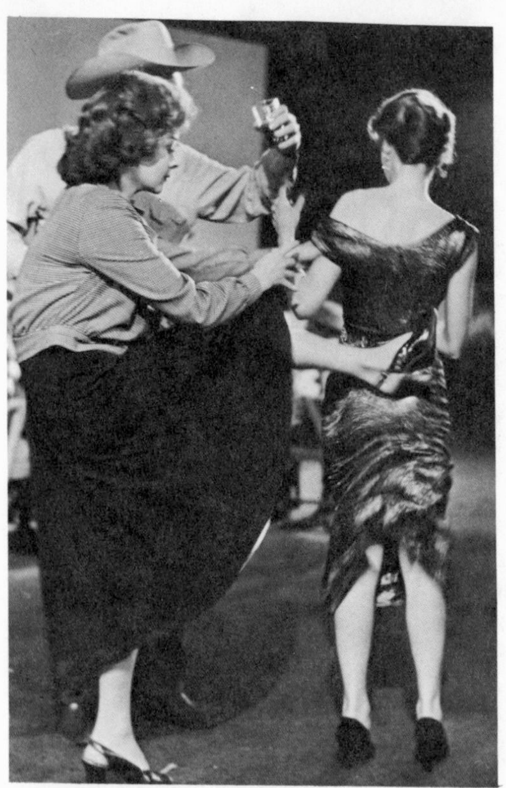

In *The Lusty Men*, Susan administere a swift kick to barfly Eleanor Tod CREDIT: MOVIE STAR NEWS

Treating a native as Robert Mitchum looks on in *White Witch Doctor*. CREDIT: THE MEMORY SHOP, INC.

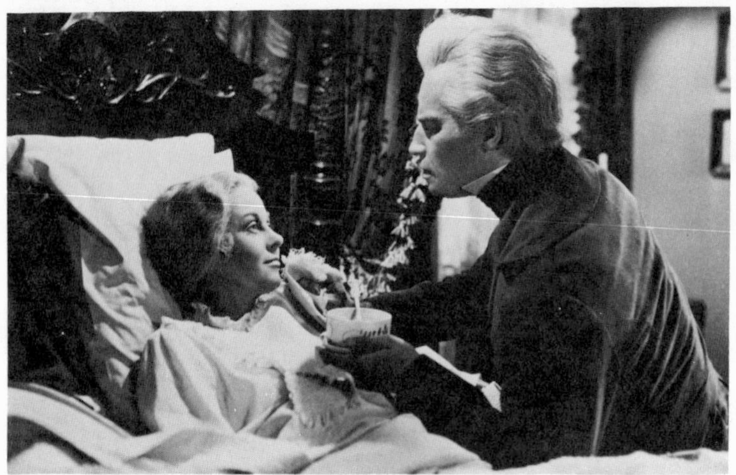

Heston was a Hollywood newcomer when he played Andrew Jackson opposite top-billed Hayward's Rachel in *The President's Lady.* CREDIT: THE MEMORY SHOP, INC.

Susan's scheming Messalina seduces Christian Victor Mature, but is redeemed by the time *Demetrius and the Gladiators* comes to an end. CREDIT: THE MEMORY SHOP, INC.

With Richard Widmark and Gary Cooper in *Garden of Evil*—Susan's first picture with Cooper since *Beau Geste*. CREDIT: MOVIE STAR NEWS

Scarlett O'Hara takes to the jungle (with Tyrone Power) in *Untamed*.

Clark Gable was Hayward's *Soldier of Fortune*. CREDIT: THE MEMORY SHOP, INC.

For a romantic publicity still the stars of *Soldier of Fortune* strike an uncomfortable pose in front of a fake sky. CREDIT: PICTORIAL PARADE

The Barker clan, less than two years before the breakup. CREDIT: THE MEMORY SHOP, INC.

old desks—first seat on the right. With the entire student body of forty-five hundred waving good-bye, Susan climbed back into her limo and sped away. As soon as she was out of sight, Susan lit up, threw her head back and sighed. It's wonderful coming back, she thought, but even more wonderful to leave.

Back at her Hampshire House suite on Central Park South, Susan invited some of her old teachers and their spouses over for tea. Photographers clicked away as Susan poured from a fifteen-hundred-dollar silver tea service. Jess, meanwhile, hovered about in the background. As they left, one of the women complimented Susan on her choice of a mate. "You have such a nice husband," the woman gushed.

Susan was caught off guard. "I'd rather," she replied with a faraway look in her eye, "have a successful one."

She also invited Church Avenue buddy Bob Emslie, Martin's brother, and his wife over to gossip about the old Flatbush gang over drinks. But the primary purpose of this trip to New York was to publicize *With a Song in My Heart* and let loose with a few opinions of her own. It was an election year, 1952, and stars were not hesitating to line up behind either Dwight Eisenhower or Adlai Stevenson. Susan refused to go along, although she now seemed to be leaning toward Ike. "Actors," she loudly declared, "should stay out of politics. Just because you can play a scene doesn't mean you know a damn thing about the issues, or that you have the right to sway others."

Not that she wasn't public-spirited. That Christmas Susan sparked a Yule "gift lift" to G.I.'s fighting in Korea. With the aid of the Junior Chamber of Commerce, she managed to convince the Hollywood community to donate presents that were then shipped to the front. "There are a hundred thousand United Nations troops fighting that war," said the flame-haired Santa, "and I want every one of them to have at least one package to unwrap on Christmas Day." She fell short by thirty thousand gifts, but the avalanche of mail from grateful servicemen made it well worth the effort.

Susan's experiences on the home front were less gratifying. Jess had not had a job since the 1950 stinkeroo *The Milkman* when Susan stepped into the part of Andrew Jackson's spirited second wife, Rachel, in *The President's Lady*. Rachel had married the President before her divorce was finalized, and as a result was reviled by the public as a wanton woman. Jackson was played by nervous newcomer Charlton Heston, so in awe of his costar on the film that twenty-seven years later he could scarcely recall anything of the experience other than the fact that Susan was "a great and gracious lady" who did what she could to help him along. Away from the cameras she was—as with nearly all of her coworkers—aloof, almost frigid. On the job, however, she was given to livening up the proceedings. After spending three hours being made up, she emerged a wizened old woman for the final scenes.

"What have they done to you?" Heston asked in mock horror.

"Remember, Mr. Jackson," Susan replied, "you took me for better or worse."

On *The Lusty Men* she had been no less quick. In an on-screen tiff, Robert Mitchum had the line "My, but you're small with your shoes off."

"You're small with yours on," Hayward ad-libbed.

The President's Lady brought Susan yet another unexpected honor. Her pipe-puffing in several key scenes prompted the International Pipe Smokers organization to proclaim her "the girl we'd most like to go up in smoke with."

White Witch Doctor reunited Mitchum and Hayward in the spring of 1953, but the freeze between them on the Hollywood set was enough to cause icicles to form on the plastic jungle plants. Mitchum kept his distance, but Susan found herself being pestered by a hairy creature of a different sort. One scene had a local witch doctor envious of Susan's "magical" powers as a missionary nurse placing a deadly tarantula on her cot. The independent-minded spider somehow managed to get away from its handler and crawl up Susan's arm. Wide-eyed with terror, Susan screamed and tried to brush the monster off. In her panic she fell to the floor, tearing several shoulder ligaments.

"Isn't that carrying realism a bit too far?" the studio doctor asked as he tended to her injuries.

"They assured me," replied Susan, "that it was a reliable tarantula."

Once *White Witch Doctor* was out of the way, Susan and Jess deposited the twins with her mother and headed for a second honeymoon in Europe to celebrate their ninth anniversary. It was more of a last effort to hold their shaky marriage together.

They bought a Jaguar and motored through Italy, Spain and France. The trip lasted three months, winding up in Paris. There Susan was stopped by a little girl while strolling along the sun-dappled Champs-Élysées. "Oh Maman, voici Jane Froman!" Such moments were rare, however, as Susan and Jess bickered and battled from the Prado to St. Peter's Square.

They had been home barely two weeks when the Battling Barkers' Vesuvian tempers finally erupted into violence. The twins were present for the event, as was a houseguest: Sarah Little's younger sister Martha, whom Susan had instantly invited to California when she learned that Martha had developed cancer. There was another witness to the goings-on that night: Lodie Swain, the next-door neighbor's chubby black maid. The seamy details would make headlines for weeks when Susan, Jess and Lodie Swain took the stand during pretrial divorce hearings the following February.

The three versions of what had happened that torrid summer night differed greatly. All made for melodrama. With dour-faced Superior Court Judge Herbert Y. Walker presiding, Susan told her story in response to questioning by her attorneys, Martin Lang and Milton A. Rudin:

Q. What time of the day or night was it?

A. Well, it was late at night, because my husband had gone out to get the late editions of the newspapers; it was on his return.

Q. Who was at home on that night, July 16, 1953?

A. My husband and myself and my houseguest.

Q. Where were the boys?

A. And my children were upstairs.

Q. All right. And it was after dinner then, late at night, about eleven or twelve at night?

A. Yes. We had been talking before this.

Q. What were you doing on that occasion?

A. I had been studying, and Mr. Barker had been watching television.

Q. Studying what?

A. My script, or a script. I can't remember right now whether I was working on something at the time or preparing.

Q. When Mr. Barker went out for the late editions of the newspapers, where were you at the time he came back?

A. In the living room.

Q. Can you describe what happened on that occasion?

A. Yes. As I said before, we started to argue. We argued

about most of the things we've argued about in the past. I remember one thing: that I asked Mr. Barker for a divorce, because I said to him, under the circumstances, that I felt a divorce might be the only solution to these problems. He said I would never get a divorce.

Q. Did you discuss the question of employment, or his not working?

A. Yes; this was part of our argument.

Q. And the effect on the children?

A. Yes.

Q. Give the conversation, please.

A. As well as I can remember, it wound up in the fact that he said to me I'd never get a divorce. And I said, "If you don't love me, and don't want to do what I consider right, why do you want to hang on?" And he said, "Well, you're a good meal ticket."

Well, when he said that, I didn't understand, and I looked at him, and I said, "I don't understand you. I think you're very queer."

Q. What did he do?

A. And he walked over to where I was sitting and he slapped me.

Q. In the face, Mrs. Barker?

A. Yes.

Q. Go ahead; proceed.

A. I was frightened. I said, "Don't." So he slapped me again. I tried for him not to hit me. He threw me on the floor, and pulled off my robe, and proceeded to beat me.

Well, when my husband was beating me, I tried to get loose from him, first of all, because it hurt; secondly, because there were children in the house, and Martha Little, who is not well. I didn't want to disturb them. But when he beat me, it hurt, and I was crying.

So finally I got loose and ran out of the house into the

back garden. I just wanted to get away. Mr. Barker caught up with me; he forced me back into the house. I was struggling with him, and he hit me again.

Q. Where did he hit you, do you remember? I know it's tough, but we've got to do it.

A. I don't remember where he hit me; he hit me wherever he could.

Q. What were you wearing, by the way, Mrs. Barker?

A. I was wearing a terrycloth bathrobe.

Q. And what underneath that?

A. Nothing, I sleep in the raw.

Q. All right. Then he was dragging you back in the house. Continue the story.

A. When he continued to beat me, I had to get help. I ran to the telephone. I was going to dial the operator, call the police, or anything I could.

Q. What happened?

A. He came after me and knocked the telephone out of my hand, and he said, "I'll cool you off," whereupon he yanked me by the arms and dragged me out again, back through the garden and up the steps to the swimming pool.

Q. And what did he do then?

A. He threw me in.

Q. And will you relate what happened after he threw you in?

A. Well, as I said, I was wearing this terrycloth robe, and it's pretty full. It's a big, pink, voluminous thing, and when I hit the water, the water soaked it up, and I went down. It's hard to get up because there are many folds in the garment. I got up to the top, and I started screaming again, because I was afraid, whereupon he pushed my head under the water.

Q. Were you in fear of your life?

A. Of course I was.

Q. And what did you do after he held your head under the water—pushed it under?

A. I suddenly realized that I was not dealing with a person who was quite themselves. I knew that he was so highly enraged that he wasn't responsible for his actions that night.

Q. So what did you do?

A. So when I came up the second time, I kept my mouth shut, and didn't make any noise. He said, "Now get back into the house." So I went quietly.

Q. What happened to the terrycloth bathrobe?

A. That was soaking wet; and as I said, it was very heavy. It was left by the poolside.

Q. And you therefore had to go into the house without any clothes on at all?

A. Yes.

Q. What happened then? Proceed. You walked in with Mr. Barker behind you?

A. Yes. I walked in the house with Mr. Barker. He pushed me into the bedroom, and he said, "Now stay there." Naturally, by this time I was pretty scared, and I knew I had to get out and get help somehow, because I didn't want to stay in the same house with him. So I went to the closet and threw on whatever clothes I could find . . . There's a little door that leads out of the bedroom, a side door, so I didn't have to go out around again through the den where I thought he might be. I opened the door quietly and walked through the garden, and then, as I remember it, around by the kitchen door, because that leads out into the driveway, and freedom. I got as far as the kitchen door, and it was suddenly—I hate to tell these things.

MR. LANG: I don't know what else we can do.

A. It was suddenly opened by Mr. Barker. He said, "Where do you think you're going? Get back in there." At least I think that's what he said; it's hard to remember . . .

The Court: You can't remember exactly. The Court wouldn't believe you if you gave me the exact wording. Give it as near as you can recollect.

The Witness: He grabbed me and threw me into the kitchen ahead of him, and that was lucky, because he threw me with such momentum that I could race to the front door. You go through the kitchen and the dining room and the hallway to the front door. And I opened it, and I ran out, and I ran down the driveway, and he caught up with me, and started to hit me again. He said, "You're not going anywhere."

Q. Proceed.

A. At this point, of course, again I was screaming for help. I was screaming the man's name next door. It was dark outside, and I was screaming for help from the man across the street, anybody.

The next thing I remember, he tried to get me into the house, and I refused to go, and I was struggling with him, and he threw me over the hedge and I was down on the ground, and he still kept beating me. And that's all I can remember until Martha came out the front door, and she yelled, "What's going on?" because—

Q. "Martha" was Martha Little, your houseguest?

A. That's right. She came out the front door, and she ran over and said, "Stop it! Stop it!" Well, when she said that to him, he stopped momentarily, and I ran back into the house and grabbed the telephone, because I was going to call the police. He ran back in after me, and again knocked it out of my hand. And then suddenly, I don't know, there was a commotion outside, and I ran out, and the police were there. I said, "Would you please call me a taxi?" I told the policeman—

Q. By the way, do you know who called the police?
A. No, I don't; I never reached them.
Q. Proceed. What happened?
A. So, when I asked the policeman to call me a taxi, I must have looked a mess. I said I wanted to go to my mother's house. So they called me a taxi. They offered to drive me in their squad car, but I said that wasn't necessary. So they called a cab, and I got in it, and Miss Little came with me, and we went over to my mother's house . . .
Q. You spent the night at your mother's house?
A. Yes. And then I tried to reach your office in the morning, and I wasn't successful, so I called Mr. Wood, my business manager, at his home, and asked him would he go back to the house with me and ask Mr. Barker please to leave. Also, my brother came with me.
Q. And you went back to the house the next morning?
A. Yes.
Q. With Mr. Wood and your brother?
A. Yes, and Miss Little.
Q. And Mr. Barker left the house that day?
A. Yes, he left the house that day.
Q. It was after that that you filed your Complaint for Divorce, and asked for a restraining order?
A. As soon as I could reach your office, one of your attorneys came to my home; I explained to him what happened.
Q. And did you secure medical treatment for your injuries?
A. Yes. I was X-rayed, and taken care of.
Q. And can you describe what your injuries consisted of as a result of what had happened the night before?
A. You want a description of how I looked?
Q. Yes. What were your bruises, contusions?
A. Well, I had a black eye, I guess you call it; bruises on

the left side of my face, on the temple, the jaw, the nose. I thought my jaw was broken. The eyeball was injured—it was all bloody. My body was covered with bruises, mostly on my "fanny" (indicating), and my feet and legs were scratched and bleeding.

Q. What was that from?

A. From being dragged up the steps and down the steps, and being knocked against things.

Q. And how long a period of time did it take before the visible evidences of your injuries cleared up?

A. Well, that black eye lasted quite a while.

THE COURT: That still doesn't answer the question about how long.

Q. [By Mr. Lang] About how long?

A. I don't know; I didn't keep count of it.

Q. About a week, or two weeks?

A. Two weeks.

Q. Now, Mr. Barker did not live at the home from that time on, did he?

A. He did not.

Q. Did he come to take the children with him on occasion?

A. Yes, he did.

Q. Would you, on those occasions, see him?

A. Yes, sometimes I would.

Q. And he would not stay at the house, however?

A. No.

Q. Just come and get the children, and bring them back?

A. That's right. Or if he wanted to pick up any of his clothes, or things like that.

Jess recalled that fateful evening differently:

Q. [By Sammy Hahn, Barker's lawyer] . . . Let's begin with the fact that you were out, and then you came home about a certain hour, and let us start from there . . . What happened?

A. . . . We went home, had our usual drinks before dinner—never less than two . . .

After dinner I was sitting in front of the television set for a while, and the programs were dull, and I left it. Mrs. Barker wasn't studying a script, because she wasn't working at the time, and there were no scripts, to my knowledge, that had been sent to her. She had just finished a picture . . .

Q. You know about scripts?

A. I should know; I have worked with them enough.

Q. You studied the scripts with her?

A. Always.

Q. And you advised her?

A. Yes, I did.

Q. And what else do you do helping prepare for the work of a star?

A. To give her every bit of knowledge I have had in the years in the theater, and what I have had in the motion picture business.

Q. Did you attend interviews with her?

A. I was frequently present in interviews with magazines and newspaper people. Quite frequently Mrs. Barker would ask me to join her, providing, as she termed it, the "light touch."

Q. Did you have to advise her about costumes at the studios?

A. I was with Mrs. Barker on practically every picture she started on the costumes, and I saw the tests made, suggested camera angles, anything connected with her work.

Q. In addition to that, you bought the groceries for the house?

A. I bought the groceries for the house.

Q. And you bought the supplies, and maintenance for the house?

A. I did to the best of my ability.

Q. And raise the children?

A. That I did to the best of my ability.

Q. All right. Now, tell us what happened from there on. You say she was not working?

A. Mrs. Barker was sitting in front of the television set when I went to get the newspapers . . . Mrs. Barker . . . started reading . . . I had a newspaper . . .

Q. And what happened? What was done by you or her?

A. There was a discussion about families in general in Hollywood—not gossip—just in general, about this person, and that person, which is the way many of our conversations started out. During the course of the conversation, something was said where a remark about my mother was brought into the conversation. Why it was there, I don't know.

Q. What remark did she make about your mother?

A. Well, it isn't very pleasant. It was about an incident I told her about when I was a child. "Possibly," she said, "that's what's wrong with you." . . . after the mention of my mother, I sat in complete stunned silence; and Mrs. Barker gave me all of the bad things that she could think about me.

Q. What did you do then?

A. I sat on the couch. I stayed right there wondering why a woman that I had all the respect for in the world should say that to me, the father of her children. Mrs. Barker leaned across me to get a cigarette, and said right in my face, "Besides, I think you're queer." And with that, I think I said, "You're not going to get away with that." And I slapped her, and the struggle was on from then on.

She struggled back. I tried to quiet her down, and by this time Mrs. Barker got hold of me, and hit me very hard in the left arm, in the muscle . . .

Q. Then what happened? How did you get to the swimming pool?

A. Mrs. Barker ran outside; I brought her back inside. I let her back inside; and I gave Mrs. Barker a spanking . . .

I asked her to please keep quiet, the children were upstairs, and I picked her up, carried her and put her into bed, and covered her . . . And Mrs. Barker got up again, and ran outside, and I said, "If you don't keep quiet I'm going to cool you off."

Q. What did you do to cool her off?

A. I picked Mrs. Barker up, carried her to the pool, and dropped her in.

Q. Which side of the pool did you drop her in, the nine feet deep or the three feet deep?

A. It's approximately four feet deep . . . The robe, by the way, that she was wearing, slipped right off.

And I said, "Now are you cooled off?" And Mrs. Barker was still screaming, and I helped her out of the pool, and took her back in the house. Mrs. Barker never entered the parkway area gate in the nude—never . . .

Q. Did you ever drag her?

A. I never dragged Mrs. Barker. Mrs. Barker fell on a couple of occasions pulling away from me, yes . . .

Q. You did not try to drown her as she says?

A. No, Mr. Hahn. I helped Mrs. Barker out of the pool . . .

Q. Then you went back in the house, and what happened then?

A. Mrs. Barker was in the room for quite some time, and I was in the den, and in the state I was in I decided to take a walk in front of the home.

I was sitting outside by the driveway which has the drain, and Mrs. Barker came out fully dressed with a coat on: I mean fully dressed apparently to the eye, with a scarf over her head. She had the dog in her arm, and she was going down the street in the dark . . . I tried to get her back, and there was a struggle . . . I took her to the front door, and asked Mrs. Little to please put Mrs. Barker to bed, and she said, "I will."

Q. That's the first time you saw Mrs. Little that night?

A. That's the first and only time I saw Mrs. Little until she left shortly after that with Mrs. Barker . . . Mrs. Little opened the door and was waiting.

Q. And then the police arrived?

A. . . . I sat on the front doorstep, or stoop, and sat there until the gentleman walked up to me in uniform and said, "What's the trouble here?" And the only word I spoke to the gentleman was, "Domestic."

Q. Did you at any time throw her over a fence of some sort?

A. I did not.

Q. Did you at any time hear her scream loud and long, "Don't kill me, don't kill me?"

A. I don't remember that.

Q. Did you try to kill her?

A. No, sir, I did not.

Q. Did you try to do her any physical harm other than what you say you considered she deserved, a spanking?

A. I did nothing else, Mr. Hahn. I left the home in the hopes that the home would be reunited and perpetuated . . . I was back on a Tuesday with flowers. This is the first occasion . . .

Q. You brought her flowers for your and her anniversary?
A. I did.
Q. She accepted them?
A. Yes.
Q. She appreciated them?
A. She thought they were lovely . . .

Neighbor Lodie Swain got an eyeful:

Q. . . . you could see from your bedroom into the area in which the pool is located?
A. Yes.
Q. All right. Now, on the night of July 16–17 of 1953, did anything occur which you remember at this time?
A. In the early morning of July 17, I was awakened with a loud scream—a lady's voice. And then I got up out of bed with the loud scream still on. Then I went back to my bathroom and I went straight to the back kitchen door, and I stood in the doorway looking and listening.
Q. At this time of the morning were there lights on in the yard of the Barker home?
A. There was two lights, big headlights, in the backway.
Q. And did you see anything at that time? . . .
A. I saw a lady run by out of the gateway, the back of the house, and she didn't have on anything. If she did, it was very sheer to me.

A few minutes after she was in the house, I heard a loud scream, then they ran outside in the backway, direction of the pool, and I heard screaming real loudly, and she was screaming, "Don't kill me; don't kill me" and "Somebody help me; somebody help me; please don't kill me." I heard a man mumbling, said, "You're going to sign that deal." She said, "No, no." And I heard a big splash as if something bumped in the water, and she was screaming and struggling. And then I heard conversation out near the pool, but I couldn't see, so I just heard the mumbling. I couldn't understand what they were saying otherwise . . .

Q. And did you go back to bed?

A. I stood there for a little while, and then I laid back down. And later, in the early morning, I heard a man in the backway, two men, talking. I didn't even get up to see who it was.

Q. Now, did you recognize any distinctive part of the person you saw running—the lady; was her hair noticeable to you in the light?

A. It was kind of red—reddish-like . . .

Q. Was the person you saw Mrs. Barker?

A. I would say she was.

MR. LANG: Thank you very much. You may cross-examine.

MR. HAHN: Did you notice that naked lady again?

A. . . . I saw her twice.

Q. All right. Now, after you saw her run into the door, when did you see her again?

A. When she ran out the back door next to where I am.

Q. Did you notice her for just about a second again?

A. She was running so fast I guess it was a second.

Q. And that lady was still naked?

A. Yes.

Q. Where did the naked lady run after she got to the driveway?

A. In the direction of the pool. I don't know where she ran after that.

Q. That's the last you saw of the naked lady?

A. That's right.

Q. When did you hear somebody yell, "Don't kill me, don't kill me"—after she ran to the swimming pool, or when the naked lady ran through the door the first time?

A. When she ran back to the swimming pool.

Q. That's the first time you heard a lady say, "Don't kill me?"

A. No. She was just hollering when I was awake. I was awakened with a scream; that's what I told you.

Q. Yes, and with screams, "Don't kill me?"

A. Yes, when she ran back to the pool, and there was some slaps like that . . . Then I heard her hollering, "Don't kill me . . . somebody help me . . ." Then I heard a man's voice say, "You're going to sign that deal," and she said no, and splash, he throwed her in the pool, and there was a scrambling, and scrambling, and that's the way it was . . .

Q. A scrambling over a deal?

A. In the water.

Q. Did you go over there and look?

A. No, I didn't go over, because I didn't want to interfere.

Q. Did you call the police?

A. I didn't call the police, because I didn't want to interfere . . .

Q. . . . When you saw the naked lady run in the house, and when you saw the naked lady run out of the house in the swimming pool, you didn't see a man follow her?

A. Yes, there was a man following her, but I didn't look at that second. He was sure following . . .

Q. Now, when the man's voice said, "Sign the deal," where was that?

A. That was outside.

Q. Outside, when she ran out the first time or second time?

A. The second time.

Q. Well, how soon after she ran out toward the swimming pool did you hear a man say, "You'll have to sign this deal?"

A. It wasn't long afterward, because that's when the most screaming was.

Q. About how long?

A. About a few seconds. I don't know just how long it was, but it wasn't very long.

Q. How long did this yelling, "Save me; don't let him kill me," go on?

A. It went on quite a while, because I don't see why somebody in the neighborhood didn't hear beside me . . .

Q. How long did they talk quietly in the swimming pool, in that direction, after the screaming stopped?

A. Quite a while, I guess, because I went and laid down.

After the July 17th shenanigans, Susan turned her attentions to Ned Marin. Her longtime friend and agent was dying of a brain tumor, and Susan took it upon herself to pack Marin up, grab Gregory and Tim and fly the whole group to Honolulu for much-needed R&R. On her return, Susan received a call from Jess. "Do you mind," he asked, "if I take the boys down to Studio City and see your picture, *White Witch Doctor?* We promised them they could see it." Pouring herself another round from a frosty pitcher of scotch, she declined his invitation to accompany them.

Jess brought the kids back at 6 P.M. and discovered that Susan was entertaining wealthy neighbors John and Thelma Dorsen. Jess joined them for cocktails by the pool, but after a few minutes he told the Dorsens that he wanted to talk to Susan alone. The guests returned to the house, drinks in hand, while Jess mixed himself a martini.

"Jess," asked Susan, "will you please be sort of quick

about it, because dinner is ready, and I don't want any delay."

"I want to talk about us . . . about getting back together."

Susan nipped the idea of reconciliation in the bud. She was not in the mood right now—not when she had the Dorsens and the children waiting in the dining room to be served dinner.

"Let's talk about this some other time, not tonight," insisted Susan. "Now why don't you leave?"

"Goddamnit," he shot back. "I'll leave when I get good and ready to leave." The action moved into the house, where Jess sat in an overstuffed chair and Susan on a small loveseat. While Jess hammered away at their obligation to stay together for the sake of the children, she walked to the dining room table, lit a cigarette and returned. She looked at the burning end of the lighted Chesterfield. "I ought to push this right in your eye," she threatened.

Jess laughed. "You haven't got the guts," he taunted her. With that, Susan made a jab for Jess's face. He knocked the cigarette out of her right hand with his left. Susan's screams brought the Dorsens running. The twins watched from the dining room.

"The son of a bitch hit me," Susan told Thelma Dorsen.

Jess grabbed his wife by the shoulder and sat her on the couch. "What is the matter with you?" demanded Jess. "This girl claims she's been hit. Would you take a look and see if she has a mark on her? She's got sensitive skin; it would show."

Susan answered this challenge to her truthfulness by throwing a glass of Chivas Regal in his face.

"Will you please tell the truth?" begged Jess as he wiped the drink from his face with a napkin.

"You hit me!" she screamed, storming about the room. "You hit me!"

"Please tell the truth. The children have heard you, for God's sake. I'm not going to leave the house until you tell the truth." Susan was not about to change her story, and a defeated Jess stormed away.

The Susan Hayward-Jess Barker divorce follies went into previews in November, when the court ordered them both to visit a conciliation commissioner in children's court to determine just who would get custody of the children while the divorce itself went ahead. Commissioner Margaret Harpstrite, a severe-looking matron who wore her dark hair in a bun, mentioned to her boss, Judge Georgia Bullock, that the interesting case of the movie star and her estranged husband was about to come on the docket. "Fine," said grandmotherly Judge Bullock. "Let me know when they come."

No sooner did Mrs. Harpstrite call to tell the Judge that the Barkers had arrived than the white-haired Judge hurried upstairs to have her picture taken with the famous couple. Mrs. Harpstrite was shaken. "She had to be in the picture," cried Harpstrite, "so let her take the case herself! I won't hear it!" Susan, facing the most traumatic experience of her life, found herself in the bizarre position of having to calm down the conciliator. "You take the case," she said, gently stroking Harpstrite's hair. "I like you." But the conciliator could not be conciliated. Their lawyers trailing behind, Susan and Jess walked downstairs to Judge Bullock. The Judge promptly sent them right back. "It isn't fair," Harpstrite still insisted. "She sits down there on the podium and I do all the work. It just isn't fair. I work so hard so many nights and go without lunch all the time and she comes in and has her picture taken and gets all the glory."

After another abortive trip to Judge Bullock's chambers, they managed to calm Harpstrite down. After she heard what Jess and Susan had to say, Harpstrite decided that Susan should take the kids during the week and Jess would have them on weekends. To even the score, a United Press photographer snapped some additional photos of the Barkers and Harpstrite—without Her Honor. Was there really a chance for a reconciliation, asked a reporter as the pair hurried out of the courthouse toward separate cars. "It takes two to tango," answered Susan.

As wrought-up as she had ever been during the nine and a half years of their tempestuous marriage, Susan nonetheless went back to a Twentieth Century-Fox sound stage to film the final scenes of *Demetrius and the Gladiators*. Her distraction was painfully evident to costar Victor Mature. At one point he turned to director Delmer Daves and muttered, "Jesus, she acts like she's a hundred years old." On the screen, however, she portrayed the Roman Emperor Claudius's evil wife Messalina to Technicolor perfection. Making her entrance in a sedan chair borne by Nubian slaves, she kicks things off by ordering Mature, a peace-loving Christian, sent to the arena the next day to kill or be killed. She manages to win Mature over briefly, but after a fling at her seaside Temple to Venus it is she who sees the error of her ways. Not only did Susan get the opportunity to float from marble palace to Coliseum in diaphanous gowns of green, blue, white and amber, she also got to supervise the ruination of virgins (one of which was played by Twentieth Century-Fox rookie Anne Bancroft), sentence her own uncle and cousin to death and throw wine in St. Peter's face. She had had ample practice at home for that last scene.

The morning after the reconciliation fiasco, Barker went ahead and filed a countersuit asking for a share in

$1,293,319 of his wife's assets. Susan was livid. After all, in 1951, she had grossed $163,692 while he brought home a piddling $318.75. He did a little better the following year with $346.50, but then Susan pocketed $211,376.50. She left the matter with her lawyers and took off for Mexico to make the so-so *Garden of Evil* with Gary Cooper. She had never been a particular fan of Coop's aw-shucks style, and though he charmed the rest of the cast and crew the hero of *For Whom the Bell Tolls* and *High Noon* left Susan cold. Whenever she did go out during the filming of *Garden of Evil,* it was with Assistant Director Stan Huff. Merle Oberon's wealthy third husband Bruno Paglai gave a New Year's Eve party in Acapulco at which the main topic of conversation was Susan's upcoming divorce. To everyone's shock, Susan actually attended with Huff. It was 8 P.M., and the bash had gotten underway at Paglai's impressive seaside villa. "Well," said Susan, now accustomed to the silence that fell over a room whenever she entered it, "where do ya eat around here?" Director Henry Hathaway, also among the guests, explained that a light buffet was to be served later. With that, Susan picked up her coat, threw it over her shoulder and headed for the door. "Then good-bye. A girl's gotta eat."

That evening there was an urgent message waiting at Susan's hotel. Her mother was baby-sitting Greg and Tim back in Sherman Oaks, and had called to say that Jess had moved into the house, claiming that both women were not capable to care for his sons. Susan telephoned her attorneys and the next day Jess was slapped with a contempt of court citation and told to return the care of the children to Mrs. Marrener.

In the weeks before the pre-divorce hearings, the screen's most lusted-after woman had no trouble finding solace in the arms of Hollywood's most desired bachelors. Ruggedly handsome, silver-haired Jeff Chandler (Ira Grossel back in the days when he had carried her books home from school in Brooklyn) took more than a brotherly interest now that he was temporarily unattached from his second wife, Marjorie. Seldom seen on the town, they preferred to furtively meet at the bachelor pad he had rented when his marriage seemed to dissolve. There they did more than share memories of the good old days along the Gowanus Canal—despite Ellen Marrener's heated denials that her daughter was involved with any men during this trying period. Their affair soon died a natural death. Chandler, deciding that his marriage was worth saving, moved back in with his wife.

In early 1954, Howard Hughes was a very busy man. He oversaw not only the operations of his flagship Hughes Tool Company, but his very own airline—TWA—as well as RKO. Hughes had already done what he could to make busty Jane Russell a star in *The Outlaw*—including inventing a special cantilevered bra to accentuate her attributes. Still, he had ample time to add Susan's name to a growing list of conquests which at one time or another included Billy Dove, Ginger Rogers (to whom he was engaged), Joan Crawford and Katharine Hepburn.

It seemed only appropriate, then, that his ostensible reason for visiting Susan at her home was to discuss script changes in their upcoming RKO epic *The Conqueror*. Hughes made the point of never wasting an entire day on just one woman. He would have breakfast with Ginger, share lunch with Jane Russell and pay an afternoon "call" on Joan before pulling up to Susan's driveway in his silver Duesenberg. Lankily handsome, his chin covered with stubble and a hat pulled over his forehead, he smiled warmly when Susan opened the door and beckoned him inside.

Susan was excited by Hughes in a way she had never been by Jess. He was powerful, mysterious. As she walked ahead of him, he was impressed by how much more voluptuous she seemed in person. Her hip-rolling walk always made it look as if she were climbing stairs—straight to the bedroom. And the hair! Hughes had had affairs with redheads before, but none quite so red.

Hughes was introduced to the twins by Susan as "Mr. Magic." She explained that "his name is Magic" because "he flies airplanes and does many things." Hughes was not particularly warm toward children, but he mustered enough interest in Greg and Tim to offer them a ride in one of his planes. He never made good on the promise, but it did not matter to Susan. Hughes was tall, dark, powerful, oddly domineering. They dined at Ciro's on two occasions, but for the most part Hughes and his newest stayed out of public view. There was no doubt that she would have married Hughes—had he asked. As was the case even then, however, publicity was Hughes's nemesis. Once he was finally subpoenaed to testify at the divorce trial, Hughes closed the Hayward chapter of his romantic life and turned to the one titled "Jean Peters."

The pre-divorce hearing began February 25, 1954, and as expected, the tawdry recollections of Susan's midnight sprint across the front lawn and the cigarette-in-the-face incident made headlines. FILM BEAUTY TELLS OF FLEEING IN THE NUDE blared the New York *Daily News*. The Los Angeles *Times* trumpeted: SUSAN HAYWARD FLED NUDE FROM HUSBAND. Wearing a high-collared beige suit with mink sleeves, Susan dabbed away a tear with a black-gloved hand that still held a cigarette. Several times, Susan broke down on the stand and at one point a five-minute recess was called so that the distraught witness could regain her composure. She even admitted for the first time that she had repeatedly lied to reporters about the stability of her marriage. On returning from her vacation with Jess in Europe, Susan had told interviewers that things were going swimmingly even though she knew her marriage was over and had all but resolved to divorce Jess. Once on the stand he pulled no punches, describing Susan as "an icy woman" and an "absentee mother." Jess, undaunted in his desire for reconciliation, tried to corner Susan whenever and wherever he could—on the stairs of the courthouse, in the hallways, in the courtroom itself. It was all to no avail; Susan remained as remote and unreachable as she usually did with her co-workers. To give the court a look at the scene of the dunking episode, Susan (in dark glasses, the ever-present pearls and a wide-brimmed white hat) and Jess went along on a tour of the house on Longridge Avenue. While the presiding judge, clerks, lawyers and reporters looked about the property, Susan toyed absentmindedly with a sailboat in the pool.

The divorce finally came down to whether the prenuptial contract separating their incomes meant that Jess was entitled to no more than his $5,000 savings account. Barker's lawyers argued that, because they filed joint tax returns, he had made a substantial contribution to the household's finances. Mrs. Nayma Gilmore, a tax expert who had prepared the couple's returns for years, testified that she had filed the returns jointly only after Hayward stated that she was happily married and intended to tear up the prenuptial agreement separating their incomes. (The agreement was never destroyed.)

Still, Susan was anxious enough to wash her hands of Jess that she offered him $100,000 to be paid as alimony. The figure was acceptable to the Barker camp, but in the lump-sum form of community property as opposed to alimony. Jess was suddenly too prideful to accept alimony from his soon-to-be-ex-wife. Rejecting Susan's pretrial offer of a settlement, Barker pressed for what he saw as his rightful share of community property. The result: Susan walked away with her $1,293,319, custody of the children and a $3,500 bill for court costs that she was more than happy to pay. Jess got the family station wagon.

In the closing months of their marriage, Jess was not without his own shoulder to cry on. Yvonne Doughty, then twenty-three, was an attractive brunette who had just finished a supporting role in Marlon Brando's *The Wild One* when Jess met her at her mother's restaurant in the San Fernando Valley. From that moment on, Jess confided totally in young Yvonne. Jess told her he had to bring Susan flowers every time he wanted to make love, that she was cold and he was lonesome. Yvonne may have thought it strange for a man she had just met to reveal so much of his personal life, but she crumbled anyway.

That evening Jess and Yvonne went out, and the next night they slept together. The following morning they rented an apartment, and for a year—except for one two-week period in the summer of 1954 when he visited Timothy and Gregory—they lived together. And even during that brief time, Jess brought the twins to meet Daddy's "friend" at the apartment.

Yvonne did Jess's laundry, cooking and housework, but when it became clear that he had no money to help pay the rent, she moved back in with Mother. The following April, she called Jess and they drove down to the beach together. It was there, with the moon casting an otherworldly silver glow over the pounding Pacific surf, that she broke the news: their baby was due in December.

Jess was predictably belligerent—until Yvonne promised that she would not make any public announcement. She did more than that. Four months later, Yvonne filed a paternity suit naming Jess as the father and demanding a hefty sum in child support.

The courts ruled that, despite his claim that he had broken up with Yvonne in November of 1954 and therefore could not be responsible, Jess should fork over a nominal $50 a month in child support until the case could come to trial.

It did not take long for Yvonne to up the ante to $200 a month, but Jess claimed that he had assets of only $9.34 and was forced to "eat in cheap restaurants." The paternity trial was every bit as much of a circus as the Hayward-Barker divorce had been. At one point in the proceedings, Yvonne screamed, "I hate you!" at hapless Jess, who was ordered by the presiding judge to stand next to the child so that their facial characteristics could be compared. Eventually, it was decreed that Jess was indeed little Morgana Ruth's father. They were never told by their mother, but Tim and Gregory suddenly had a half-sister.

Susan read the news with a mixture of sadness and vindication; her worst fears about Jess had, she felt, been confirmed. Ellen viewed the whole affair with unabashed glee. "I married for love and security but got neither," Susan confided to a friend. "I married a man who wasn't in love with me. I bore his children. I did everything I knew to make the marriage work. Then I had to spill my personal life from coast to coast to keep my sons. I'm divorced and I never wanted to be divorced." Now, at least, she had no doubts that she had made the right decision.

Dirty Harry

None of the cast and crew could have suspected when shooting began on Howard Hughes's $6 million epic *The*

Conqueror in Utah that it might be the most important production of their lives. Hayward, whose affair with Hughes would come to an abrupt end before the completion of the film, undertook the project as something of a lark. Leading man John Wayne saw playing Genghis Khan as an opportunity to break out of his Western-and-war-movie rut. Director Dick Powell, a fine actor who would show promise behind the motion picture and television cameras, viewed *The Conqueror* as the professional challenge of a lifetime—an assignment that would get him as far away from Busby Berkeley as it would get John Wayne away from Howard Hawks and John Ford. Veteran troupers Agnes Moorehead, Pedro Armendariz and Thomas Gomez had all played with Hayward and Wayne before. If the two greatest stars in the Fifties firmament were willing to gamble on Hughes's improbable script, they were willing to go along.

It had actually begun a year earlier—on May 19, 1953.

At 5:05 A.M. this crisp spring Saturday, a dry lake bed at Yucca Flat, Nevada, cracks like a Wedgwood plate beneath the hammerblow of an explosion. The searing orange fireball rises against the blue Georgia O'Keeffe sky, then evaporates into a strangely beautiful, lavender-blue mushroom cloud. The five hundred residents of sleepy St. George, 145 miles away across the Utah border, are awakened twenty seconds later as the earth undulates beneath them. It is a familiar feeling; nearly everyone turns over and goes back to sleep.

For those men whose job it was to set off atomic bombs in the Nevada desert, the detonation scheduled for this morning seemed at first as routine as any of the other eighty-seven nuclear explosions that would take place there between 1951 and the 1963 test-ban treaty. The device itself—at 32 kilotons packing several times the wallop that razed Hiroshima—was affixed to the top of a hundred-foot concrete-and-steel tower. Structures of cement, stucco and wood dotted the blast area, so that photographic equipment could record the eerie process as roofs were peeled back like the tops of sardine tins and walls vaporized within a fraction of a second.

But something would happen to make this particular atomic test tragically different. At almost the instant the device exploded, a sudden and unexpected wind shift swept a cloud of intense radiation toward St. George. Within three hours a gray ash fell, coating the locals' lawns and pastures and playgrounds, discoloring their clothes and burning their skin like lye. "Dirty Harry" was America's worst nuclear accident, but there was no warning for the people of St. George until 10 A.M., nearly five hours after the blast. For most, warning never came; the Atomic Energy Commission would choose to downplay the incident, allowing the deadly fallout to silently take its toll in lives and suffering over the next three decades.

Almost one year to the day after Dirty Harry—long after pigs and herds of sheep had fallen dead from the effects—Susan Hayward arrived with costars Wayne and Moorehead, actor-turned-director Powell and hundreds of other cast and crew members to begin filming Hughes's own $6 million disaster, *The Conqueror*. Hayward and the others were unaware of Dirty Harry, or of the ten other atomic tests conducted afterward that had added layer upon layer of radiation to the already highly contaminated terrain. Instead, they were interested in getting *The Conqueror*—doomed to artistic and commercial failure as soon as it was conceived by Hughes as a means of dethroning King of the Epics Cecil B. De Mille—over as fast and as painlessly as possible.

Wayne was incongruously cast as Genghis Khan, who

stops Hayward (in the equally unlikely role of the Tartar princess Bortai) en route to her wedding and winds up conquering her for himself. Wayne seethed at having to utter unintentionally comic lines like "You er beootiful in yer wrath" and "My blood says take this Tartar woman!" No less outrageous was the task assigned to Hayward. Flame-haired as always, but "orientalized" with slanting eyes and exotic teardrop earrings, Hayward's Bortai finally admits, "To reach his arms I would betray my people into Mongol bondage"—but not before performing a suitably suggestive ritual sword dance (which took her six weeks to learn) that climaxes with one of Bortai's sabers quivering in a wooden beam just inches from the great Khan's face. Where the Duke spent much of his time fuming over this drivel, his old friend and frequent costar found herself constantly dissolving in laughter. "Me, a red-haired Tartar princess!" she cracked to Wayne between takes. "I look like some wild Irishman stopped off on the road to Old Cathay!" When she wasn't cracking wise for the cast and crew, she sewed, read or chatted with members of the local Chivwit Indian tribe who were being employed as "Mongol" extras.

However absurd the plot of *The Conqueror*, it was nowhere near as bizarre as the real-life drama in which they were unknowingly entwined. Over the next quarter of a century there occurred among the people of St. George a shockingly disproportionate number of birth defects, as well as a surge of leukemia and of thyroid and other types of cancer.

The Conqueror would take two years to complete, and though it had been launched before *Garden of Evil* would not be released until immediately after *I'll Cry Tomorrow*, in 1956. Once the majority of the exterior scenes were shot in Utah, everybody packed up and returned to RKO in Hollywood.

To compound the danger to the unsuspecting visitors from Hollywood, a caravan of trucks was loaded with tons of red earth from the Utah location—soil that, it was later suggested, contained the seeds of death—and brought back to Hollywood for exterior scenes actually shot inside the RKO studios. For two full years the cast and crew was exposed to the radioactive menace, spread out on the floor of the indoor sound stages by Mexican gardeners.

It would be less than a decade before *The Conqueror* began to claim its unsuspecting Hollywood victims. Noted character actor Pedro Armendariz, Wayne's brother in the film, shot himself in June of 1963 at the UCLA Medical Center after learning that he had acute lymphatic cancer. Five months later, Powell succumbed to the disease. Art Director Carroll Clark developed prostate cancer not long after, and at about the same time makeup chief Webb Overlander had a cancerous lung removed. Character actress Jeanne Gearson would eventually develop skin cancer. Moorehead died from a malignancy in April, 1974, and Wayne's heroic fifteen-year cancer battle came to an end with his death on June 4, 1979. Hayward waged her own fight against a brain tumor and defied medical odds for three years before joining the list of victims on March 14, 1975. Ironically, the Brooklyn spitfire who had always demanded control of her own personal and professional destiny would never know the true source of her illness, the reason for her death. Surely no one was better qualified to play—or live—the bittersweet role.

It came as a surprise to no one—with the possible exception of producer Hughes—that *The Conqueror* was a dismal failure both critically and commercially. Ultimately, the movie would have the dubious distinction of being listed among the "50 Worst Films of All Time." Hughes did not share that opinion. When he finally sold RKO, he bought back *The Conqueror* and Wayne's equally unmemorable *Jet Pilot*. Price: a cool $12 million. During his final hermetic years of psychosis and drug addiction, he sat alone in his room with the windows taped shut, watching these and a few other pictures over and over again.

Joan Crawford, Lana Turner and Susan's onetime nemesis, Jane Wyman, had scratched for the lead opposite Ty Power in *Untamed*, a Henry King-directed Technicolor adventure set amid the struggle of Dutch settlers to wrest African territory from hostile natives. Even though Zanuck had turned over the production reins at Twentieth Century-Fox to Buddy Adler, there was no doubt about who would get the role of Irish-lass-turned-jungle-fighter Katie O'Neill. Again, Susan filmed her scenes from the comfort of a Hollywood sound stage. Power, in the meantime, was becoming accustomed to being upstaged by La Hayward.

At a Bel Air party in 1950, Clark Gable had been holding forth with his usual tricks—the King's most disconcerting habit was popping out his false teeth, then lapsing into an all-too-convincing imitation of Gabby Hayes. Eddy Duchin and Hoagy Carmichael traded off at the piano, accompanying Bing Crosby and Judy Garland as they warbled a duet. Charlie Chaplin sat sipping a scotch and soda, pausing to reminisce for anyone who would listen. Before the evening was over, everyone would become sufficiently bored to start playing "The Game," a form of charades with very complicated rules. Gable, Bogart, Ty Power, James Stewart and Henry Fonda loved The Game; it gave them the opportunity to make funny noises, hop around on one foot and generally enjoy behaving like children.

A hush fell over the crowd when a vision in violet breezed into the room: the sparks between Gable and Hayward were enough to bring the rest of the festivities to a breathless standstill. Gable instantly recognized that famous come-hither look, but nearsighted Susan could not even see that he was in the room, much less intentionally send him romantic signals. After exchanging a few pleasantries with the host, she spun around and was out the door. Gable, dismayed, went back to removing his choppers.

Now, five years later, Susan and Gable were formally introduced. The occasion was their first and only film together, *Soldier of Fortune.* Grace Kelly had forgone the role at the last minute to marry Prince Rainier of Monaco, and Buddy Adler at once saw Susan as the logical alternative. Gable was already packing for Hong Kong, and his new leading lady was so excited at the prospect of actually going on location for six weeks with the twins that she did not anticipate trouble from Jess. He moved quickly to obtain a court order prohibiting her from leaving the country with Tim and Greg. The grounds: such a trip would subject them to danger and disease. Rather than leave the kids behind, Susan returned to the Fox lot to shoot her scenes.

VII

Tomorrow Comes Today

All Hollywood lined up for the role of the torch singer reclaimed by Alcoholics Anonymous in Lillian Roth's million-selling autobiography *I'll Cry Tomorrow*. Jane Wyman (would she never learn?), Ann Blythe, Julie Harris, Jane Russell, Shelley Winters, Rhonda Fleming, Jeanne Crain, Grace Kelly, Eva Marie Saint, Piper Laurie, June Allyson, Jan Sterling, Dana Wynter, Barbara Rush, Jean Simmons and Janet Leigh were all in the race at one time or another. Allyson—Dick Powell's wife and now at her peak as a box office draw in her own right—seemed to have the job sewed up. *I'll Cry Tomorrow* director-designate Chuck Walters and screenwriter Helen Deutsch were old friends from her days on Broadway in *Panama Hattie* and *Pal Joey*. No sooner had they taken on the project of making Lillian Roth's life come to life on screen than they were hard at work trying to make *I'll Cry Tomorrow* (a takeoff on Scarlett O'Hara's closing line in *Gone With the Wind*, "I'll think about it tomorrow"), a vehicle for Allyson.

When they were at last finished tinkering with the story, Walters and Deutsch marched into the office of MGM chief Dore Schary. It was then they learned that Susan, who owed MGM a film, had brought the property to Schary in the first place. Hayward had argued that Roth's candid memoirs, written in collaboration with Gerold Frank and Mike Connolly, "combine the best elements of my two favorite films, *Smash-Up* and *With a Song in My Heart.*" Schary went ahead and secured a verbal option from Roth, who had Susan in mind for the role even before the book's completion. Then Susan put together a package for MGM that included Lawrence Weingarten as producer, Walters as director, Deutsch as writer—and Susan as star. Included as featured players in Susan's proposal were Jo Van Fleet, Richard Conte, Eddie Albert, Albert's wife Margo (best remembered for the scene in which she shrivels in the snow while escaping from Shangri-la in *Lost Horizon*), Don Taylor and Don Barry—a Hollywood womanizer who was destined to act out a nasty little offscreen scenario with Hayward not long after *I'll Cry Tomorrow*'s completion.

The script submitted by Walters and Deutsch was clearly tailored to June Allyson and not to Susan Hayward. Schary rejected it out of hand and called Susan for suggestions. Scanning the scene, Susan honed in on the man who had done a magnificent job directing Shirley Booth in her Oscar-winning *Come Back, Little Sheba* role and Anna Magnani in Paramount's *The Rose Tattoo*—Danny Mann. And Jay Richard Kennedy was a much-talked-about recent addition to the local colony of screenwriters. Susan hired them both. Much to their chagrin, Walters and Deutsch had maneuvered themselves out of a job.

There was no question in Roth's mind who was best suited to play her on celluloid. Like Froman, Roth lobbied vocally for Hayward to take on the assignment. On her own, Susan hopped aboard a flight to Las Vegas and caught Lillian's act several times at El Rancho Vegas on the strip. Five nights in a row, Susan sat at ringside or discreetly in the back, committing every gesture, every nuance to memory. Several weeks later, Susan paid a call on Roth at her bungalow at the Beverly Hills Hotel. She arrived wearing a pair of black silk Chinese pajamas with a coat thrown over them. They talked for hours, and by the time Susan left Lillian did not know who was imitating whom. "We were both as emotional about things," Roth wrote in her sequel, *Beyond My Worth*, "so that when we faced each other it was almost like looking into a mirror; I was looking at Lillian and she was looking at Susan."

As had been the case with Jane Froman in *With a Song in My Heart*, Susan was resigned to hearing someone else's voice coming out of her mouth in *I'll Cry Tomorrow*. Eager to find the right voice, she met with MGM's multi-Oscared musical director Johnny Green. The composer-arranger-conductor sat down at his Steinway and began noodling as Schary and a couple of studio executives looked on. Green ordered the man in the control booth to start recording and asked Susan to sing a few notes. If they were to come up with the right "voice double" for the star, Green had to know what her precise vocal traits were. Susan froze. She refused to sing a note until everyone except for Green left the room. When they were alone, Susan claimed she was an off-key shower singer and that she really didn't know any songs. Fumbling for something appropriate but not too intimidating, Green came up with a well-worn copy of the Harold Arlen standard "Let's Fall in Love" and handed it to the star. He led off in a low key, and after a few bars began singing in his own somewhat winey pitch. Susan merely stared at him in utter dismay.

"Don't just stand there," Green demanded. "Make a sound, *any* sound. Fart!"

Susan exploded with laughter, then began singing along. Green almost fell off the piano bench. Susan was shaking like an aspen leaf but had a perfect sense of phrasing, rhythm and line. The sounds came naturally. She was no less surprised with her performance, and in a rare moment of abandon kicked off her high heels and belted out several choruses.

Green took the recording directly to Schary, and after they listened to it together, Green leaped to his feet. "Susan's voice is full of imperfections," he conceded, "but her voice has real beauty. She's a powerhouse musical talent." Schary agreed. By using her own singing voice, Susan would, he reasoned, add at least $3 million to the domestic gross of the film and probably even more abroad. Susan was to do all her own singing in *I'll Cry Tomorrow*, and production would be delayed eight weeks while she spent time with a vocal coach to bring out the best in this untapped musical talent.

The pressure was on as it had never been before. Now that her own distinctive singing voice would be filling theaters, Susan had taken on the burden of sounding as convincing as she acted and looked. Added to her grueling schedule of script conferences, fittings and rehearsals were three hours a day of physically and emotionally taxing voice lessons.

So much hinged on the outcome of her forty-ninth picture. For her entire professional career, Susan had struggled to keep her private life out of the papers. Now that the sordid details of her marriage to Jess and her affair with Hughes had been dragged through the papers, she had to regain her self-esteem. *I'll Cry Tomorrow* offered Susan the opportunity to show that she was beholden to no man. She had found the property, had fought for it and won it. Now she was working harder than ever before to make it work—to make *I'll Cry Tomorrow* the definitive portrayal of one woman's near-fatal collision with fame and the bottle, not to mention Susan Hayward's finest 117 minutes on the screen.

Enter Jess, fresh from a minor part in Warner's *Kentucky Rifle* and wanting to talk over their mutual interest in the twins' future. Understandably hesitant at first, Susan eventually acquiesced to a secret meeting on neutral ground, with her lawyer present.

Swathed in mink, Hayward settled her five-foot-three-inch, 110-pound frame in the back seat of her chauffeur-driven limousine and peered from behind rhinestone-rimmed sunglasses through the window at shoppers scurrying into Mays, Bullocks and the other stores strewn the length of Wilshire Boulevard. As her driver turned the car right onto the long, palm-lined drive leading to the Ambassador Hotel, Susan noticed that her diamond ring—the one she had paid for herself when John Carroll jilted her a dozen years before—cast flecks of sunlight on the Cadillac's interior. She turned her hand slowly and watched the kaleidoscopic patterns change. The limo came to a stop behind the hotel's main building, in the carport of one of its private bungalows. She pulled on a pair of pale jasmine gloves like a boxer getting ready to enter the ring.

Jess was waiting inside. He looked particularly tanned and fit, she thought, but Susan wasted no time on trading compliments. She was still steaming because he had prevented her from taking Greg and Tim with her to Hong Kong. How dare he imply that she was an unfit mother, she demanded. He could, he replied, because she was—an absentee movie star mother who left her offspring in the care of servants or her mother while she slaked her unquenchable thirst for power in Lotusland. The meeting, not altogether surprisingly, quickly dissolved into a verbal slugfest, with Susan's hapless lawyer acting as referee.

Afterward, the press, still hungering for more juicy tidbits concerning the year's messiest divorce, cornered Jess after the "secret" powwow. "Susan will never talk to me unless she wants something," he carped. "She won't speak to me when I come to pick up the boys. She won't even let the servants talk to me. The children see this and other things, and it has to be bad for them. I admit I blew up at the finish of the meeting. We had gotten absolutely nowhere. I said some unpleasant things, but they had been on my chest for two years."

Susan shut the door forever on further discussions with Barker. "I have my reasons for not seeing Jess alone," she explained, warning that they were now "diametrically opposed people" who resorted to violence when left alone. Nor did she have any qualms about her conduct as a mother or the emotional well-being of her children. "The boys," she declared, "are in better shape than they have ever been before."

Less than forty hours after her rambunctious session with Jess, Susan returned from a pleasant dinner with Darryl Zanuck at the Mocambo and tucked Greg and Tim into bed. The maid was already asleep in her room, and Susan left a note for her on the kitchen table asking to be awakened at 11:30 the next morning—Tuesday, April 25, 1955. The note was signed "Miss H."

Susan's hands shook as she pushed aside the mink that hung in her closet, searching for her blue silk pajamas. Wrapping herself in a white quilted robe ironically appliquéd with little red hearts, she went to the medicine cabinet for the only thing that could now soothe her nerves.

Susan's friend and physician Stanley Immerman had prescribed a mild sedative for the times when she felt tired and moody—but he had no way of knowing that she was taking two and sometimes three times the prescribed dosage, and that the cumulative impact of these barbiturates was to merely make her more depressed and more dependent. Nor did Dr. Immerman know that Susan had fortified herself with another prescription for sleeping pills from a different doctor.

Despite her heavy reliance on these small yellow tablets, Susan had somehow managed to hoard two full bottles—enough for a lethal dose. Why had she hoarded them? Perhaps she wanted to be assured of having an ample supply as her need grew. Or perhaps she had long planned on doing what she was about to do this bleak April night.

Opening the cabinet, Susan stared straight ahead at the two cotton-stuffed bottles with the white plastic caps. A glass smudged with fingerprints and toothpaste had been left upside down on the bathroom counter. She picked it up, washed it off and filled it from the tap. She took two of the tablets, as prescribed by both doctors, and returned to the living room to curl up on the couch with her shooting script of *I'll Cry Tomorrow*. Roth's own desperate story mingled in Susan's mind with her own. Would she, like Lillian, always be manipulated by men? She had managed to keep her personal life out of the papers for a decade, but now it was a sideshow in which she was the star freak. The weeks of the trial had been a nightmare, with photographers relentlessly pressing in, lightbulbs flashing, and notebook-clutching reporters demanding to know every sordid detail. "Poor Susan Hayward," one reporter wrote. "Some Hollywood stars spend a lifetime transgressing and often stay undetected. Whereas Susan has always taken pains to maintain a sequestered personal life.

So wouldn't you know that the rare instances when she slipped would be discovered and detailed on front pages around the world."

Susan felt that her life was a shambles, and Jess had made it clear that things would never return to normal as long as she retained custody of the twins. The battles, the bitterness, would go on forever. Susan was thirty-six years old, and the pressures on her were not unlike those that would later kill another star in her late thirties, Marilyn Monroe. Both had given too much of themselves to Hollywood, both felt that they had been psychologically raped.

Sinking further into this quagmire of despair, Susan put down the script and walked slowly, deliberately toward the bathroom. This time, she stood at the washbasin and systematically took the tablets, two by two, until both bottles were empty—at least thirty in all. Just as calmly, she went back to reading the script, making the necessary marginal notations in red pencil.

It took less than twenty minutes for the pills to begin to take effect. Her head was already swimming by the time she reached page 61. It was on that page that Lillian Roth tells her mother not to worry about her drinking—that no matter what happened, Mom would be taken care of. Susan circled the dialogue again and again in red, then staggered toward the telephone. A sense of panic gripped her, triggered by the lines pertaining to Roth's mother but heightened by the disorienting effects of the pills themselves. Her fingers fumbled on the dial, but somehow Susan managed to place the call.

Across town, Ellen Marrener was startled awake. The clock on her night table read 3 A.M. Not quite alert, she answered the telephone in a sleepy, half-conscious voice. The person on the other end sounded equally groggy, though her voice was tinged with a disturbing urgency.

"Don't worry, Mother," Susan slurred, "you'll be taken care of."

Ellen tried to get her daughter to explain precisely what was wrong, but Susan kept repeating the same reassurances. Then she started to cry uncontrollably. Her voice became high and hysterical—as if she were horrified that someone might dare to suggest that Susan Hayward, the famous movie star, might not provide for her mother after her death.

"Have you taken something, Susan?" Ellen asked to no avail. "Hang on," Susan's mother pleaded. "Oh God, hang on!" The phone went dead.

Ellen wasted no time in calling Wally. He had always been his little sister's protector; maybe now he could protect her from herself. He was fast asleep, but within seconds was out the door and into his car for the twelve-minute drive to Susan's. Ellen then called the Los Angeles police. "I'm Susan Hayward's mother," she said, "and I think my daughter is going to commit suicide." There was a pause while Lieutenant Charles Glazer weighed in his mind whether or not this was a crank call. "Where does she live?" he demanded. "3737 Longridge, in Sherman Oaks," Ellen quickly replied, repeating it once before she slammed down the receiver and headed for the door herself.

Van Nuys detectives G. W. Wilkerson and Kenneth Brondell arrived at the front door of Susan's stately home within fifteen minutes of receiving Mrs. Marrener's call. They rang the doorbell, then, not getting any response, began calling her name. "Susan? Susan!" yelled Wilkerson. A vague "Yeah, yeah" was all they heard, then silence.

Acting swiftly—both men had handled suicides before—they forced open a French door that opened onto the patio and went in. The house was ablaze with lights. Cautiously, they made their way into the living room. There, sprawled on the floor, was Susan Hayward. Beside her was the script, the key words circled in red. She was unconscious. An ambulance had been called by the police, but Susan was breathing so hard and with such difficulty that they decided not to wait for it. Wally had arrived within minutes, and helped the detectives carry his sister's limp body to the squad car. They raced through the streets to North Hollywood Receiving Hospital, where photographers were already waiting to snap Susan being carried out of the car and into the emergency room, a tongue depressor hanging from her slack lips. Was she dead a photographer asked. In a matter of seconds, the detectives thought, she would be.

The doctor on duty took Susan's pulse, respiration and blood pressure. He checked her glazed eyes, then clamped her tongue to keep Susan from biting it or gagging while they pumped her stomach. There was so little time, and for a moment the doctor doubted whether he could save her life. Once her stomach was pumped, they examined the contents. The dosage was lethal, but there was no way of telling how much had already been absorbed into her system. By now Susan had sunk into a deep coma. Her life was ebbing away.

Shortly before dawn, an ambulance pulled up to the emergency room entrance. Dr. Immerman had ordered Susan's transfer to Cedars of Lebanon in Los Angeles. An ocean of photographers surged toward the dolly, but the object of their attention was oblivious to the volley of popping flashbulbs. An oxygen mask was over her face, and her red hair was now streaked with gray. Wally followed the ambulance in his car. Both MGM and Twentieth had dispatched emissaries to Cedars, where Immerman had her registered as "Mary Brennan." All visitors were banned—even her mother. Susan's agents wasted no time in trying to contact their prized client, but Immerman barred the hospital door. A brief statement was issued: Miss Hayward was overworked, tired and had argued with her ex-husband over how to raise their children.

Two thousand miles away on a promotional tour for *Kentucky Rifle*, Jess Barker collapsed when he heard the news. "Oh, my God!" he moaned to his *Kentucky Rifle* co-star Chill Wills before breaking down, "I love her. I love her." Wills told reporters: "It's a shame that people in love have to have this happen to them. He's been carrying the torch for her so long and she's still in love with him."

Once he had recovered, Barker locked himself in his hotel room and called Dr. Immerman in Los Angeles (wire photos run in hundreds of newspapers the next day would show him on the telephone, sobbing hysterically). Within hours, Barker was winging his way to California. "BARKER RUSHES TO SUSAN'S SIDE" blared the front-page headline in the New York *Daily News*, accompanied by a photograph of an unconscious Susan being carried to the squad car by detectives Brondell and Wilkerson; a cigar was clenched in Brondell's teeth. "If she hadn't gotten treatment right away," Wilkerson told a transfixed public, "she would have been a goner."

Two days later, Susan had slept off the effects of the pills and had regained her composure enough to at least talk with her mother. "I feel so ashamed," she admitted—not so much because the official police records now showed that her overdose was a "probable suicide attempt," but because she had somehow lost control of her life. It was just an accident, she insisted to a doubting Ellen. Wally believed her; suicide was something totally out of character for his strong-willed sister.

Friday morning, Susan, looking as though she had never heard of sleeping pills, made a typical Hollywood exit from

Cedars of Lebanon. Surrounded by a platoon of studio press agents and greeted by an army of photographers and reporters, she was wheeled to the door (a hospital rule required that all outgoing patients leave in wheelchairs) by a smiling attendant. Beaming like the starlet of fifteen years before and clad in a white silk dress emblazoned with tiny strawberries, she looked as if she was about to step onto a set. In a sense, she was. As soon as the wheelchair rolled through the doorway, its white-gloved occupant sprang to her feet and hopped into a waiting studio limousine (which had been commandeered from a miffed Bette Davis)—but not before the assembled newsmen got off a few questions. She told them that she was most eagerly looking forward to a reunion with her sons. Would she get back together with Jess, even though she would not even let him visit her at the hospital? "You know what the lady said," she smiled.

The lady, of course, said no.

VIII

And When She Was Bad

When he picked up the morning paper and read that Susan had taken an overdose, Danny Mann was stunned. He had dismissed as gossip all the rumors that Susan and Jess were still waging emotional war on one another. While she was holed up incommunicado at the hospital, Susan spoke on the phone only to her mother and to Mann—if for no other reason than that she wanted to assuage any fears he and MGM might have that she might bow out of *I'll Cry Tomorrow*. Mann had an appointment to see Susan the morning after she arrived home from the hospital. But as he pulled up in his battered Pontiac he saw that he would have to make his way through scores of newsmen. Once he got inside the house, it was like entering the eye of the hurricane. All was quiet and calm. Waiting alone in the living room, he spotted the *I'll Cry Tomorrow* script on the coffee table and picked it up. There, circled in red, was the line: "Relax, Ma. I'll always be able to support you." At that moment, Mann, hearing footsteps behind him, turned to see Susan coming down the stairs—floating, really—in a cloud of pink organdy. She looked recharged, revitalized, stunning. It was time to go back to work.

The next several weeks of shooting were therapy for

Susan—an emotional catharsis that would keep her from again trying to take her life. Every day of shooting, before she would go onto the set, Susan sat alone with Mann and listened intently as he described the scene and the emotions she would be called upon to summon. Then they talked about the tragic circumstances of Lillian Roth's life —her insatiably ambitious stage mother, the death of her fiancé, her decline into alcoholism, her chronic victimization by men. They had already done ample research: Susan, Mann and the producer Lawrence Weingarten had visited jails and hospitals and AA meetings to, as Susan put it, "know that woman's life and what it had been." But these private talks with Mann struck a raw nerve with Susan. Once she began sobbing, Mann could tell she was ready for the scene. If anger was called for, she often worked herself up into a rage, kicking doors and throwing things until she had built up the necessary head of steam.

For his part, Mann did his best to insure authenticity—even at the risk of angering his star. He would not let Susan get her hair curled, as she had requested, or use lipstick or makeup when the scenes called for her to look as if she were headed for Skid Row. In the middle of a take, if he felt her hair was not sufficiently mussed, he stopped the camera, splashed water on Susan and matted her hair down with his hands. For the hospital scene in which a nurse pours Roth her first drink, Mann tricked his star by substituting the real thing for the colored water that was supposed to be used. The cameras were rolling as the nurse poured four fingers of Bourbon into a glass, then handed it to Susan. She raised it to her mouth, still not knowing it was real whiskey. The grimace that resulted once it hit her lips was genuine, and Susan the actress reacted instinctively—she leaned back on the pillows and downed the entire thing.

The result was what many believed to be one of the

greatest films of the 1950s—certainly the most effective movie about female alcoholism ever made. With it, Susan came up off her knees personally as well as professionally. No one was more moved than Roth herself. "Susan's performance was magnificent," she said after previewing the movie in Chicago. "My throat tightened as I suffered with her. I began to fill up with tears." Roth was not sorry that she had held out for Susan over June Allyson—and neither was MGM. Not only was Susan universally praised for her acting—"A great performance" proclaimed *Variety*, "Gut-wrenching," concurred *Time*—she was suddenly an overnight singing sensation. The Hollywood press once had trumpeted GARBO TALKS! with the advent of motion picture sound; headlines now read HAYWARD SINGS! Indeed, from Susan's throaty rendition of Roth's trademark "When the Red, Red Robin Comes Bob, Bob, Bobbin' Along" to "Sing You Sinners" to "Happiness Is Just a Thing Called Joe" and "I'm Sittin' On Top of the World," Susan displayed as much, if not more, vocal talent than the original. An LP and a single were released from the film, and each made it onto the charts.

Susan, delighted and surprised by the response to her singing, made it quickly known to *South Pacific* director Joshua Logan that she would "do anything" for the part of Nellie Forbush in the film. "Anything?" he asked. "Will you test for it?" "Never." Mitzi Gaynor got the job.

Photoplay's readers voted Susan best actress of the year. *Redbook*, *Look* and a slew of other magazines bestowed on Susan their awards. Susan was the only American among the winners at the Cannes Film Festival. No sooner did she get off the plane at Cannes than she made the columns again. "Where are the men?" she asked reporters. "Not actors. I said men!" At the awards ceremony itself, Susan,

Not a word is exchanged as Susan walks past Jess in a courthouse corridor. Their divorce trial turned into a media circus. CREDIT: THE MEMORY SHOP, INC.

As the court visits the scene of their spectacular row—the Barkers' house on Longridge Avenue—Susan does her best to avoid Jess. CREDIT: THE MEMORY SHOP, INC.

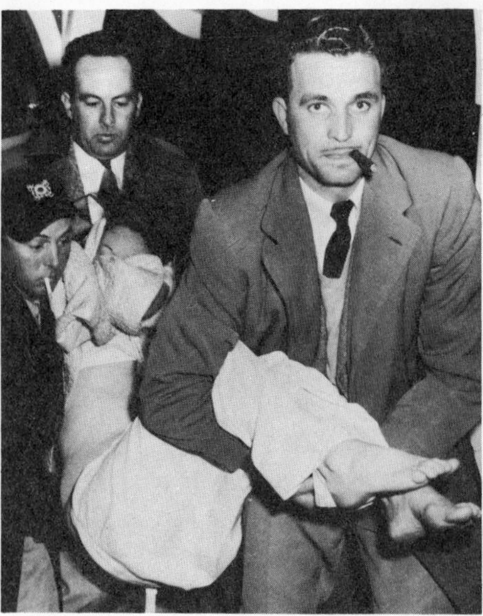

Wally (left) and Detectives Wilkerson and Brondell carry Susan's limp body from her Sherman Oaks house. CREDIT: WIDE WORLD PHOTOS

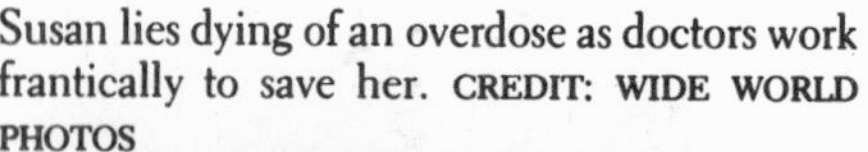

Susan lies dying of an overdose as doctors work frantically to save her. CREDIT: WIDE WORLD PHOTOS

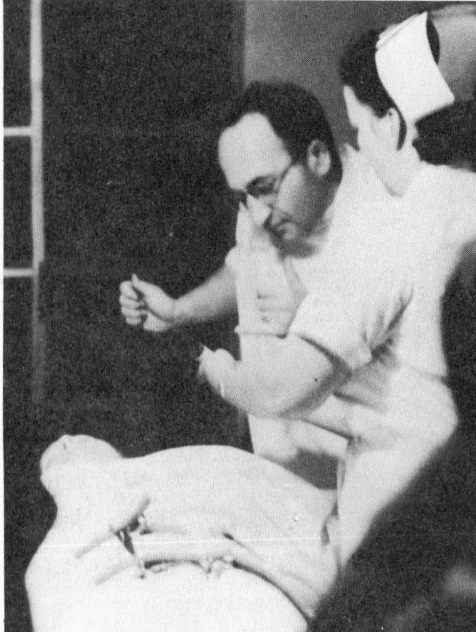

Brondell and Wilkerson arrive at Hollywo Hospital and take Susan from police car emergency room. CREDIT: WIDE WORLD PHOT

Four days after her suicide attempt, the s makes her Hollywood exit from Cedars Lebanon Hospital. CREDIT: WIDE WOR PHOTOS

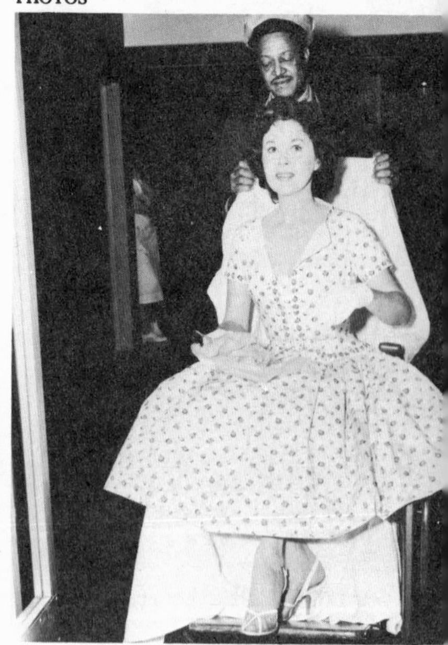

As Lillian Roth at her peak, doing a rousing rendition of "Sing You Sinners" in *I'll Cry Tomorrow.*

With the real Lillian Roth at the 1955 premiere of *I'll Cry Tomorrow.* **CREDIT: PICTORIAL PARADE**

Mom seemed a sure winner for *I'll Cry Tomorrow* when she brought Gregory (left) and Timothy along for the 1956 Academy Award ceremonies. CREDIT: PICTORIAL PARADE

san, Dick Powell and John "Genghis" ayne: marked for death on location in Utah *The Conqueror.* CREDIT: PICTORIAL PARADE

Mr. and Mrs. Eaton Chalkley turned heads at the 1958 Foreign Press Awards Dinner in Los Angeles. CREDIT: PICTORIAL PARADE

Taming General Kirk Douglas in *Top Secret Affair.* CREDIT: MOVIE STAR NEWS

The toughest cookie at the penitentiary—as condemned murderess Barbara Graham in *I Want to Live!* CREDIT: THE MEMORY SHOP, INC.

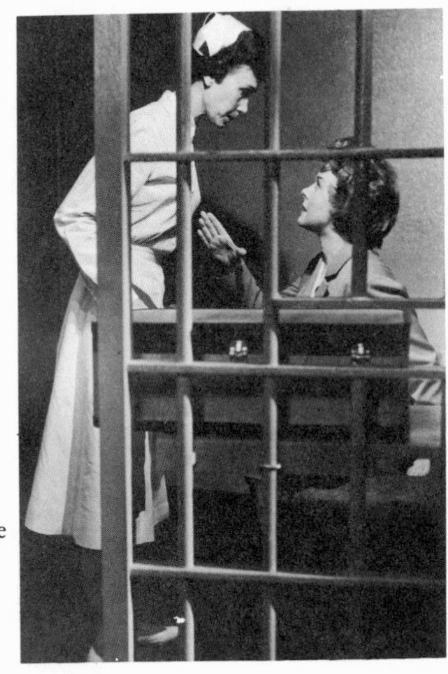

I Want to Live's prison nurse, Alice Backes, faces off with Susan.

The winner! With Best Supporting Actor Burl Ives (for *The Big Country*) and David Niven, Best Actor for *Separate Tables*. Not shown: Wendy Hiller, Best Supporting Actress, also for *Separate Tables*.

still the most popular actress in the world, got a fifteen-minute standing ovation. Susan never hesitated to give Mann credit, and to proclaim him "the best goddamned director anywhere." She knew that Mann's lucky number was 9, so when his birthday rolled around on August 8 she saw to it that a gigantic crystal bowl filled with 99 long-stemmed roses arrived at his door.

Susan was a shoo-in at the Academy Awards—or at least so it seemed. Even Mann, who had also directed Oscar-nominated Anna Magnani in that year's *The Rose Tattoo*, felt Hayward was the odds-on favorite in her fourth try at bat.

Driving the only Pontiac in a sea of Rolls-Royces, Mann had such difficulty getting his car attended to that he nearly missed the presentations. From his vantage point in the theater, he could see both his stars—Hayward, smiling confidently, and a pensive, almost moody Magnani. Susan was confident enough to have already invited scores of friends to a catered victory celebration at her home. Escorted to the ceremonies by Timothy and Gregory, she registered no emotion as Anna Magnani's name was read as Best Actress of 1955. For the first time in anyone's memory, the applause came close to being drowned out by groans of disbelief. She went through with the party, managing to mask any signs of disappointment. Once the guests left, she dissolved in tears.

Susan sought solace in the arms of Don "Red" Barry, the chunky star of a dozen Republic Westerns, the shoot-'em-up Red Ryder series, and a bit player in *I'll Cry Tomorrow*. It was yet another liaison she soon came to regret. Dropping into Barry's house unannounced at 11 A.M. for coffee, blond starlet Jil (*A Twinkle in God's Eye*) Jarmyn was greeted by Barry at the door. He was wearing maroon pajamas. Suggesting that her visit was ill-timed, Barry barred the door, but Jarmyn pushed her way in to discover Susan in bed, clad in blue-and-white pajamas.

"Get that two-bit whore out of here!" screamed Jarmyn.

"Who is this girl?" Susan yelled.

Before anyone had a chance to answer, Susan attacked Jarmyn, batting her over the head with a wooden clothes-brush and tearing the buttons off her blouse. Barry, who had once been engaged to Jarmyn briefly, separated the two and went into the kitchen to make coffee. Within seconds, Susan took her lighted cigarette and shoved it at the terrified Jarmyn.

"Cut it out or I'll start screaming!" yelled Jil as she retreated to the living room.

"Go ahead and scream," snarled Susan. "I don't care what you do."

Jil fell backward over a couch, then slammed into a coffee table as she made her getaway from her enraged pursuer. Barry, who had once showered Joan Crawford with $50,000 in furs and jewels during a brief romance, returned to find Jil gone and Susan simmering.

Jarmyn wasted no time filing an assault-and-battery complaint against Susan—the publicity certainly wouldn't hurt Jil's career—and Susan was once again answering questions in court. "Where did the fight start?" the District Attorney asked. "I could say I was in the dining room," replied Susan, "but I will tell you it was in the bedroom." She went on to say that she couldn't recall exactly who struck the first blow, but allowed that it was probably her. "That girl," testified Susan, "walked in and made an insulting remark to me. I'm red-haired and Irish and have quite a temper, you know." Barry's gallant reaction: "Look, I'm in the middle of this."

Under pressure from studios very keen on protecting

their $12 million-plus investment, Jarmyn eventually agreed to drop the charges—but not before Susan's children were dragged into the drama. Jarmyn had hired Jess Barker's lawyer, Sammy Hahn, to represent her in the assault-and-battery proceedings. "This incident," Hahn said ominously, "might help Jess's appeal to get back his children." Given Barker's own less-than-exemplary private life, however, the Battle of Barry's Bedroom was not enough to tip the scales in Jess's favor on the question of custody.

In the end, Marlene Dietrich got off the best line about the scandal. Recalling that both women had originally claimed going to Barry's for a spot of coffee, Dietrich cracked, "Zat Barry sure must make good coffee!"

To eradicate the last vestiges of her life as Mrs. Jess Barker, Susan, smartly attired in a honey-colored silk suit and matching coat, appeared in Judge John L. Ford's Superior Court to officially have her name changed from Edythe Marrener Barker back to Edythe Marrener. The Judge asked her why she wanted her original name restored. "Well, Your Honor," she answered, "my business affairs have been conducted under that name in the past and will be in the future. It will be less confusing." Judge Ford granted the request, and Susan left the courthouse with her last remaining tie to Jess—save for the children—severed.

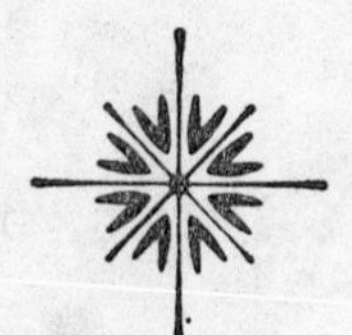

EATON

"What do you do?"
—Cop to Susan in
I Want to Live
"The best I can."

"I've done both, lost
and won. And believe
me, winning is best.
By far."
—Susan

IX

The Prize

"Reliability, tenderness, strength—and an equal income." These were the qualities Susan now said she was looking for in a man. She found them in Floyd Eaton Chalkley. Born in Washington, D.C., to a working-class family, he worked in the local drugstore, played sandlot ball and eventually earned a law degree at Georgetown University. Chalkley, well over six feet tall and solidly handsome in a Ward Bond sort of way, joined the Federal Bureau of Investigation during World War II. When the war was over, Eaton was one of two hundred cut from the ranks of G-men when Congress refused to grant the appropriations requested by then-director J. Edgar Hoover. Chalkley capitalized on the firings. He picked up a number of the best agents who had been let go and started his own D.C.-based investigating agency. He installed security systems in large industries throughout the country and, continuing his law practice, accumulated wealthy and famous clients to push him into the millionaire category—all in the span of five years.

In the fall of 1956, Chalkley, who had been a bachelor since he had divorced his first wife in 1950, decided to buy a Cadillac dealership in the sleepy Georgia town of Carrollton, some forty miles outside Atlanta. He told his old boyhood chum Vincent X. Flaherty, now a columnist for the Los Angeles *Examiner*, that he knew he had a good investment. But he fretted that he was invading strange territory; he didn't know anyone in Georgia. Flaherty did: Susan's old "Uncle Harvey" Hester, good-natured owner of Aunt Fanny's Restaurant in Atlanta.

Flaherty decided to bring Uncle Harvey and Eaton Chalkley together, so he invited them to a party at his Beverly Hills home. Eaton brought an attractive young girl. "Uncle Harvey" came with Susan Hayward. The party wound up at the Mocambo, where Susan sat out most of the numbers because Harvey hated to dance. Eaton was equally miserable. Flaherty nudged his old friend. "Hey Eaton, why in the world don't you dance with Susan?" Eaton balked. "Oh, she doesn't want to dance with me." Finally, Flaherty literally shoved Eaton into Susan's arms. "Mix in, pal, mix in!"

The handsome ex-G-man and the flame-haired movie star discovered they had much in common—particularly a love for horses (Susan had learned to ride before she was married to Jess) and baseball. Around World Series time, both could be found cheering in bleachers at Yankee Stadium (though Susan also made her annual pilgrimage to watch the Dodgers in her native Brooklyn). Susan and Eaton were inseparable over the next few months. He took her to see his Mt. Vernon-like estate in Virginia, and as he did for all his guests, pridefully pointed to the long and sharp rise in the terrain which vividly marked the earthworks where Robert E. Lee's troops had fought a bloody battle against the Union Army of General Meade.

Eaton was also an avid game fisherman, and primarily to satisfy that passion he had purchased a waterfront home on ritzy Nurmi Drive in Fort Lauderdale. But the place Eaton planned to make his true home was Chalmers

Farms, his four-hundred-acre estate in Carrollton, Georgia, with its glass playhouse and man-made lake. There was much more room for riding, and it was only an hour's plane ride from Ft. Lauderdale and fishing. Susan fell in love with all of it—Georgia, Florida, riding, fishing—and Eaton.

Most of the time during their courtship, however, it was Eaton who flew to Hollywood to be with Susan. Distance meant nothing to him. Before boarding a plane for Kentucky to catch the Derby or for California to see the Rose Bowl, he merely phoned ahead and said, "I'll see you in a couple of hours." Susan basked in the attention. Although Howard Hughes's *The Conqueror* was an unmitigated critical and financial disaster, it kept Susan in the public eye through 1956, allowing her the time to be choosy about the next part she would undertake. Perhaps she was being a bit too persnickety; Susan turned down the title role in *The Three Faces of Eve*, the part which brought an Oscar to relative newcomer Joanne Woodward.

"Women are only hard until they meet the right man and fall in love," Susan mused to a friend. "Any woman would put love before a career." And Susan did when Eaton asked her to elope with him. In a last-minute panic, Eaton called up his old chum Vince Flaherty. "Look at me," he told Flaherty. "I go and come when I please, my businesses are doing fine. I can knock off work and go fishing whenever I want—or take in a Rose Bowl game. Nobody's asking, 'When are you coming home, dear?' or 'Where have you been?' Am I crazy to be getting married again?" Not to Susan, was Flaherty's reply.

Now that he managed to shore up his resolve, Eaton prevailed on his boyhood pal to help them elope—before he "chickened out." "Do you know anybody in Phoenix who can help us have a quiet wedding?" Flaherty called attorney Neil McCarthy, whose close friend was Frank

Brophy, a wealthy Phoenix banker. McCarthy was en route to his ranch. Eaton wanted faster action, so he picked up the phone and called Brophy himself. Brophy arranged everything, but Eaton suddenly realized that he had forgotten something. He rushed down to Rodeo Drive and bought a diamond wedding band. Once back, he packed his bags and took off to collect Susan.

The next day, Flaherty was to meet them both in Phoenix. "Please be there," Eaton pleaded anxiously. For the first time ever, Flaherty saw his always-calm friend trembling. "I'll call you as soon as I arrive," he reassured him. Flaherty did; this time Eaton's tone had escalated to near-hysteria. When he went to get a marriage license, the man at the bureau said he would have to wait the mandatory forty-eight hours. Frank Brophy was once again asked to intervene, but this time he declined. Flaherty cancelled his flight from L.A. to Phoenix and booked a later flight, but late Friday night Eaton called to say that the city of Phoenix actually had granted him and Susan a special writ waiving the forty-eight-hour waiting period. Even though Eaton was a devout Catholic, they were married in a brief civil ceremony that evening—February 8, 1957. He was forty-seven, she was thirty-eight.

Susan was transformed. She promptly sold her properties in California for $1 million and packed for Georgia. Still, she had committed herself to play Clare Booth Luce-like Dotty Peale, a magazine tycoon out to tarnish the medals of spotless hero General Melville Goodwin (Kirk Douglas) in *Top Secret Affair*. Humphrey Bogart and Lauren Bacall had been slated for the parts before Bogart's death, and Susan felt that what her career needed now was an injection of romantic comedy.

Unfortunately, the chemistry between the two was not magic; *Top Secret Affair* made a reasonable profit, but Susan herself deemed it "a bomb." Yet never did she look happier or more attractive. Recalled character actor Roland Winters, who had a supporting role in *Affair*, "I and everyone on the set was overcome by the unwaning desire to get into her drawers. She was the most gorgeous female I had ever seen." All crass remarks aside, Susan was glowing now. She had discovered with Eaton the kind of quiet contentment that made her all but forget her career. Eaton gladly took on the responsibility for being stepfather to the twins. He was no stranger to family life: his son and two daughters lived with their mother outside Atlanta.

Home for the Chalkleys was the estate at Carrollton. A seventy-five-year-old red clapboard farmhouse at the gate was the first thing any visitor saw; it had been converted by Chalkley to a guesthouse. The emerald-green pasturelands were crisscrossed by a latticework of whitewashed fences, and a score of horses could be seen grazing beneath the hot Georgia sun. At the end of the winding, half-mile-long driveway stood Casa Chalkley, an unassuming, one-story air-conditioned structure faced with granite from nearby Stone Mountain and roofed with crushed white Georgia marble. Surrounded by pines, the house faced Chalkley's mirror-like fifteen-acre man-made lake. Inside the floors were of black Georgia slate, and the walls were constructed of tongue-and-groove logs, painted white. Susan made the wide entrance hall into something of a mini art gallery, covering the walls with her favorite Moderns and Impressionists.

Susan's pride was the huge fireplace in the living room, which also extended into the bedroom on the other side of the wall. Eaton had installed a clever panel device on the raised hearth so that the bedroom and living room could be connected or divided by the fireplace at will. Facing on the lake, the yellow-and-white master bedroom was adjacent to Susan's dressing room, with its pink walls and pink marble countertops. As well as being a place to dress, this small room served as Susan's studio whenever she felt like painting.

The kitchen, run by Susan's stately-looking black maid Curly Crowder, opened out onto a bright, glass-enclosed breakfast room. Here the twins, who shared a pine-paneled bedroom on weekends and holidays only, downed their Wheaties before being driven back to Georgia Military Academy in College Park, some thirty minutes away. Perhaps because Susan was an absentee movie star mother, Tim continued to be something of a troublemaker. Greg, always more even-tempered than his brother, was already on the road to becoming a veterinarian—as far away from the phony world of premieres and Oscars and p.r. flacks as he could get. Both, however, enjoyed life at Carrollton and begged their discipline-minded mother to let them visit whenever they could. There was every reason for them to. Not only were there horses to ride, but a glass-walled playhouse on the lake complete with indoor barbecue, a dressing room for swim parties, a player piano—and Mom's gleaming acting trophies.

For the first time since her earliest Brooklyn days she felt warmed by the genuine affection of her neighbors. The townsfolk of sleepy Carrollton (its population then numbered around 10,000) viewed her simply as Mrs. Chalkley, and for once she enjoyed *not* being fawned over as a movie star. Shortly after arriving there, the newlywed Mrs. Chalkley was getting ready to walk out of a drugstore when a man behind the counter, puzzled by her accent, asked if she came from England.

"No, I'm from a place called Brooklyn," she replied.

"Where's that?"

"That's up North."

"Oh, I see. Well, I knew you weren't from anywheres around here."

Calling itself "The City of Opportunity," Carrollton

boasted the campus of West Georgia State College, a granite, neo-Grecian county courthouse and narrow streets lined with pines, elms, willows and dogwood. The Little Tallapoosa River emptied into muddy Lake Carroll, which gave the town and the county its name. The dignified but unpretentious brick and clapboard homes in the center of town gave way to tin-roofed shanties on the city's edge, but these in turn were replaced by sprawling farms as one got further into the country. It was here, seven miles from the courthouse, that Eaton built his idyllic world for Susan.

She still owed Fox eight pictures over the next six years, but it took a desperate plea from a man to whom she felt she owed a great debt to finally drag Susan away from her personal Shangri-la. Walter Wanger, broke and determined to expose the criminal justice system after his own jail term over the shooting of Jennings Lang, had sent Susan the two-hundred-page outline for *The Barbara Graham Story* by Pulitzer Prize-winning San Francisco *Examiner* reporter Ed Montgomery. Graham was a beautiful San Francisco bargirl who, many believed, was wrongly convicted of murder and sent to the gas chamber at San Quentin after a slanderous media campaign against her.

Susan was fascinated by the contradictory traits in the personality of this woman who had an extraordinary impact on everyone she met. She was first a juvenile delinquent, then a criminal—arrested on bad check charges, perjury, soliciting and a flood of misdemeanors. But somewhere along the line, Susan noted, she had managed to be a caring wife and mother. Susan read Barbara's letters—often literate, sometimes profound. She loved poetry and music, classical as well as jazz.

Yet none of this seemed to square with the picture drawn by newspapers at the time of the trial. Reporters, Montgomery in particular, had originally branded Graham the "Tiger Woman" and "Bloody Babs"—a ruthless, amoral killer. Susan studied the final transcript and decided that, although Barbara Graham was probably in the room at the time Mrs. Mabel Monahan was murdered and not at home as she had claimed, she was not guilty of the crime. Susan knew from personal experience that the press could be destructive, and in the tragic case of Barbara Graham it literally had killed an innocent woman. Barbara had had no way to fight back, but by portraying her on the screen Susan did.

Without a finished script, Susan agreed to do the film. Solely on that pledge from Susan, Wanger got the financing he needed. Robert Wise was directing it for Joseph L. Mankiewicz's new Figaro, Inc., production company.

The title was now *I Want to Live!* Wise knew that Susan was ideal for the difficult role. She could convey the difficult childhood, the grinding poverty of her early years, her betrayal by a variety of men, the hard-boiled exterior that masked a quivering mass of insecurity. They even bore a close physical resemblance to one another. But the director, who would go on to win Oscars for his direction of *West Side Story* and *The Sound of Music,* knew all the stories about the star's temperament. He would eventually discover that she was one of the most cooperative actresses in the business, but not before having a head-to-head confrontation even before shooting began.

Always intently concerned about the way she looked on screen, she had requested through her agents her own cinematographer: Stanley Cortez, who had made her captivating in *Smash-Up* and *Top Secret Affair.* Wise sent back word that he wanted "Curly" Linden, whose grainy, documentary style would give *I Want to Live* an authentic look. Linden had also photographed Susan, but she stuck to her original choice. A summit was arranged by Susan's agents in Wise's office. They both made their arguments, but when the dust settled no verdict had been reached. Several days later Susan, persuaded by her agents to concede this point, sent a message to Wise to go ahead and use Linden.

It was the only disagreement between the director and his "temperamental" star. During the first week of filming, Susan was confined to her Beverly Hills Hotel suite with the measles. Once Susan was back on the set, however, Wise was totally impressed by her professionalism. She came in day after day—on time, of course—discussed the scenes, rehearsed them and nearly every time performed them before the camera without a hitch; a minimum number of retakes were required. Susan, as always, had done her homework—visiting women's institutions with Wanger and actually sitting in the gas chamber where Barbara Graham's life had ended three years before. Still, she stuck to the script religiously, only occasionally asking to change a word or phrase if it seemed particularly uncomfortable to her. Wise and Susan never got to know one another personally—she always retired between takes to play cards with her hairdresser or wardrobe women in her trailer—but it did not matter at all to Wise. He was getting brilliant work from one of the finest talents the business had to offer.

Something happened, however, to shatter Wise's euphoria. The day's shooting was to be devoted to Barbara Graham's trial, and 250 extras were on hand for the courtroom scene. But Susan, for the first time during the shooting, was not on hand. Wise dispatched a studio search party, but no one—not her agents, not Wanger, not even her husband—knew where she could be found. Exasperated, Wise finally sent everyone home. It was not until that evening that Wanger called Wise with the answer. Florence was at it again. As she was getting ready to leave for the set, Susan received a call that her sister, by now twice-divorced and a habitué of downtown L.A.'s less fashionable watering holes, was in trouble. Susan, as she had done several times before, personally intervened on Florence's behalf—though it did little to improve relations between them. The next day Susan arrived at work on time. She offered no explanations or apologies, and since it was a potentially touchy personal problem, Wise did not think it necessary to make an issue out of it. Susan had proven herself a dedicated and thorough professional; her absence clearly could not have been helped. Shooting resumed on schedule.

Susan did not consider *I Want to Live* her best effort; she was proudest of *I'll Cry Tomorrow*. But the story of Barbara Graham as filmed by Wise was a searing indictment of capital punishment—the most graphic ever attempted on film. Wise himself had, once again for the sake of authenticity, witnessed an actual execution at San Quentin. As with all Susan Hayward movies, the star was the magic ingredient. Susan's portrayal, described by the New York *Times*'s Bosley Crowther as "shattering" and Paul V. Beckley of the New York *Herald-Tribune* as "a master drawing," veered from tough (Cop: What do you do? Graham: The best I can.) to tender, particularly when Graham is visited by her little boy while surrounded by hostile reporters.

So realistic was Susan's death scene—Barbara had reacted to a matron's suggestion that she take a deep breath to hasten her death from inhaling cyanide with "How would *you* know?" but took the advice—that Wise and half the crew burst into tears even as the cameras rolled. During one crowd scene filmed in Los Angeles' barrio, Susan was warned by Wise to be careful of some tough-looking characters inching their way to the periphery of the mob. "They're Park Avenue compared to the kids I grew up with," she cracked. Ironically, the experience did not leave Susan particularly sympathetic to the cause of the abolition of the death penalty. "My only feelings about capital punishment," she replied when asked to state her opinion on the hot topic, "are simply that if somebody murdered the man I loved and didn't get the death penalty, I'd murder him myself!"

Susan was due for another devastating personal blow shortly before the release of *I Want to Live!* Her mother, who had suffered from cardiac difficulties, died of a massive heart attack at Mt. Sinai on April 14, 1958, with Susan at her bedside. She was sixty-nine. All three children attended the funeral at the Chapel of Pierce Brothers Beverly Hills mortuary. Ellen's death was not enough to patch up the bitter differences between Florence and her movie star sibling. Wally, caught in the middle, clearly sided with Susan. As soon as the brief ceremonies under the hot California sun came to an end, each Marrener child went a separate way. Ellen's ashes were left behind in a cardboard box with a vault number attached. Two years later, Florence took the opportunity to further humiliate Susan by charging in a rambling magazine interview that Susan was so callous and self-centered that she did not bother to have her own mother's ashes placed in a proper urn and shipped back home to Brooklyn for interment. In reality, Ellen's youngest and closest child was so shattered by her passing that she could not bring herself to deal with this final grisly detail. Grief was to be a familiar companion for Susan that year; at about the same time her mother died, Eaton's son was killed in the crash of a light plane.

Susan was up against her stiffest Oscar competition ever in 1959: Shirley MacLaine in *Some Came Running,* Deborah Kerr in *Separate Tables,* Elizabeth Taylor in *Cat on a Hot Tin Roof* and Rosalind Russell in the classic *Auntie Mame.* It was her fifth time out, and Susan was more determined than ever to hear her name read when the envelope was opened. By the time Oscar time rolled around, she had already won the Hollywood Foreign Press Award, the New York Film Critics Award and the Golden Globe.

On the night of Monday, April 6, Susan and Eaton climbed into their limousine for the drive from their Beverly Hills Hotel bungalow to the ceremonies at the Pantages Theater. Wally appointed himself chauffeur. As she stepped out of the car and onto the red carpet, a deafening roar went up among the thousands of fans who strained at the police barricades. Swathed in scarlet ("That's what they call red when I wear it," uttered Susan in *I Want to Live!*), Susan made her entrance slowly on Eaton's arm. Once inside, she shed her coat to reveal a strapless black satin gown with matching gloves. She was the essence of confidence—and she was petrified. Walter Wanger tapped his favorite actress on the shoulder and handed her a coin-sized religious medal. On one side was a religious figure that Susan thought was St. Christopher. On the other side was engraved "To Susan—Best Actress and Best Friend. W.W."

Minutes after Kim Novak presented David Niven his Best Actor Award for *Separate Tables*, the envelope was torn open and the announcement made that—at long last—Susan had won the coveted golden statuette. Bolting out of her seat, Susan ran down the aisle and onto the stage. She clutched Oscar with her right hand and allowed herself only a moment to admire his expressionless, gleaming face. After the obligatory nod to old friend Walter Wanger—whose professional judgment had once again proved right—Susan delivered the closing line of her brief acceptance speech in the sultry, smoky voice that was now one of Hollywood's most recognizable. "I won," she said, "for my three men"—meaning Eaton and the twins. This moment of triumph culminated nearly three decades of clawing in Tinseltown. Once back in her seat, she leaned over to her husband and whispered, "Finally, dear, I've climbed to the top of the dungheap."

Seven rows away, Walter Wanger sighed with relief. "At last we can all relax," he told his wife Joan Bennett. "Susie's finally got what she's been after for twenty-five years."

In fact, the whole affair was somewhat anticlimactic. Susan saw the bitter irony in the fact that, now that she indeed had what she had been striving for all those years, she no longer needed it—at least not in the same desperate way she had before. Eaton had filled up all the gaps in her life, and Susan now could not wait to get back to Carrollton and her sons.

Before they could, however, Susan and Eaton had to act out the final scenes of her triumph. A phalanx of police preceded them as they left the Pantages, and for a time it looked as if they might not make it through the throngs gathered outside the Beverly Hilton—site of the Academy Awards dinner. Once inside the ballroom, Eaton and Susan were seated at the edge of the dance floor with old chum Vincent Flaherty and his wife, Bob and Delores Hope, Walter Wanger and his wife Joan Bennett. "I couldn't have made *I Want to Live* without Susan," he candidly told reporters who gathered around the winner's circle. "I wouldn't have attempted it without her." Susan returned his praise. "If Walter has anything for me, I'll do it. I feel I owe him so much."

Louella Parsons, still a power in gossip-hungry Hollywood, plodded toward the victor, her ample girth enveloped in what seemed to be several hundred yards of yellow chiffon. Susan girded herself, then held her trophy high so that her former boss on the vaudeville circuit could see it. The old gang had taken to calling the old dreadnought "Mom."

"Well, Mom," Susan chirped, "I won!" Ever the reporter, Louella asked if, like a good mother, she had talked with the kids on the telephone. "Not tonight," the star answered. "It's much too late, but both the boys were allowed to stay up at school to watch the awards on television. They were sure I was going to win—more sure than I was—and for their sake as well as for Eaton's, I'm glad they were right!" Perhaps more than anything, she confided, "I want Eaton to be proud of me." Eaton wasted no time in saying that he was prouder of the job she was doing as wife and mother. As for the hoopla, he was clearly uncomfortable. Shrinking back to the shadows, trying to avoid the ever-present cameras, he huffed, "Goddamnit, why do they want a picture of me? I didn't win anything." Yet the winner, fatigued by the attention, was no less addled. "I'll be glad," she sighed to Flaherty as the flashbulbs popped, "when we get back to the hotel so I can talk things over with Eaton . . ."

Susan and Eaton stepped on a Georgia-bound plane two days later, both ecstatic to be heading home. She already had her next two films, a potboiler called *Woman Obsessed* and *Thunder in the Sun* (a tepid shoot-'em-up with old Flatbush chum Jeff Chandler) in the can. And though she still owed Fox five pictures, the studio's titian-haired money machine was now ready for a few months of uninterrupted domesticity. The Chalkleys, ever mindful of the value of Southern real estate, bought six hundred acres of Alabama farmland.

While life still centered on Carrollton, the Chalkleys spent more and more time in Fort Lauderdale, where they struck out on deep-sea fishing expeditions that sometimes lasted for days or even weeks. In the canal behind their sprawling, palm-lined house with its circular drive and wrought iron fences bobbed the Chalkley fishing fleet: an 18-foot Boston whaler (christened *Li'l Susannah*), a 38-foot sport-fisher (*Big Susannah*) and a converted 55-foot shrimper (*Oh, Susannah*). The various Susannahs plied the sport fishing waters between Cape Cod and the Bahamas, and for once Chalkley found his match. When Susan reeled in a 69-pound kingfish, she was the only soul aboard the *Oh, Susannah* who was disappointed. "I was shootin'," she shrugged, "for a white marlin."

There was no doubt that Susan Hayward was ready to retire from acting, were it not for commitments made prior to her now-blissful marriage. As long as she had to work, Susan and Eaton reasoned, why not do it on their own terms? The couple formed Carrollton, Inc., and were soon running a mini-empire that not only encompassed Eaton's own previous investments in car dealerships and real estate, but also a National League baseball franchise for Atlanta and a production company that would give Susan an even larger share of the action on any screen project she might choose to undertake. Yet she was more than eager to let the corporation run itself. Mrs. Chalkley, at forty-two, preferred to fish, ride, travel to Ireland for The Hunt and throw out the first ball of the season for her husband's team, the Atlanta Braves. Next, Eaton obtained the American League pro football franchise for Atlanta and set out to build a suitable stadium.

"Miss Hollywood? Not on your life!" she once told a startled AP reporter. "There are no agents, no phone calls telling you there's a great script you should read. You'd be surprised how unimportant the movie world seems when you get away from it." Even when she returned to make the dismal *Marriage-Go-Round* with James Mason and Julie Newmar in 1960, Susan was never mentally far away from the red clay of Georgia. In the midst of a bull session on the set filled with show business gossip, everyone stopped when Susan chimed in with her big news: "One of our cows dropped a calf today." The transformation was complete.

Eaton did not confine himself to home. Indeed, he took an active part in helping Susan find better roles and secure juicier contracts. They may have diversified their interests, but that did not mean that the Chalkleys took lightly the millions Susan still stood to reap as one of the industry's few remaining name-over-the-title leading ladies. Often in the West on business of his own—among other things, he was the attorney for California's giant Sunkist growers—Eaton frequently dropped in unannounced to watch silently from the sidelines as his wife filmed a scene. As soon as work was over, the pair would disappear for dinner alone at Chasen's or the Brown Derby before he hopped the next plane back to Carrollton or Ft. Lauderdale. Whenever she returned home from work on a film, Susan was always greeted by a dozen yellow roses.

Susan, herself a lapsed Episcopalian, respected the fact that Eaton was a devout Catholic. He attended Mass nearly every day, and as one of the South's leading men of substance made sizable contributions to the Church that made him friend and confidant of cardinals and bishops. Eaton's quiet devotion to his faith, Susan soon came to feel, was an inner source of strength. It had begun to occur to her that she, too, might be able to tap this wellspring of the spirit. But Eaton had never discussed her conversion, and she felt awkward bringing it up lest it seem patronizing. For now, she was content to be an interested spectator.

Father Michael Regan knew little of what the topic of conversation would be when he was invited to lunch with

Atlanta's archbishop at the Carrollton home of Mr. and Mrs. Chalkley. The bishop and Chalkley had been friends for years; the cherubic white-haired Regan was comparatively new to the area and was slightly intimidated by the idea of dining in the home of the county's leading citizen and his still-glamorous movie star wife. He was delighted to find that both were seemingly unaffected, affable and genuinely interested in seeing the tiny diocese flourish in a sea of fundamentalism. More than 90 per cent of the region's inhabitants were rock-ribbed Protestants—a fact vividly attested to by the dozens of white-steepled Baptist, Methodist, Presbyterian and Episcopal churches that lined Carrollton's narrow roads.

After all had finished their elegantly simple cold chicken lunch, Eaton leaned back and told the bishop and the priest why they had been invited. Some nights before, Eaton recalled, he had dreamed that a Catholic church stood across the road from his estate. It was built of flagstone and glass, and was clearly visible from the white wrought-iron gate and stone wall that guarded the entrance to his estate. Chalkley felt it was nothing less than a divine message, and told the clergymen that he was willing to put up $75,000 toward its construction. Susan chimed in that she would help raise the difference. His Excellency the bishop and the good father thought it was an excellent idea, though Regan returned to his own parish and promptly forgot about it. Three years later, the flagstone and glass church with its vaulted wood ceilings, tiny chapel and community center was completed. The altar, a scaled-down replica of the one in the Atlanta Cathedral, was donated by the President of Cadillac out of deference to one of his most important dealers. Our Lady of Perpetual Help Church opened its doors to parishioners for the first time in 1965. The resident priest: Father Michael Regan.

Hollywood faced the new decade without the artistic nourishment of its finest actors. Bogie was gone; Coop, Gable and Tracy soon would be. They were rapidly being replaced by such antiheroic types as Marlon Brando, Dustin Hoffman and Warren Beatty. The decline of the powerful studios also gave rise to a new breed of actress who reflected the impact of both the sexual revolution and the emerging counterculture. By the end of the 1960s, names like Streisand, Fonda, Farrow and Loren would become as familiar to moviegoers as Garbo and Dietrich had once been. A few of the great ladies had managed to hang on, if only barely. Joan Crawford and Bette Davis would revive their careers with the horrific *Whatever Happened to Baby Jane?* Ingrid Bergman would lay low until a variety of interesting roles came along in the 1970s, and Katharine Hepburn would continue to burn as brightly as ever in a wide variety of challenging and memorable roles.

Susan entered the new era, however, with only a handful of real contemporaries—Marilyn Monroe, Judy Garland, Grace Kelly, Audrey Hepburn and Elizabeth Taylor. Two were destined to self-destruct; one abdicated her Hollywood career to marry the Prince of Monaco; another retreated into semi-retirement as a doctor's wife; and the last seemed intent on making headlines for the remainder of the century. In the fierce competition for roles, it was Elizabeth Taylor who gave Susan her greatest challenge—and in more than one instance producers who had wanted Hayward had to settle for Liz.

The *Marriage-Go-Round,* though filmed in 1959, constituted Susan's first 1960s release. More significantly, the Technicolor comedy wiped the slate clean as far as Susan and Fox were concerned. The studio paid her $400,000 and cancelled the three films that remained on her contract. With this film, she had fulfilled her obligation to the studio. Clearly, Susan had no regrets. Darryl Zanuck's ouster as head of the studio in 1956 meant she had lost a powerful ally there. In an interview with Associated Press reporter Bob Thomas, she made it abundantly clear that no love was lost. "Let's face it," she sneered, "what have I done here in the last five years? The studio has nothing planned for me. They used to plan things when Darryl Zanuck was in charge. But since he left—nothing. It's the old question of being a stepchild everyone takes for granted."

Susan lamented that most of her big hits of recent years had been while on loan to other studios on a straight salary. Hence *I'll Cry Tomorrow*'s then-impressive gross of $8 million in its first six months of release did nothing to bolster her bank account. Things were different with *I Want to Live!*—her percentage of the profits amounted to around $500,000.

Once again, she seized the opportunity during the Thomas interview to sing the praises of her new-found home and life with Eaton Chalkley. But she would be spending most of the next couple of years in California, filming three pictures in quick succession: the third version of Fannie Hurst's classic tearjerker, *Back Street; Ada,* with Dean Martin; and something called *To Thank a Fool* opposite British actor Peter Finch. After that? "I'm not saying I'll quit," she hedged slyly. "But I'll certainly work less often, and only when it's something *I* really want to do." Besides, she told another columnist, "I don't miss Hollywood at all—not even my psychiatrist. The career doesn't interest me very much, and more and more I ask why I make any pictures at all."

Ada was as good a reason as any. Based on the Wirt Williams novel *Ada Dallas,* this MGM black-and-white drama dealt with a naïve country-western singer, Dean

Martin, who is maneuvered into the governor's mansion of a small Southern state by a bunch of unscrupulous back-room boys. Their boss: Wilfrid Hyde-White, who, like most British actors, found little trouble slightly altering the cadence of his speech to sound authentically southern. What Hyde-White and the rest of Martin's corrupt cabinet had not counted on was Ada, the shady lady of the evening that Martin met at a whorehouse and in a decidedly imprudent moment decided to make his wife.

Once again paired with her favorite director, Danny Mann, Susan got the chance to play a hellcat not unlike Barbara Graham in many ways. In Ada's case, unbridled personal ambition gives way to a curious sort of honor and morality when, after getting herself made Martin's Lieutenant-Governor, she suddenly decides to single-handedly wrest control from Hyde-White's band of bandits and hand it back to the people. Thus going from bitterly cynical to embattled to brave, Ada is transmogrified from villainess to erstwhile heroine.

Susan tore into the meaty role with abandon. Now at her lowest weight in years (103), she looked years younger than in her last few pictures. Again, Susan had several delicious scenes, memorable for their pyrotechnics rather than, as with the same year's *Back Street*, tugging at the heartstrings. Uncertain of herself at a tea she has given for society women at the Governor's Mansion, the state's new First Lady makes a genuine effort to get along. But when she is pressed sadistically by her smug guests, Ada flares—"That's right. I'm a sharecropper's kid from off the Delta Road!"—and proceeds to give the stunned ladies a blistering dressing down. When she views the movie for the first time at a special showing, Susan is delighted when the audience bursts out in applause once Ada has finished her tirade. Soon paying moviegoers all across the country were doing the same. Susan could not have asked for a better vehicle than *Ada.*

Back Street gave Susan the opportunity to display her flip side to best advantage. Producer Ross Hunter, who was rapidly gaining a reputation for this kind of film, had Susan in mind from the outset, but she resisted on the grounds that she did not really have to struggle—that she was merely the melancholy victim of events. But the persuasive Hunter managed to convince her to take the part. If any story were perfectly tailored to Susan's talents, it was the Hurst tale (first brought to the screen with Irene Dunne in the lead in 1932 and nine years later with Margaret Sullavan) of star-crossed love. Cast as a corn-fed, optimistically cockeyed Midwesterner, Hayward, now more alluring than ever, falls in love with serviceman John Gavin. He goes off to war (needless to say without marrying poor Susan), so she migrates to New York and loses herself in her work—high fashion design. Soon, she becomes "rae" ("all small letters, very chic"), queen of couture on two continents.

Lavishly dressed by Jean Louis, Hayward seems content to pursue her ambitions—until she bumps into Gavin on Fifth Avenue. He is married to boozer Vera Miles and has a son and daughter, but Susan cannot keep the old flame from rising anew. Their back street affair begins, culminating in what may be the weepiest scene of its kind: When Gavin and Miles are killed in a car crash, their two now-orphaned darlings come to ask if they can visit Daddy's friend every now and then. She embraces them. The scene is reflected in a drawing that still hangs on "rae's" wall—the sketch she drew of him back when they first met during the war. Susan's tear ducts work overtime, as do the tear ducts of everyone in the audience. A definite three-hankie flick, *Back Street* did not rouse the critics. But it did keep the cash registers ringing across the country—enough to make it one of the top ten grossers of 1961. Two decades later, it is still one of the most frequently run (and most-watched) late-night offerings on television.

While Susan was winding down *Back Street*, sister Florence was living a melodrama of her own making. Destitute and on welfare, Florence appeared before Judge H. Eugene Breitenbach to fight for custody of her two children—Larry, then 17, and a four-week-old infant born to her the previous Christmas Eve. Neither of Florence's two ex-husbands, tennis pro Udo Zaenglein or mining engineer John E. Dietrich, were willing to help. Nevertheless, it was obvious that the public's attention would be focused on Florence's famous, hardhearted sister—even though they had not seen each other since their mother's death nearly three years before. "I saw Susan at the funeral," a wide-eyed Florence told reporters. "I haven't seen her since then. Our only communication has been through attorneys."

Indeed, it was Susan's lawyer, Dean Johnson, who issued a simple statement on the actress's behalf: "This has been a long, drawn-out situation, and Miss Hayward and her husband, Eaton Chalkley, prefer not to discuss it."

Anyone who picked up the Los Angeles *Mirror* and saw the article with its photograph of a disheveled Florence could not help being stricken by the uncanny family resemblance. It was almost as if there were two Susan Haywards—one achieving wealth and fame by depicting the tortured lives of unfortunate women, and the other actually experiencing such a life.

"I'm worried sick for fear they will take my children from me," Florence sobbed to the papers. "My baby is still in General Hospital but I want them both with me. That's where children belong—with their mother." She pointed out that, to complicate matters, her son Larry suffered from a heart ailment and required special care. "He doesn't belong in a foster home," she declared. "They won't know how to take care of him!"

What Florence needed now, she said, was a job. "I can sew and I can do general housework and I can work as a saleswoman," she said, her voice tinged with desperation. "If someone would only give me a job I could earn money enough to support my two children."

Susan said nothing. She had long since washed her hands of her bothersome sister, and once her mind was made up there was no changing it.

Eaton and Susan were anxious to get back to Ireland for The Hunt, so when MGM offered them a free trip to the Old Sod for *I Thank a Fool* they were eager to go—perhaps too eager. The film, directed by newcomer Robert Stevens, was one of several that Susan did that ironically touched on a gruesome subject with which she would become all too personally familiar—terminal illness. She was a janitor's daughter who worked her way through medical school, then blew it all by giving her dying lover a lethal injection to end his pain. Peter Finch, the prosecutor who put her behind bars for eighteen months, is waiting at the prison gates when she is finally released; he feels contrite, and wants her to nurse his mentally disturbed wife (Sean Connery's then-spouse, Diane Cilento).

As it turns out—though the tale is so murkily told that it is difficult to be certain—Cilento dies from an overdose of sleeping pills, and Susan is obviously the prime suspect. Or did Finch hire her just to rub out his irksome wife and pin it on the convicted murderess? Neither, it develops. Cilento did herself in, but her father had tampered with the evidence to make it look like murder because he could not cope with the idea of his daughter taking her own life.

Throughout the on-location shooting in Ireland, Susan and Eaton holed up in a rented castle of their own, miles from the rest of the cast and crew. When they were well into filming, Stevens was summoned to Susan's dressing room. Eaton quietly introduced himself, then disappeared. The star was having some difficulty with the script. She suddenly could not accept the idea of portraying a woman who had committed euthanasia; mercy killing was something that she strongly opposed. She did not want it to appear as if she were endorsing it.

Stevens was speechless at first. Then he reminded Susan calmly that this had been the story from the beginning. Surely she must have known when she first agreed to do *I Thank a Fool* that the main character's status as a convicted mercy killer was crucial to the entire plot. Of course, Stevens failed to note that Eaton had not closely examined the script until now, and on reflection felt that it denied his Roman Catholic principles. Euthanasia, he told Susan, was simply sin. And Mrs. Chalkley was listening to him closely on such matters. Still, they had all gone too far down the road to alter the plot of *I Thank a Fool*—though any change would have almost certainly been for the better.

Susan came face-to-face with the issue of mercy killing as soon as she returned home to the United States. Her lifelong friend, Jeff Chandler, had been on location in the Philippines filming *The Maurauders* when he injured his back. During the last four weeks of shooting, he was virtually crippled. Once back in Los Angeles, he underwent surgery on May 13, 1961, for a ruptured spinal disk. Five days later he was rushed into emergency surgery at Culver City Hospital for severe internal bleeding. He was operated on again on May 27.

Chandler, who had parlayed his rugged good looks and prematurely silver hair (it had turned gray in his teens) into movie stardom as Cochise in *Broken Arrow*, had wasted away from 200 pounds to perhaps 140 when Susan visited him. He was bleeding to death internally, and was receiving constant transfusions just to keep him alive. Chandler was in agony, but Susan managed to control her emotions while she visited his hospital room. "Why don't they just let me die, Susie?" he begged. "I just want to die."

He did, after wavering between "critical" and "fair," on the night of June 17. Marjorie, who had finally divorced him two years before on the grounds of mental cruelty, was at his bedside. His divorced parents, Phillip Grossel and Ann Shevelew, were in the corridor outside his room, as was his secretary, Mrs. Laura Burgess. "They told us we didn't need to come, that there was nothing that could be done," Mrs. Burgess said. "But we wanted to be there anyway." The autopsy showed the cause of death as septicemia, or blood poisoning. He was forty-two.

The moviegoing public was stunned at the news of the tragedy, coming only seven months after the sudden death of Clark Gable and barely one month after Gary Cooper's passing. But for Susan, who had known Chandler when he was little Ira Grossel carrying her schoolbooks back in Brooklyn and had loved him in a more mature way when both were caught in the throes of divorce, it was a shattering blow. She was upset enough to take a stiff belt of Jack Daniel's and chain-smoke her way through a pack of Chesterfields by way of steeling herself for the midafternoon funeral services at Temple Isaiah in West Los Angeles. Once the services were over, she wept in Eaton's arms.

Susan's next film role was not exactly calculated to perk her up. It, too, would prove to be disturbingly prescient. Susan traveled, this time without Eaton, to England for *Summer Flight* (the title was eventually changed to *Stolen Hours*), the Daniel Petrie-directed remake of Bette Davis's classic 1939 tearjerker *Dark Victory*. Considering the fate that was destined to befall Susan, the United Artists production seemed an uncanny choice at this juncture. Whereas Davis (with an able assist from George Brent and Humphrey Bogart) played a shrill, spoiled society girl who falls in love with the doctor who diagnoses her brain tumor and learns to come to terms with her own death, Susan is vulnerable and warm throughout. *Time* magazine, however, saw it differently:

> Brain tumors can be beautiful. On Hollywood's form sheet, a woman with a brain tumor can be practically certain that she will win the love of a handsome and successful doctor and live out her days in his tender loving care . . . Susan was miserable before she got her tumor. All she had was money and the things that supply it or require it: oil wells in Texas, a stately home in England, lots of yachts and a pack of International Jet Setters baying after her heels. She didn't have love. She didn't have a rose-covered cottage by the sea. She didn't have a brain in her head. But one day out of a clear sky she was told she had a tumor on it.
>
> Overnight, her life was changed. She met a handsome Harley Street specialist (Michael Craig) who fell madly in love with her. She had a lovely operation and came out of it feeling just fine. They get married and settle in Cornwall. True, there was a ser-

> pent in her paradise. She knew that in a year her tumor would return, that one day suddenly she would be blind, that a few minutes later she would be dead. But death too can be beautiful, especially in Deluxe Color.

Such caustic commentary aside, Susan brought her own special fire to *Stolen Hours*. At the outset, she is fun-loving —Chubby Checker spent a week teaching her the twist for a party sequence that was cut—but not at all sarcastic, as was the case with the Bette Davis rendering. And when Craig, who has surreptitiously tried to diagnose her illness at a party, blurts out that he is really a physician, Susan simmers. The doctor lists several symptoms before he points out that something is wrong with her sense of direction. She promptly throws her drink square in his face. "What do you think of my sense of direction now, Doctor?"

The final scene, in which she sends her doctor-husband along to deliver a baby even though sudden blindness has alerted her to the approach of death, tears at the heart. She is in the midst of throwing a party for some local children, and she asks one of the little boys she has befriended to help her up the stairs to her bedroom, where she quietly drifts away. In real life, Susan had no intention of going so quietly.

Time notwithstanding, many of the reviewers lauded Hayward's efforts in *Stolen Hours*. "Superb," wrote the New York *Herald-Tribune*'s Robert Salmaggi. "Tears will cause a lot of mascara to streak, and the men may fight a tight throat as well."

In less secure days, Susan might have let such a depressing story and the recent death of Jeff Chandler get to her in much the same way that she had veered toward suicide during the making of *I'll Cry Tomorrow*. But now she had

Eaton. At Shepperton studios outside London, she quietly retreated to her dressing room between takes to knit. As always, she returned to her hotel room to find a dozen yellow roses from the man she loved.

While Susan calmly worked on the projects for which she could whip up some enthusiasm, producers clamored for her services. There was talk of retooling a television version of *Rain* originally intended for Marilyn Monroe so that it would fit Susan, and separate studios had her on their drawing boards for the movie version of Tennessee Williams' *Sweet Bird of Youth* and his *Night of the Iguana.*

Susan was Walter Wanger's original choice to play the title role in his monumental and controversial *Cleopatra.* Twentieth Century-Fox, on Wanger's urging, offered her the role. Susan was intrigued enough to talk it over with Eaton. Both agreed that she could handle the assignment, but was Susan physically right for it? Clowning around with a kerchief, she created an ersatz pharaonic headdress and paraded up and down before Chalkley in their Carrollton living room. They enjoyed the laugh, but it was obvious to both Eaton and Susan that, although redheaded, delicate-boned Claudette Colbert had pulled it off three decades before, today's moviegoers were no more willing to accept a redheaded Susan as Cleopatra than they were to accept her as Bortai the Tartar princess in Howard Hughes's *The Conqueror*. Susan politely turned down Wanger's offer to play the Queen of the Nile, but she had a candidate of her own to suggest: "How about Elizabeth Taylor?" Wanger thought that was not a bad idea—not bad at all.

X

Fasten Your Seat Belts

Ever since she was a teenager slouching in the balcony of Flatbush's Glenwood Theater, Susan had held Bette Davis in awe. Davis had admired Susan's work ever since they met briefly on the set of 1938's *The Sisters*, in which Davis starred and Hayward had a now-you-see-me-now-you-don't bit part. So when Joseph E. Levine signed them both up to do his Embassy-Paramount version of Harold Robbins' best-selling soaper *Where Love Has Gone*, of course, everyone was in for a dandy time.

Wrong. The experience turned out to be a replay of the Bette Davis-Joan Crawford wars that had raged on the set of *Whatever Happened to Baby Jane?* barely two years before. Davis had won that battle, and she was not about to be upstaged at this late date in her career. What she had not counted on was the simple fact that, even more than Crawford, Susan was champ in a land of blood-spattered brawlers. As Davis's Margot Channing warned in *All About Eve*, "Fasten your seat belts. It's going to be a bumpy night." But bumpy for whom?

No one knows just who threw the first punch, but neither seemed particularly anxious to avoid conflict. From the outset, director Edward Dmytryk knew he would have his hands full; both movie queens were blatantly suspicious and jealous of one another. Davis came on strong, perhaps because she had more reason than Hayward to be upset. For one thing, Susan had just finished retooling her favorite film, *Dark Victory*. ("There are some pictures that should *never* be remade," she growled.) Over the years, the two had constantly been compared—and now for the first time they would be acting head-to-head in a film. There was also the matter of the MGM limousine that had been snatched away from Davis eight years before so Hayward could make her exit from the hospital after trying to kill herself. The *coup de grace:* for *Where Love Has Gone,* Susan Hayward—not Bette Davis—was top-billed, and Davis was cast as Susan's mother!

For her part, Susan was not about to knuckle under to any slight—real or imagined.

Where Love Has Gone closely paralleled the sensational stabbing death of Lana Turner's lover Johnny Stompanato by Turner's daughter Cheryl Crane. In this case, however, Susan played a lubricious sculptress—not a movie star. Cast in the unenviable role of Hayward's murderously jealous fifteen-year-old daughter was an appropriately sullen Joey Heatherton. Davis, alas, was forced to wear a blue-white wig—undoubtedly, she delighted in telling everyone, because it was the only way in which the audience could be made to believe that she was Susan's mother. Once again "pagan to her fingertips," as she had been billed at the beginning of her career, Susan easily out-acted the wooden Davis.

It was not for want of Davis's trying, however. Bette always arrived hours early on the set. One day in the first week of shooting, director Dmytryk dropped into Davis's trailer to discuss how that day's scenes would be filmed. He had disliked the script from the beginning, but felt that with the cooperation of the players he could revise it as the shooting progressed. Davis could not have agreed more. They huddled over the script as the trailer filled with Davis's cigarette smoke.

Susan arrived a few minutes before 9 A.M. and, with hairdresser in tow, glided toward her trailer. As myopic as ever, she could not see the crew members straining to catch a glimpse of her. "Jesus," sighed a cameraman with a nudge to his gawking assistant, "she still looks goddamn terrific." At that moment, the door to Davis's trailer swung open in the distance. Dmytryk and Davis had agreed on some basic changes in the script, but Bette was not about to make it look like a joint effort.

"Boys!" she yelled to the crew, her voice resounding through the studio like coal down a steel chute. "Everything's changed. This is the way we're going to do things today." Dmytryk winced. He would have objected to Davis's take-charge attitude on the spot had he seen Susan, stopped dead in her tracks a hundred feet away. The cameraman saw the developing disaster. "Oh-oh," he muttered. Susan registered not a trace of emotion. The incident was only the first of many, and when Susan felt threatened she fought back.

The boys in the front office shot to their feet when Susan Hayward finally stormed in. "Look, gentlemen," she told them, "either we shoot the script I signed to do, or I take a walk." That afternoon Dmytryk got a call from the head of production. "Susan wants to shoot that script," said the voice at the other end, "and she's got us. No more changes." Round one to Susan. Bette steamed.

They came out swinging again toward the climax of the film. As the selfish, manipulative mother whose main interest is wresting custody of granddaughter Joey from Susan, Davis did not like the way her death scene was written. A hasty conference was called with Dmytryk. Susan listened patiently. "If the mother has to be shown as a monster," she begged, "at least give me one scene being really monstrous to the daughter so people will really believe it. Besides, I can't do the suicide in less than two pages of dialogue." Susan dug in. In the end, they flipped a coin to decide which character would have to die. Susan lost—and won the suicide scene. Reluctantly, Susan wound up running into her studio at the conclusion of the picture and stabbing herself with her artist's knife.

The compromise made little sense, both actresses agreed. Davis would always insist that her suggested changes could have saved *Where Love Has Gone*. "Unfortunately," she shrugged years later, "Miss What's-Her-Name didn't see it that way, and she did get top billing, so . . ."

Dmytryk, who also directed *The Carpetbaggers*, remembered what it was like being caught in the middle: "Susan was frightened of Bette, who can come on very, very strong if she likes. And much as I like her, Bette didn't help any."

Where Love Has Gone did neither star justice, but among those who saw it there was little doubt that Susan acted her nemesis off the screen.

Susan spent the mid-1960s immersed in her homelife with Eaton. Days were filled with riding (they now had five horses—three palominos and two racehorses), gardening and painting when she could in her little studio off the master bedroom. They bred cattle for slaughter—there were no milk cows—and Susan even raised her own chickens, though she became so attached to them that when it came time she could not bring herself to eat them. "I'm very bad in the kitchen," she had to admit anyway. "If I have to cook for myself, I'll go to Nate 'N Al's and buy a bottle of herring. But opening the bottle presents a problem for me."

As it had been for years, the real domestic loads were carried by Curly Crowder, the Chalkleys' tall, high-cheekboned housekeeper. Curly was devoted to Susan, and vice versa. "Mrs. Chalkley told me she liked the simple people," Crowder later recalled. "They was more sincere, she said. And whatever they say, they be really meaning. Town's people liked Mrs. Chalkley too because she was a down-to-earth person. They accepted her."

Susan happily participated in Eaton's various business ventures, entertaining his clients and partners whenever the need arose. Mrs. Chalkley took particular interest in his new Atlanta football franchise. "The plan," she eagerly told anyone who would listen, "is to build a stadium with a built-in hotel with suites having balconies overlooking the stadium so that guests won't have to leave their rooms to watch the games—just step out on the balconies! Oh well," she quipped, "I'll probably be very busy parking cars."

The twins were clearly headed in different directions. Quiet, self-assured Gregory was now studying veterinary medicine at Atlanta's Auburn University. The hell-raising Timothy was sufficiently smitten by show business to toy with the idea of becoming a cinematographer. She still did not see very much of them, but was always pleased to get a progress report.

If she was an absentee mother, at least now she was a full-time wife. Susan even went on the stump for the various charities Eaton had long contributed to. Chalkley himself appeared healthy enough. His only real brush with serious illness had been serum hepatitis from a botched blood transfusion during World War II. But his strong religious conviction made him a believer in philanthropy. While opening a resort at Lake Spivey, Georgia, for the benefit of Carrollton's Tanner Memorial Hospital, Susan shared the platform not only with Eaton but with Georgia's governor and several of the state's top health officials. When her turn to speak came, Susan jumped up and walked to the microphone. She had only managed to utter a few words before she noticed a slight titter rippling across the audience. Was it something she had said? Eaton whispered the reason from his seat behind her: Susan's petticoat had fallen down around her ankles. With suitable flair, she merely stepped out of it and let Eaton pick it up gallantly. It was a full two minutes before the crowd—and Susan—managed to stop laughing.

At about this time, Eaton's various charitable activities brought both him and Susan into contact with lifelong bachelor Ron Nelson. The Pensacola, Florida-born Nelson reacted to his own bout with heart disease by devoting himself completely to raising funds for heart research as president of the Broward County Heart Association in Ft. Lauderdale. Lean, handsome Nelson and Susan hit it off instantly, in large part because soft-spoken Nelson had little interest in Hollywood. The fact that he seemed never to have heard of *I'll Cry Tomorrow* or *I Want to Live!* intrigued Susan. Nelson was clearly not a celebrity hound. In those early days of their friendship, Nelson marveled at how truly happy Susan seemed to be. The Chalkleys were, without exception, the happiest married couple he knew.

ALONE

"I'll go out the way I came in."

XI

No More Yellow Roses

Indeed, Susan was on top of the world physically, emotionally and professionally when her old chum from *House of Strangers*, producer Joseph Mankiewicz, called asking if she would agree to star with Rex Harrison, Edie Adams, Capucine, Cliff Robertson and a newcomer named Maggie Smith in a romp called *Anyone for Venice?* The catch: Susan would have to travel to Italy, where the modern-day version of the timeless Ben Jonson classic *Volpone* was being filmed. (Actually, the film was mostly shot in Rome.) It was the fall of 1965, and Susan had not made a picture in two years. Now, she figured, was the time. Besides, it was an excuse for a second honeymoon. Before they left, the Chalkleys caused a minor ruckus when they tried to renew their passports. Although Susan wore a nondescript white sundress and sunglasses, she was recognized by a clerk and a near-riot ensued.

Anyone for Venice? was released as *The Honey Pot*, but under any name it seemed destined for oblivion at the box office. The movie featured Rex Harrison as the wily, eccentric millionaire Cecil Fox, who summons his three ex-loves to his lavish palazzo so they can brawl over his nonexistent fortune while he supposedly lies dying. Adams was the

Brooklyn-born Hollywood bombshell, Capucine played a princess and Susan portrayed Mrs. Crockett "Lone Star" Sheridan, an oil-rich Texan wealthy enough in her own right to be more concerned about Fox than his money. Hayward, who is mystifyingly rubbed out rather early in the film, gets off the memorable lines while elbowing out the Princess ("Hold on to your crown, Highness,") and movie star Adams ("You too, Lowness"). Maggie Smith, as the hypochondriacal Lone Star's nurse, attracted most of the attention in her first major role.

Between takes, Susan and Eaton reveled in each other's company. St. Mark's Square and the Grand Canal glistened romantically in the autumn sun. In Rome, where the cast and crew spent most of their time, Eaton and Susan seized every opportunity to share a pasta lunch on the Via Condotti or visit the Vatican. The Chalkleys managed to wangle a private audience with Pope Paul VI. On an earlier trip, his predecessor, John XXIII, had presented Susan with a giant onyx crucifix.

Susan's romantic dream was shattered one morning in mid-October when Eaton woke up in agony. He was weak, drained. The hotel physician examined him and came up with a diagnosis that both Eaton and Susan had feared: Chalkley's World War II case of homologous serum jaundice—a viral form of hepatitis caused by a botched blood transfusion—had inexplicably returned. Mankiewicz readily agreed to shoot around Susan while she flew back to the States with her husband. Eaton entered Ft. Lauderdale's Holy Cross Hospital, and for the next several days Susan was constantly at his side. Amazingly, the jaundice went as quickly as it had come, and as soon as Eaton was out of danger and released from the hospital with a clean bill of health, his wife returned to Rome to finish the picture.

Susan called Ft. Lauderdale several times a day to talk with Eaton, and every day when she returned from work a dozen fresh yellow roses awaited Susan in her hotel room. On December 20, while Susan was preparing for a scene, word came that Eaton had been readmitted to Holy Cross. It was not an emergency, she was told at first, but seven days later his condition had worsened. She rushed to Eaton's bedside. "I'm dying honey," he told Susan, clutching her hand. She was shocked that his grip was so weak. She told him he was being silly, but when Eaton asked to be taken home to the house on Nurmi Drive to die, she humored him.

Susan was talking to Eaton at 7:30 A.M. Sunday, January 8. Chalkley was secure in his Catholic faith, but told Susan he worried about what would happen to her soul once he was gone. If they ever were to meet in an eternal afterlife, he told her, Susan would have to become Catholic. Sobbing gently, she told him she would. The attending physician, Dr. Leonard Erdman, watched Susan shudder as she realized that Eaton was dead. She rushed into the bathroom, locked the door and yelled and yelled and yelled until the rage had left her. After ten minutes she walked out, totally self-controlled. "Okay Doc," she said to Erdman, wiping the tear that nestled in the corner of her right eye, "what do I do next?"

Funeral arrangements were made quickly. The same night, Susan and Eaton's sister, brother and sister-in-law visited Ft. Lauderdale's Baird-Case Funeral Home to view the body. Immediately afterward Susan and William Chalkley left for Miami International Airport to accompany the casket to Washington, D.C., for services there, then on to Carrollton for burial. Susan left the Baird-Case funeral home wearing a full-length mink. A scarf covered her head, and she wore no makeup. Curly Crowder followed on a later flight. Eaton was laid to rest in front of the church he had built, Our Lady of Perpetual Help. There was a place for Susan beside him. "He was the strongest man I ever knew, and the tenderest," she said of her late husband. "He was rugged and he was fair. Quite a man." For the first time, there were no yellow roses waiting for her when she got home.

Mankiewicz told Susan that it was not necessary for her to return to the *Honey Pot* set in Rome, but the star insisted. "My husband wouldn't have been very proud of me," she said, "if I hadn't finished what I'd already started."

Susan's old costar in *Reap the Wild Wind* and *The Forest Rangers,* Paulette Goddard, was having lunch with her husband Erich Maria Remarque, author of *All's Quiet on the Western Front,* by the pool of the Rome Hilton when the familiar woman in black walked up to them. "Susan!" exclaimed Goddard, "what are you doing in Rome?"

Susan was pleasant, but numb. "I've just lost my husband," she told them. Remarque sympathized with the sad, beautiful lady. Goddard found her as enigmatic as ever.

Six months after Eaton's death, Susan was quietly baptized a Catholic by Eaton's old friend Father Daniel J. McGuire in a secret ceremony at Sts. Peter and Paul Church in East Liberty, Pennsylvania, just outside Pittsburgh. Speaking to no one, she received her first communion and after Mass stole away. She was recognized by the entire congregation, yet no one bothered her. The wall around her was invisible, but it was nonetheless a wall. "I sure as hell hope there is an afterlife," she told Nelson. "I want to see Eaton again."

Susan had to sell off the house and properties in Carrollton and in Alabama—even the house on Nurmi Drive contained too many painful memories of her happy life with Eaton. Plunged into deep mourning—"Like an eighteenth-century Spanish widow," old friend Martin Rackin once put it—Susan would over the next five years try everything from game fishing to African safaris to motorcycle racing to erase the painful memory of "the happiest ten years of my life. When you say ten years it sounds like a long time," she explained, "but when you live it and are truly happy, it's only a moment."

Her constant companion now was Mate, her oversized and affable black Labrador retriever. Mostly she drank. In public, Susan downed Jack Daniel's and Johnnie Walker Black Label on the rocks. At home, she drank doubles and she drank them straight. And when the Bourbon and the scotch were gone, she turned to potent Beefeater martinis in brandy snifters the size of goldfish bowls. Ron Nelson, now her closest friend and constant escort, begged to know why she was doing this to herself. "Simple," she said, snapping her fingers just as she had done when she portrayed a swozzled Lillian Roth in *I'll Cry Tomorrow*. "I drink for one reason: to get blown away."

Still, Nelson managed to corral a weary Hayward into working on behalf of his Broward County heart fund. Others who tried did not always escape unscathed. At one point a local civic type paid an unannounced visit to Susan's home and paused in the middle of her pitch to compliment Susan's taste in decorating.

"What did you want to see me about?" Susan snapped, lighting up a filter-tipped Newport.

"Joining the association."

"What's it cost?"

The woman answered, and Susan stood up. "Fine, I'll join. Send me a bill and can the chitchat. It bores me."

With the exception of Nelson, who never took her support for granted, Susan shunned the entrenched Ft. Lauderdale social set. After all, she growled to Nelson, no one wanted to really get to know Susan Hayward the human being. "It's either the name or the money. That's what they want. Or they want me to be a monkey on a goddamn stick and I'm tired of that. If they want me, they've gotta pay me." With that ultimatum, the ladies of Ft. Lauderdale and the city's most celebrated resident grudgingly came to a separate peace.

If the good people of Ft. Lauderdale did not want to cough up for their redheaded "monkey on a stick," Hollywood expressed willingness to pay—and pay plenty. Susan turned down a dozen major parts, including that of Mrs. Robinson in *The Graduate.* The role, which eventually went to *Demetrius and the Gladiators* bit player Anne Bancroft, not only required the actress to seduce her neighbor's son but to appear nude—if only for a don't-blink-or-you'll-miss-it moment. La Hayward deemed it unsuitable. "I don't want to go doddering around making faces in front of a camera until I'm playing grandmother parts," she insisted. "I don't find the idea of retiring abhorrent at all."

So why did she agree to replace Judy Garland in Jacqueline Susann's loathsome *Valley of the Dolls?* "Itchy feet," shrugged Susan. Again, she took on the assignment—the first since Eaton's untimely death—to bail out an old friend, this time *My Foolish Heart* director Mark Robson. Garland, at first confident that the role would earn the Oscar that had so long eluded her, gradually became intimidated by her breezily confident young costars Barbara Parkins, Patty Duke and Sharon Tate. Judy began to retreat into a haze of booze, pills and paranoia. After ten days and not one foot of film on her, Judy Garland was summarily fired. Garland had called author Susann and

Susan and her old Brooklyn childhood chum Jeff Chandler, scrapping in *Thunder in the Sun*—their only film together. CREDIT: THE MEMORY SHOP, INC.

Buttering up Governor Dean Martin in *Ada*. CREDIT: MOVIE STAR NEWS

Kleenex stock went up when Sus starred in the classic Fannie Hurst soa er *Back Street*. CREDIT: MOVIE ST NEWS

Between takes in Ireland, the Chalkleys and Susan's costar in *I Thank a Fool*, Peter Finch, catch up on gossip. CREDIT: PICTORIAL PARADE

Michael Craig helped Susan come to terms with a brain tumor in the sadly prophetic *Stolen Hours*. CREDIT: MOVIE STAR NEWS

It was the battle of the legends when top-billed Susan starred with Bette Davis in *Where Love Has Gone*.

Shortly after Susan filmed these scenes of *The Honey Pot* in Rome with Cliff Robertson and Edie Adams, Eaton fell gravely ill. CREDIT: MOVIE STAR NEWS

Patty Duke and Susan scratch it out in *The Valley of the Dolls*. CREDIT: MOVIE STAR NEWS

Angling for marlin aboard *Li'l Susannah*. CREDIT: PICTORIAL PARADE

Mame, 1969.

Proud mother at Gregory's graduation from Auburn (Alabama) University, June 1969.

Susan defends a defiant Lee J. Cobb in *Heat of Anger.*

Susan already suspected she had a brain tumor in 1972 when she took on the role of a widowed physician treating a young cancer patient with the help of Darren McGavin in ABC's *Say Goodbye, Maggie Cole.*

A last good-bye. Leaving the Academy Award ceremonies in April 1974 after her final public appearance. CREDIT: PICTORIAL PARADE

complained that she could not get anyone at Twentieth Century-Fox to return her calls. "Jackie," she pleaded, "I'm a star, aren't I?"

"Yes," answered Susann.

"Well, where did everyone go?"

Director Robson considered Bette Davis, Jane Wyman and Tammy Grimes as replacements for the Ethel Merman-type "Old Ironsides" character Judy had been chosen to play. But everyone agreed that Hayward was better qualified to play the musical stage star who stays on top by firing any young talent who looks remotely like a threat—a classic survivor in the Broadway jungle. Susan agreed to do it, on the following terms: that she would get top billing, that Garland would be paid full salary—no questions asked —and that whatever Garland got, Susan would get double.

How did she feel about replacing Garland? "I don't know the circumstances of Miss Garland's leaving the part," she shrugged. "We don't read the columns out there in Ft. Lauderdale. We're just plain people." She did not get away with that coy routine for long. "She's such a talent," Susan said of Garland, "such a fine actress. I guess I don't understand these things. I've enjoyed every minute of my career. It isn't art for me, it's work, and damn good work, but it's never been my life. There are other things *vastly* more important to me."

Thus while Judy had felt threatened by the younger actresses working on the film, Susan went about her business cheerfully, knowing that she would collect $50,000 for two weeks' work. The first day of shooting marked Susan's return to her home studio, and Fox's publicity machine was not about to let the milestone slip by without notice. With dozens of reporters, columnists and photographers present to record the event, Barbara Parkins piped up, "Now let me introduce you to one of my costars, Miss

Susan Hayward." One of my costars? The set fell silent at such bald-faced effrontery. Not that it bothered Susan in the slightest. As the set was cleared to begin the day's work, Robson found his eyes riveted on Susan. She was still the compact (103 pounds, 36½-24½-35) powderkeg he had directed almost twenty years before. The face, still taut beneath the makeup, did not betray the fact that she was nearly fifty. "Ready, Susan?" he asked while the cameras moved into place. "Ready?" She laughed. "I was *born* ready." Anyone who had known her just five years before would have been startled to witness Susan breaking up a quarrel on the set of *Dolls*. "Gentlemen, gentlemen," she soothed. "It's *just* a movie."

If *Valley of the Dolls* was memorable for anything, it was the scene where a drunken Neely O'Hara (the Judy Garlandish neurotic played by Duke) confronts Hayward's character, Helen Lawson, in the ladies' room. Lawson had once had Neely fired, and now it was time for the young star to take her revenge. "Get away from the door," Hayward orders Duke. "I got a *man* waitin' for me."

"That's better than the fags you're usually stuck with."

"At least I didn't marry one," Hayward fires back.

With that both stars bare their talons and attack one another. When Duke grabs at Hayward's hair, she winds up pulling off her red wig. Beneath it is a head of white stubble. "It's a wig, it's a wig!" Patty exults triumphantly, holding it aloft like a dead rabbit. With Hayward in hot pursuit, she locks herself in a stall. "My God!" screams Hayward as the toilet flushes. "She's throwing it in the can! I'll kill her!"

"How do you like that," laughs Patty. "You can't even flush it down the john!"

When the stunned powder room attendant ("What a terrible thing to do, and you such a great star, Miss Lawson") shows her the back way out, Susan decides not to give rotten little Patty the satisfaction. Putting a kerchief over her head, the sequin-suited Hayward calmly says, "I'll go out the way I came in." And she does.

Maybe Susan better understood the personality of Helen Lawson than the character's creator. "Helen doesn't remind me of any one, but a kaleidoscope of many," mused Susan. "She's a human being, she's understandable. All of her actions spring from a motive, a cause. She does the only thing she knows how to do—but woe betide anyone who gets in her way. Helen's not typical," she went on in a classic understatement. "Most women are much more soft. Women *are* soft. They're only hard till they meet the right man and fall in love. Then it all changes. Any woman would put true love before a career."

Jacqueline Susann herself, whose own courageous bout with cancer would later parallel Susan's in some ways (in fact, at one point they were both being treated for cancer at the UCLA Medical Center at the same time) conceded that Hayward did a "good job," but the author had wanted Bette Davis from the start. Besides, she and Susan did not get along. "One time in Ft. Lauderdale she had some people to meet us," Susann once related, "and she asked me to be nice to them. I was. But it wasn't like someone saying to you 'I just love these people; they're my friends.' It was a command. I've seen Susan do parts where she was warm and lovable, but in person she's sort of an iceberg."

Jacqueline Susann's feelings notwithstanding, the general consensus was that La Hayward walked away with the picture—such as it was. "Amid the cheap, shrill, and maudlin histrionics of Patty Duke, Sharon Tate and Barbara Parkins," wrote the New York *Times*'s venerable Bosley Crowther, "our old friend Susan Hayward stands out as if she were Katharine Cornell. Her aging musical comedy celebrity is the one plausible character in the film." The experience back on familiar turf was a relatively pleasant one, but Susan was anxious to collect her pay and depart. "More and more, Hollywood is an unhealthy place," she told reporters. "I don't like it here. So sue me."

Once back in Florida, Susan found a new hobby to add to safaris, motorcycling, marlin fishing and astrology—politics. A middle-of-the-road Democrat in the Forties and Fifties, she had grown increasingly conservative since her marriage to Eaton. And, living as she was in one of Ft. Lauderdale's most severely restricted communities, perhaps a touch anti-Semitic.

Whatever her prejudices, Susan was wary of actively campaigning on behalf of candidate or party. She had made that abundantly clear back in the 1950s when she condemned her fellow actors for using their influence to swing support behind either Dwight Eisenhower or Adlai Stevenson. She felt the same way during the Kennedy-Nixon battle of 1960. As the 1966 elections approached, however, Susan did an about-face—at least on the state level. She was so impressed by Florida's dashing Republican gubernatorial candidate Claude Kirk that she agreed to stump for him.

Susan began her brief flirtation with the GOP by registering Republican and causing a ruckus at the Broward County voter registration office. Kept busy signing autographs on the crowded courthouse steps, Susan was handed a business card by County Commissioner R. R. Humphries, a Democrat. "If there is anything I can do for you," he said, "please call on me." Susan just smiled. "Thanks, Commissioner," she said, nodding politely. "But I'm still registering Republican."

The high points in the Kirk campaign were a series of elegant fund-raising dinners at which Susan was the star attraction. Several were held at Ft. Lauderdale's Pier 66 Tower. "Like Mr. Kirk," the Hollywood legend told rapt diners who had plunked down a hundred dollars a plate, "I was a Democrat and now I'm a Republican. Like Mr. Kirk, I finally saw the light, and I don't like what the light exposes."

Not surprisingly, the debonaire, divorced Kirk was almost instantly linked romantically with the South's most glamorous widow. Kirk squired her about for a time, but in fact their relationship remained purely platonic. "She was a wonderful friend in the campaign," Kirk said of Susan following his landslide victory. "I've seen her on a couple of occasions, and if you can be a friend after a couple of hours . . ."

Kirk tried to downplay their friendship, but at another hundred-dollar-a-plate dinner held in honor of the Governor-elect at the Galt Ocean Mile Hotel, she was as close as Florida had to a new First Lady. Nearly all of the women wore the short fashions of the day, mostly sequined, glittery or even plastic sheaths cut off at or above the knee. There was an audible gasp as Susan made her entrance in a floor-length green-and-lavender chiffon Empire gown trimmed with green velvet bows. A tier of the same emerald green velvet fell from each shoulder in panels that cascaded to the knee in front and to the floor in back. And there were the ever-present gloves, this time sleeves of tourmaline satin stretching to the elbow.

After Kirk's inauguration, his main drawing card returned to life alone on Nurmi Drive. The drinking continued, and on more than one occasion Ron Nelson found himself trying to sober up his famous pal. Still a fighter, Susan was not beyond making a scene at a local restaurant, being dragged home by Nelson and then thanking him with a barrage of blistering insults and even a flying ashtray or two. Fortunately, none found their mark. Susan never apologized. Instead, Nelson would invariably receive a call from Susan the next morning. "Don't I just piss you off?" she would laugh, then invite Nelson to go along on one of her frequent fishing trips. Nelson, with a tendency toward violent seasickness, usually tried to weasel out—almost never successfully. Susan's nickname for Nelson: "Captain Tuna, Chicken of the Sea."

Nelson dropped everything one afternoon when Susan called him at the office of the Broward County Heart Association in downtown Ft. Lauderdale. She spoke in a hushed voice, but even the whisper was distinctive enough for Nelson's secretary to recognize her and put her right through. Susan was calling from a pay phone; it seemed she had gotten into a little accident in her 1969 Cadillac Coupe de Ville. Whether the little mishap had occurred as a result of the booze or her myopia or a potentially lethal combination of both did not matter. The important thing, Susan told Ron, was that the traffic cop standing a few feet away with his little ticket book had not recognized her—yet. Would he come handle things, before the policeman got wise and the papers were all over her?

Because he did not hesitate to bail her out at times like this, Nelson was sought by Susan for advice on matters both personal and professional. Such was the case when producer Martin Rackin called his old pal "Hooligan" (he also called her "Red" and "Irish") to rib her about her sedentary life. "Hey, Hooligan, how long are you going to sit there with the old folks in sun city?" Rackin was phoning from Las Vegas, where he was part owner of Caesar's Palace. "How about coming to Vegas to do *Mame* for me?" Angela Lansbury had metamorphosed from a stolid character actress in films to a blazing musical comedy star as Mame Dennis on Broadway. "Why should I go on the stage?" Susan replied. "I'm a movie gal. That's what I grew up with." Maybe, Rackin suggested, *Mame* could do for her career what it had done for Lansbury's. Nelson agreed, and after a bit of prodding, so did Susan. Rackin was relieved. "I wasn't so sure you wouldn't tell me to go jump in the river," he confessed.

It meant, of course, easing up on the Beefeater martinis and Jack Daniel's—not to mention working at a feverish pace with fabled choreographer Oona White to master the dance numbers. Susan had undergone a hysterectomy for tumors diagnosed as benign in late 1967, but nearly a year later she felt up to the physical challenge. Her voice, already a proven commodity in *I'll Cry Tomorrow*, was at this point not deemed to be a problem—even though she was being called on to do two shows a night. If she could pull this off, Susan thought, she would have a good shot at the as-yet-uncast movie role.

After three months of rehearsals in Ft. Lauderdale and New York, Director Gene Saks, whose wife Beatrice Arthur (TV's *Maude*) would later end up with the plum role of Vera Charles opposite Lucille Ball's movie *Mame*, felt confident enough to preview the show on Sunday, December 15 at Broadway's legendary Winter Garden Theater. Susan was petrified. At the last minute, the performance was canceled and more than a thousand disappointed fans were told that the star had suddenly come down with a bad head cold. In truth, Hayward was frozen with fear at the prospect of making her stage debut anywhere and under any circumstances—much less in a musical and on the Great White Way.

At about this time, Harold Clurman, her director on *Deadline at Dawn*, was lunching at the Russian Tea Room on Fifty-seventh Street when Susan summoned him to her table. He congratulated her on her upcoming production of *Mame*, but she was more interested in impressing her old boss that she didn't need the work. "I'm rich," she smiled over a drink. Clurman felt uncomfortable—and sad that the fiery Susan was now insecure and afraid.

Her cold (feet) had disappeared by the time the curtain went up on schedule on the vast stage of the cavernous Circus Maximus Theater-Restaurant at Caesar's Palace. The opening Roaring Twenties party scene called for Mame to dance on tabletops, be carried aloft by chorus boys and slide down banisters while singing the rousing *It's Today*. The instant it was over, Susan's fears vanished as the audience gave her a thunderous standing ovation.

Reviewers were ecstatic over Susan's performance, and with good reason. Unlike Lansbury and Rosalind Russell (Roz had immortalized *Auntie Mame* in the original, non-musical movie version of the hit stage play), Hayward toned down some of the brassy harshness identified with the role and replaced it with sultry sex. Her tender moments with her nephew Patrick (played by Roger Rathburn) were so moving that Rathburn found himself moved to tears by the time he had to sing his reprise of "You're My Best Girl."

The star wrapped her husky voice around such memorable *Mame* tunes as "Open a New Window," "We Need a Little Christmas" and "If He Walked into My Life." Practically the only song not belted out by the star was the rousing title tune, sung to Mame by a chorus of doting Southern folk whose admiration she has captured after one hell of a foxhunt. Since she had won over her Southern neighbors in real life, it was a most believable scene. Garnering her share of raves for a convincing portrayal of wallflower-come-to-life Agnes Gooch was Loretta Swit, later to become nurse "Hot Lips" Houlihan on the smash CBS television series M*A*S*H.

Susan bowled over the rest of the cast, as well as critics and audiences. Friendly, conscientious and undemanding, she came to rehearsals without makeup, a brightly colored bandanna covering the curlers in her hair. She still kept mostly to herself—if for no other reason, because she needed the rest.

Mame, it soon developed, was taking its toll. Because she was required to give a staggering *two* performances a night, scenes were cut so short that Mame's many elaborate costume changes—twenty in all—had to be accomplished in seconds. Susan proved to be a rather adept quick-change artist, but she was forced to cut it so close that several times she made her entrance still zipping or fastening something. Aside from the marathon dancing, there were other acrobatics required of the star; in an early scene when a bankrupt Mame is trying to earn her keep in a chorus of a Broadway musical, she is required to swing from a moon suspended high above the stage, then tries to hang on for dear life á la Harold Lloyd. "I wonder," she asked Rathburn as she sat on the couch in her dressing room with her right foot in an ice pack, "if I'm eligible to play for the Rams. God, I'm such a klutz!"

For all the physical punishment, it would be the one thing that she had taken for granted—her voice—that threatened her Vegas run in *Mame*. She began to lose it. Susan's doctors warned her in no uncertain terms that the punishment she was inflicting on her strained, untrained vocal chords would almost certainly lead to exhaustion, collapse and perhaps even more serious medical problems if she did not pull out of the show.

Nelson had flown in to catch *Mame*, and that evening

she discussed it with him. "I've never copped out on a job in my life," she said. He sided with the doctors. In truth, she was too exhausted to continue with two performances each and every night. As they walked past the closed shops that lined the arcade beneath the casino, Susan's eye was caught by a huge, almost life-size portrait in the window of a small art gallery. "What in the hell?" she hollered. The portrait was of none other than Susan, clad in a green evening gown and standing atop a hill, her red hair trailing in the wind. It might have been a poster for *Gone With the Wind*, or her own *Tap Roots*. "It looks like a goddamn Susan Hayward doll," she sneered. "Wind it up and it cries tomorrow."

The next day, a press conference was held to announce that, for medical reasons, Susan was to be replaced by understudy Betty McGuire until Celeste Holm arrived to take over the lead in *Mame*. Susan broke down before the throng of newsmen, cast and crew. "I've never backed out on a deal before," she sobbed. "I loved playing before live audiences for the first time. I've never copped out in my life and it kills me. I picked the most difficult woman in history to play twice a night. I must have been out of my mind. It never occurred to me I couldn't do it."

Perhaps for the first time, her co-workers genuinely felt sorry for her. At the conclusion of the press conference, they gave their star a standing ovation. She repaid them later that night with a pull-out-the-stops formal dinner party complete with two orchestras at one of the casino's opulent ballrooms. "I want to go out in style and say thank you in style." That she did. Among the gatecrashers, however, was the artist who had painted the Susan Hayward portrait that she so intensely disliked. He asked if she might be interested in purchasing it. Susan was too dumbfounded to be angry. She politely declined the artist's gracious "offer."

Caesar's Palace had been grossing $50,000 a night and Hayward's contract had called for a six-month run. Holm was not the drawing card Hayward was, and receipts were expected to reflect this. But to show that there were no hard feelings, the management had a little going-away present for Susan. As the dropcloth fell away from the hideous portrait that had hung in the window of the art gallery downstairs, it was all Susan could do to control herself.

Midway through the party, Susan walked up to her replacement, Celeste Holm. Some of the cast members had worked with her before and found her difficult. "I want you to know that these are great people you're working with," Susan told her. Holm nodded vaguely, then changed the subject. "I don't think you heard me right," Susan interrupted. The crowded room fell silent. "They're great people and if I ever hear of your abusing them, so help me, I'll come here and kick your ass back to Toledo, Ohio."

Before hopping a plane back home to Ft. Lauderdale, Susan and Nelson dropped in to what had been her dressing room. Taking a grease pencil, she scrawled "Celeste Who?" across the mirror, then cheerfully made her exit arm-in-arm with Nelson. It was the sort of gesture Mame Dennis would have appreciated. Getting off the plane back in Ft. Lauderdale, Susan did her best to look haggard and worn. In truth, she was thrilled to be off the hook. The next day the local papers expressed concern about her health. "Forget *I Want to Live!*" she said, laughing. "I should get an Oscar for that!"

Six weeks after returning to Ft. Lauderdale, Susan sold her four-bedroom, four-and-a-half-bath canal-front home at

220 Nurmi Drive to Mr. and Mrs. Donald S. Chapman of Mequon, Wisconsin. The sale pushed her personal worth well over $2 million, but it was not the money that motivated her. Susan was still haunted, disturbed by the memories of Eaton. She moved a quarter of a mile away to a condominium apartment in the Four Seasons, a pink neo-Moorish monstrosity with uniformed doormen and a garish crystal-and-gilt lobby.

She was more alone than ever in her two-bedroom apartment facing the ocean. The screenplays were fewer and farther between, and she refused a hefty six-figure offer from Procter and Gamble to do a television commercial. "I don't think I should stoop to brushing my teeth in public," she told Nelson.

The twins offered occasional diversion. Susan proudly attended Gregory's June, 1969, graduation from Alabama's Auburn University with a degree in veterinary medicine. Still glamorous at fifty-two in a polka-dot dress and clustered pearl earrings, Susan once again stole the show. Tall, redheaded and freckle-faced Gregory promptly set up his own veterinary hospital in Neptune Beach at the northern end of Florida. Five years later, when Greg and his wife Suzanne made Susan a grandmother, she did not seem overwhelmed with affection. Turning purple at the mention of the word grandmother, Hayward saw her grandson only every six months. "After all," she said with a shrug, "he's not my son, he's my son's son, and I try not to be a smotherer." Of course, Hayward had never been close to her own sons. Greg had learned from an early age that his was not the Mother of the Year, yet he came to accept that fact and retain a lasting love and admiration for her. They maintained a respectful distance.

Timothy was another matter; his relationship with

Susan was far stormier. When he asked her for financial support to help him land a fellowship in cinematography, she merely shook her head. Gregory had had to work his way through school at various jobs, and Mom was not about to hand Tim a free ride. No sooner had he graduated from the University of Southern California—his move to Los Angeles did not exactly please Mom—than he was drafted into the Army. One bone of contention was their conflicting taste in movies. He wanted his mother to go back to work, but publicly criticized her for agreeing to do *Valley of the Dolls*. "He digs those new-wave movies," Susan responded. "He got me to see *Blow-Up*. I didn't understand it. Tim would like me to do Fellini or Antonioni. I wouldn't know where to begin. I'm strictly old-wave." She confessed, "I guess I'm like all mothers. I want to smack him sometimes, but pretty soon I realized he was a lot taller than Momma." She stopped by to see her Green Beret son in Germany on the way to a big-game safari in Africa.

Until 1971, Susan remained a recluse. She found time to fish, to read everything from Balzac to the *New York Times* to the *National Enquirer* to the *Wall Street Journal* —and to pick up her drinking where she had left off. Once a month she would visit the only friends she felt she had in Ft. Lauderdale besides Nelson—$400,000 in cash that she kept in a safe deposit box at Fort Lauderdale's Southeast Everglades Bank. The elderly, potbellied guard would nod politely and usher her into a private room where she would pile all $400,000 in the center of the table. One time she brought Nelson along. "Why don't you deposit this or put it in bonds and collect some interest?" he asked. "Do you realize how much money you're losing just leaving this here?"

"I don't care," Susan replied, reaching for a stack of twenties. "No, I just like to touch it . . . to count it."

It was 6:30 on the morning of January 22, 1971, when Susan was awakened by the acrid smell of smoke. She had fallen asleep hours before with the help of a few stiff Jack Daniel's, and the smoldering cigarette that had dangled from her hand at last had ignited a chair. The fire spread to the rug and flames had begun to shoot up the draperies by the time Susan woke up and realized what was happening.

Calmly, coolly, she called the Ft. Lauderdale fire department and told Lt. Kenneth Nation that her ninth-floor apartment was on fire and she was trapped: the doorway leading out to the hall was already enveloped in thick, black smoke.

Panicking now, she ran out onto the balcony and screamed, "Fire! Fire!" The screams awakened Dr. and Mrs. Russell Carson, who lived one floor below. She was terrified and would have jumped if the Carsons had not both talked her out of it. They managed to convince her to drag some blankets out of the bedroom, tie them together and then onto the balcony railing. If the firemen did not make it in time, then she would try to climb down the lifeline to the Carsons' apartment.

She was about to attempt the almost-certain-to-be-fatal climb when three burly firemen led by Henry Sledge arrived. There were three locks on the door of Apt. 901, and they wasted no time chopping it down with axes. They found Susan on the balcony—covered from head to toe with soot and gasping for air. She was given oxygen, then removed and examined by a doctor. "I'm fine, but the apartment's a wreck," she said. "Nothing valuable was lost but it's a complete wreck." Susan expressed her gratitude to the fire department repeatedly: They had saved her life. For Susan, there was an element of *déjà vu.* She had been through it all before the cameras in *Smash-Up,* where the alcoholic heroine comes close to incinerating her own daughter with a cigarette she has dropped in a drunken stupor.

The incident left Susan shaken. For the first time she realized that she was on a self-destructive course, and that if she did not pull herself together there would soon be no turning back. Susan picked up the phone and called William Morris agent Norman Brokaw, a wheeler-dealer whose first big discovery back in the late 1940s had been a part-time chauffeur named Marilyn Monroe.

Susan Hayward was back in circulation—she wanted work. That meant being seen again around town, and soon the woman who had reigned at Fox throughout the 1950s was back in the public eye—attending premieres, Beverly Hills parties and other high-visibility functions with an ambitious young press agent named Jay Bernstein (a few years later he would take credit for building Farrah Fawcett into a national phenomenon). Bernstein, a good two decades younger than his biggest client, was nonetheless quickly rumored to be the next Mr. Susan Hayward. While she was once again in the mainstream, this did not mean that Hayward was off the sauce. At a seventy-fifth birthday bash for Henry Hathaway held in the ballroom of the Beverly Hills Hotel, Susan was seated next to fellow Flatbush native Rita Hayworth. The guest of honor, who had directed Hayward in *Rawhide* and *Garden of Evil,* later recalled that both were sailing. Mindful of her pledge to retire before playing grandmother parts, Susan secretly breathed a sigh of relief when the producers of a rodeo flick, *Junior Bonner*, met her and decided that she was too youthful for the part of Steve McQueen's mother (he was then about thirty-five). Ida Lupino got the part instead.

The Revengers offered Susan the threefold opportunity to get back in front of the cameras, repay producer Marty Rackin for bowing out of *Mame* and work again with her favorite director, Danny Mann. It was Mann's first Western, and it showed.

To get *The Revengers* made at all, Rackin needed a commitment from Susan. She signed for the Screen Actors Guild minimum—$487—and appeared less than ten minutes on the screen as brief love interest to fellow Paramount contract player William Holden. Actually, the part was originally intended for Mary Ure, who abruptly canceled to do Harold Pinter's *Old Times* on the London stage. It was only one of several disasters that had befallen the film even before shooting began. Costar Van Heflin (whom she had known since they played opposite one another in *Tap Roots*) had died of a sudden, massive heart attack in his Beverly Hills swimming pool and was replaced by Ernest Borgnine. Filming was postponed while Holden recovered from a case of jungle fever contracted at his sprawling Mount Kenya Game Ranch and Safari Club, and Rackin himself suffered a mild coronary. These omens might have convinced Cinema Center to drop the whole thing. *The Revengers* was a stinkeroo.

Undaunted, Susan decided that the time was ripe to pack up and return to Lotusland—"where the action is." Barely three weeks after she finished her work on *The Revengers*, her old friend and fellow tough cookie Barbara Stanwyck fell ill three days into the filming of a made-for-television movie titled *Fitzgerald and Pride* and had emergency surgery to remove her kidney.

Again, it was Susan to the rescue. *Heat of Anger*, as it

was eventually renamed, was intended by Metromedia Producers Corporation as a CBS pilot. Susan was happy to see many familiar faces from the old days: screenwriter Fay Kanin, whom she had known at Paramount and Fox, executive producer Dick Berg from Paramount, veteran actors Lee J. Cobb and Fritz Weaver, and director Don Taylor, who had played her perennially soused first spouse in *I'll Cry Tomorrow* (Taylor: "I gotta be a man!" Hayward: "What are you gonna be a man *at?*"). Comparative newcomer James Stacy, the former husband of actresses Connie Stevens and Kim Darby, was talented and cooperative. He would later lose both legs and an arm in a tragic motorcycle accident.

What Susan had not counted on was the schedule. The entire TV movie was shot in just seventeen days. Since it was the lead—her part in *The Revengers* had been just a cameo—she felt like a pianist who had not touched a piano for years. She wondered if she could still play. She was frenzied at having to learn ten pages of dialogue every day, instead of the three pages she used to do in feature films. "But I soon found I was able to handle it. Fortunately, my brain is in good shape." It was a tragically prophetic remark. Once the ordeal was over she sent her old pal Stanwyck, still recuperating from surgery, three dozen roses. "All love," read the accompanying note, "from another Brooklyn broad."

In *Heat of Anger*, the producers were counting on transforming the great Hollywood name into a bankable television commodity. Some—Stanwyck in *Big Valley*, Loretta Young, Donna Reed, Robert Young, Robert Cummings, Lucille Ball—had managed to make the transition to series of their own. Just as many had failed. Among them: Shirley MacLaine, Jimmy Stewart, Anthony Quinn and Henry Fonda. "I know it's peculiar that I should be signed for this role because movie stars haven't been doing well on TV. But I never thought of myself as a movie star," she remarked with a smile, "—just a working girl."

Susan was at last ready to take her shot. Viewers were asked to buy her as a rich, hard-boiled Beverly Hills lawyer taking on the defense of longtime client Lee J. Cobb, a gruff contractor accused of pushing his daughter's construction worker lover off the top of one of his skyscrapers. The story was serviceable enough, and it even offered a hint of sexual tension between the fresh-out-of-law school Stacy and the fifty-four-year-old Hayward. Kay Gardella of the New York *Daily News* confirmed in print what was clear to all who tuned in to Susan's TV debut: "Miss Hayward still moves around like a little dynamo." *TV Guide* heralded "the genuine excitement caused by what everyone called—almost as if it were a movie title—The Return of the Redhead."

Susan made no secret of her desire to make that return permanent. "I thought it was time for a change," she told interviewers. "If the film is a success and the powers that be want to make a series out of it, I'm ready." As it turned out, *Heat of Anger*'s hefty prime-time ratings were not enough to convince the network to pick it up, but Susan was undaunted. She had already received offers to do two more TV movies, and announced that she intended to pull up her stakes in Ft. Lauderdale and settle back in Los Angeles where she could be "near the action." Declaring that she "felt like a freak" in Ft. Lauderdale, Susan explained that she "more or less got talked into" returning to Hollywood by her agents. "Then I decided it really was time for a change," she mused. "I'd had the fishing and the boat and the heat and the humidity. Once I was back here, I began to like it again. I feel more alive here. And I'm much happier here now than I thought I would be."

Her still-firm belief in astrology was also a factor. Carroll Righter, who had been preparing daily charts for her since the 1940s, informed Susan that her moon was in the fourth house, and that a move was in order. "The stars are right for me to move at this time," said Susan, "and this is where I should move to. After all, the place is not foreign to me. I have many friends. I like it here now, and I expect to stay as long as I'm happy." She spoke only to her closest friends about her most important reason for coming back: after seven years, her deep grieving for Eaton was at long last over.

Househunting was nothing new to Hollywood's returning daughter. She had, in fact, made millions on her shrewd real estate deals. Susan was in the market for a house befitting her stature, but she retained her almost uncanny ability to ferret out a bargain. She found it at 1460 Laurel Way in Beverly Hills—a stucco-and-stone hilltop eyrie with a hidden, palm-shaded Grecian pool and a magnificent view of the city below. It was selling for a bargain $200,000, but it had been on the market for months. There were no takers, Susan learned, because the last owner's body had been found floating face down in the blue-tiled pool. Susan snapped it up in a flash. Seven years later, the house would go on the market for $725,000.

The new owner promptly set out to make the place, architecturally reminiscent of Frank Lloyd Wright, into a home. She hired a designer—Susan abhorred interior decorators and avoided them like the plague—who promptly noticed that every time her client came into the forty-foot living room she gravitated to a comfortable position on the carpeted floor in front of the fireplace. Hence furniture that was scarcely inches above floor level was chosen. "It's my house," she told friends, "so you'd better come with a good back." The predominant colors were her favorites: yellow, orange and white. Susan delighted in ordering about gardeners ("the jungle men," she called them), movers, electricians and plumbers, but as darkness fell she watched the breathtaking tangerine sunsets alone—except for her old chum Jack Daniel's. She yearned for a script that dealt with the problems of a woman alone. "Ten days ago," she told Los Angeles *Times* columnist Joyce Haber, "I was willing to marry the plumber. Not that he asked me."

Timothy, now twenty-six and an occasional visitor to the house on Laurel Way, was hired by his mother's press agent, Jay Bernstein, to work in the music department of Bernstein's firm. Susan was unimpressed. "Tim began in the mail room, for ninety minutes," she commented. "Then he went on to handle actors. He hated actors. He thought they were crazy. I said, 'Maybe that's because you grew up with one.'" Said Tim: "Right now we're trying to find a husband for Mother."

If there was any doubt that Susan was back to stay, Johnny Carson dispelled it by introducing her as "a truly great star" during the 1972 Emmy Awards telecast. Along with George Peppard, then starring in the private eye series *Banacek,* Hayward announced the awards for the Best Actor and Actress in a Single Performance. As she read the names of the nominees for best actor, their faces flashed on screen, but not fast enough. Unlike the other presenters who invariably endure such snafus in uneasy silence, Susan snapped, "I'm waiting." Afterward, she drifted off with the winners. But it was Susan the crowd remembered.

XII

She Wanted to Live

The headaches—piercing stabs that seemed to radiate from the crest of her skull—had actually begun in 1971. She had shrugged them off as being caused by too much drinking. Now, a year later, they were far too intense to ignore. Susan worried that they might be symptomatic of a liver disorder. After years of heavy drinking, she now feared that she was paying for her sins with cirrhosis. Quietly, she flew to Georgetown University Hospital in Washington, D.C., and told the attending physician what she suspected. A thorough physical revealed nothing. Finally, to determine whether or not her fears of cirrhosis were groundless, doctors prepared Susan for a liver scan. She was to be injected with a dye, and after several minutes an expert in radiography would determine how healthy her liver appeared by following the dye's course through it on an X-ray screen. The procedure was simple, without risk and not even very uncomfortable.

Moments after Susan was injected with the dye, her back arched in violent convulsions. The stunned physicians scrambled to keep her from injuring herself as she writhed and jackknifed atop the X-ray table. An hour later, she was conscious. The worried doctors told Susan what had happened: the dye obviously had hit something in her brain that was the culprit. Something was seriously wrong, and she would have to undergo more tests. Susan would have none of it. Furious, she lashed out with a series of blazing epithets. "You bastards did this to me," she screamed. "You injected me with that goddamned dye and I'm obviously allergic to it. You'll hear from my lawyers!" she screamed as she marched out. They never did, but Susan would always blame them for doing this to her.

Susan marched straight onto the set of her second television movie, this time an Aaron Spelling venture for ABC called *Say Goodbye, Maggie Cole.* Suspecting that she was suffering from cancer, Susan tackled the role of a woman doctor who returns to work in a Chicago slum after the death of her husband only to become personally involved with the survival of one of her terminal patients—a little girl dying of leukemia. Hard-bitten colleague Darren McGavin forces Maggie to "say good-bye" to both. Involving her coming to terms with the death of her husband and then the tragedy of cancer, Maggie Cole's story was not dissimilar to Susan's—a sad coincidence of which the star was very much aware.

Say Goodbye, Maggie Cole was the 1972 season's teariest offering. Susan was not immune. On June 30, she was due to go to the studio to dub the crying scene she had already filmed a week before. But it was her birthday, and the emotionally drained Hayward told producer Spelling, "I'll do anything but cry on my birthday. I'll cry," she quipped, "tomorrow." When she did, "there were tears and sobbing and I was told it was too much for television. So I cried another way." She cried four different ways before the director chose the one that was least wracking. "If they had wanted any other kind of crying," sniffed the medium's finest weeper, "they would have had to call in another actor." Between takes, Susan sobbed in her dressing room. "When a person really cries," she told Ft. Lauderdale friend Ron Nelson when he paid her a visit, "it's not pretty, so I do the real crying away from the camera."

The headaches worsened, but Susan told Nelson that she would have to be dragged back to the hospital. "Those sons of bitches think I've got rocks in my head," she laughed. "I know they've got rocks in theirs!" She preferred to talk of how happy she was in her new home, how she was so independent that she would not even let her own children stay more than three days, how she wanted to get another dog: "They're great. They don't talk back." The truth, she insisted, was that Susan Hayward did not need people. "It's a great pleasure to poke around, to stretch out on the floor and read a book or just dream. When I work, it's concentrated work. And when I'm being lazy, I'm so lazy that if something dropped on the floor I wouldn't bother to pick it up. I love the solitude, I love being alone."

Try as she might, Susan could no longer ignore the pain in her head. She returned to Georgetown University Hospital for the brain scan the doctors had begged her to undergo over a year before. When they broke the terrifying news to Susan that she had twenty cancerous lesions in her brain, she promptly told them they were crazy and flew to New Orleans to promote the just-released *Revengers*.

Reporters who came to interview the still-glamorous star in her hotel suite could not have guessed that she had just been given what amounted to a death sentence. Don Lee Keith, there for *After Dark* magazine, watched as she fought hard with a book of matches—"First one, then another flickers but fails," he later wrote—before she hurled them to the floor and accepted his offer of a light.

"The ring of a telephone catches her as she is brushing

back her shoulder-length hair," wrote Keith, "and her right hand seems frozen, momentarily, to her temple. A second ring stirs her. She goes to answer. 'I hate to pick up telephones,' she says on the way. 'It's always bad news.'"

Midway through the interview, Susan reached up to poke gently at her lower left cheek. "I'm supposed to have some work done on that tooth next week," she explained. "I had to postpone that appointment so I could come here for the premiere. I think I've got that stuff the dentist gave me in my luggage. Just a minute. I'll be right back." She disappeared into the bedroom. From behind the bedroom door came the sound of a gentle knocking, first on the wall, then the door, then on a piece of furniture. "Come here, child," called Susan, "Mother needs help." Moments later, Keith had managed to get the cap off Susan's medicine bottle and she returned to the living room.

Was she cold and aloof, as had long been rumored? "Perhaps I have given that impression from time to time," she allowed, "but I can tell you it's not true. The truth is that, in my heart, I'm a slob, really. Give me a sad book or a movie or a television show, and it's tears. I automatically start welling up and soon the flood starts. One of my sons took me to see *Love Story* and I squalled like a silly little girl. He was so embarrassed that he threatened never to take me anyplace again.

"But the reports were true about what Walter Wanger said when I won the Academy Award: 'Thank God, now we can all relax. Susie finally got what she's been chasing for twenty years.' I was glad I got the award for *I Want to Live!* because it was Walter's picture. I was devoted to that man. Here, let me show you what he gave me." Susan disappeared again into the bedroom and came back with an elaborate gold necklace. Charms dangled from it, including an ebony voodoo doll and a little ring that her mother, Ellen, had worn when she was a girl. "Ahh, here it is!" she said, holding up a quarter-sized religious medal of gold. "Walter gave it to me the night of the awards," she recalled, rubbing the medal on the arm of the sofa. "I love this St. Christopher; I've carried it around with me all these years."

"No, Miss Hayward," replied Keith, looking closely at the medal. "It's St. Geneius, not Christopher. See the little masks of comedy and tragedy over to the side?"

"Oh, no. I'm sure it's Christopher. Here, let me show you."

Susan put on her glasses, moved closer to the lamp on the table, then settled back in the sofa in disbelief. "Would you believe that I've spent fifteen years thinking this was a St. Christopher medal? Oh, well . . ."

It was time for the New Orleans premiere of *The Revengers*, and Susan slipped into a flowing white gown. The elevator doors opened, and a woman got out with her young daughter. The child stared at Susan and pointed. "Pretty lady, Mommy." Susan smiled broadly and got into the elevator. Downstairs, she breezed past a gold-braided doorman and into a waiting limousine headed for the premiere. "That's her," the doorman said excitedly, "ain't it?"

Once inside the car, Susan pulled the small medicine bottle out of her sequined silver handbag and pulled out two more tablets. The pain in her head was unbearable, even after the pills she took for her "toothache." Without water, she gulped down two more.

For the next four months, Susan blurred the pain with Bourbon and parties. But in April she collapsed while attending a birthday bash for a friend. Friends were told she was in Cedars of Lebanon Hospital. Actually, she was registered under the name of Margaret Redding at Century City Hospital. For five weeks she battled to stay alive.

When she was finally released in mid-May, the five-foot-three-inch actress weighed eighty-five pounds. Chemotherapy and radiation had robbed her of Hollywood's most famous mane of flame-red hair; her bare head was concealed by a brassy red wig like the one she had worn as the dying heroine of *Stolen Hours*. As she had after the spectacular suicide attempt twenty-eight years before, she left the hospital in a wheelchair. This time it was not to fulfill some hospital rule; she was far too weak to walk.

News of Susan's condition swept the country. The press had been told that she was hospitalized for undisclosed tests. None of her friends were told the truth—except for Ron Nelson. Dr. Lee Siegel, Susan's physician, gave Nelson his prognosis: "It could be a week, it could be a month, but she is going to die." He predicted the Fourth of July—less than two months away.

Ron Nelson arrived in Los Angeles to find that Susan had no intention of fulfilling her doctor's grim prediction. "I have died in pictures a dozen times," Susan said, shrugging, "and when it is over I just get up and walk away." She required a full-time nurse (a quietly efficient woman named Carmen Perigini was hired) and at least one additional R.N. hired from a private nurses registry. She needed help getting around, but Susan was in a feisty mood. She traded wisecracks with her affectionately smart-alecky nurse Sidney Miller, a plump Jewish lady who came close to recreating in real life the part of Thelma Ritter in *With a Song in My Heart*.

Susan asked Nelson to take her to see Carroll Righter, and when she entered the living room of his palatial Beverly Hills home he was shocked to see that she could not even stand without the help of two friends. As much a polished actor as any of his famous clients, Righter managed to conceal his horror at her rapidly deteriorating condition. Amazingly, she still defiantly refused to believe the doctors' diagnosis. Righter was not prepared for the question she was about to ask. "Well, Carroll," she asked bluntly, "do I have cancer?" He hedged, conceding only that her chart showed a decline. "But it's only a professional decline," he hastened to add. "I see that you will be alive in January, 1975."

It was more than Susan had hoped for. That night, she took Nelson to dinner at Don the Beachcomber's, where they ran into some old friends who politely pretended not to notice that her hands shook as she chain-smoked Newports. She and Nelson even made a pilgrimage to Grauman's Chinese Theater to see her footprints. The following night, they went to the Brown Derby to celebrate her fifty-fifth birthday. Close to the entranceway hangs a portrait of the star alongside those of other Oscar winners. An admiring woman seated two tables away nudged her mustachioed young husband. They agreed that, as Susan sat there in the candlelight, her face shone with a sort of timeless beauty. She looked no older than the caricature on the wall.

The next day, Susan insisted on going shopping with Nelson, having lunch at one of her favorite Mexican restaurants in Santa Monica and inviting a small circle of friends over for dinner. One night, Nelson cooked one of her favorite dishes: green noodles with tomato sauce.

While Nelson was there, Wally was felled by a heart attack and Susan rushed to his side at the hospital. Susan visited her brother every day, and Nelson was amazed at the extent to which Susan still ran her affairs. Her spirits seemed totally unsquelched in the face of imminent death. One of the hundreds of notes on which she wrote instructions for her nurses ended with "Keep smiling, Charlie."

By July 4, the day which Dr. Siegel and the consulting

physicians had set as the arbitrary deadline for Susan's life, the holiday weekend had claimed two other legends—Betty Grable and Veronica Lake. All Hollywood, adhering to the superstition that such deaths come in threes, buzzed that Susan's time was at hand. Several smaller papers even ran front-page obituaries trumpeting the news of her untimely death.

Not if she had anything to do with it. Susan had carefully planned the entire holiday. About a dozen friends were invited to a poolside picnic, and Susan bantered cheerfully with her guests. The next night, she and Nelson were off to Jack's at the beach in Santa Monica, where they dined on Maine lobster, California scampi and her favorite Beaujolais. Susan had made it through the weekend.

It came time for Nelson to leave, and Susan ferried him to the airport in her chauffeur-driven Cadillac. There was an unreal quality about the entire scene—the still-radiant movie queen in dark glasses waving good-bye to her handsome young friend from the back of a black limousine. As he boarded the plane, Nelson felt wonderful about his visit and about his best friend's condition. Yet, in the back of his mind, he feared that it was all too good to be true.

By October, Susan was so totally convinced that she was in complete remission that she set out to prove her doctors' original diagnosis wrong. She volunteered to report for tests at Massachusetts General Hospital. She then planned to spend three weeks renewing old acquaintances in Ft. Lauderdale before returning home to Los Angeles.

Nelson met her plane at Ft. Lauderdale Airport. When all of the passengers had gotten off and there was still no sign of Susan, he concluded that she had missed the plane from Boston. He was about to turn to leave when she appeared at the end of the passage with a nurse holding her arm. She wore a sable coat and dark glasses. She was dragging her right foot. "Don't touch me," she warned him.

That evening at his house on the ocean, Nelson automatically offered Susan a drink. Her nurse, thinking herself out of Susan's visual range, shook her head furiously.

"Who the hell says I can't drink?" Susan flashed. "I can do any goddamn thing I please!" She demanded Chivas Regal and Nelson sent out for it. After three stiff belts, she collapsed and had to be carried into the bedroom. It was only then that Nelson let himself cry.

Christmas arrived, and now Susan was dragging her leg more. The paralysis had spread over her entire right side, except for her arm. The reason, the doctors explained, was a large tumor on the left side of her brain that was already spreading to the right side and would paralyze her completely. Angrily, Susan called an immediate halt to all further surgery, radiation and chemotherapy. She took painkillers only in moderation. Turning to less accepted forms of treatment, Susan sought out and found a doctor who would supply her with the controversial drug Laetrile. Four weeks later, in February of 1974, she was again in remission.

Buoyed by her improved condition, Susan decided to once again defy Dr. Siegel's advice and accept an invitation to be a presenter at the Academy Awards ceremony on April 2. Her brain seizures were now occurring almost hourly and were lasting five, sometimes ten minutes. To disguise her condition, old friend Nolan Miller designed a high-necked, full-length gown of shimmering black sequins. Her paralyzed right hand was concealed beneath points of delicate black lace.

At Jay Bernstein's Beverly Hills mansion, Susan watched the Oscar telecast. Flushed and wobbly, she now regretted her decision. Was there time to call and cancel? Susan and Bernstein continued to watch on the tiny Sony in the back of Bernstein's limousine as it sped toward the Dorothy Chandler Pavilion. She trembled, shaking her head. Once there, she was met by Dr. Siegel. Immediately before her turn came to walk onstage, he gave her a massive dose of Dilantin, a strong tranquilizer used to control seizures.

Introduced as "a medical miracle," Susan Hayward walked slowly yet regally to the podium on the arm of her costar in *The President's Lady,* Charlton Heston. The crowd began rustling to its feet to give her a standing ovation, but Susan quelled any such overt display of emotion by quickly launching into the list of nominees in that unmistakable Bourbon-and-water voice. "Well," she said afterward, "that's the last time I pull that off." Later that night, she collapsed with a seizure at a small party.

Three months after she walked onto the stage at the Oscar ceremonies with Heston, Susan was at last willing to travel to Atlanta's Emory University Hospital for exploratory surgery. First she underwent physical therapy, and her progress was so rapid that doctors there suggested that her tumor might be benign. Nelson was present when Susan's grim-faced doctor came into her hospital room with the results from pathology. "If he's gonna tell me what I think he's gonna tell me," Susan told Nelson, "I think you'd better leave."

Nelson left, and seconds later heard her screams of disbelief. He went in to comfort her. "Do you want to talk about it?" he asked.

"Nothing to talk about, is there?" she said, shakily lighting a smoke. "I'm going to Ft. Lauderdale and I'm going to act as though it never happened. You know what I'd like for dinner tonight? Chicken livers cooked in mushrooms and wine." Nelson came back with her order, and they dined silently in her hospital room.

By late summer of 1974, Susan was confined to her wheelchair, her legs in braces to prevent the now-brittle bones from shattering. She could no longer turn the pages to read or feed herself; her hands shook too badly. She and Nelson stayed up nearly all night every night, watching talk shows and old movies on television. Once she turned to him and muttered, "The night has a thousand eyes, doesn't it?"

The comment sent a shiver up Nelson's spine. "Are you afraid?" he asked.

"Let's put it this way," she replied. "I feel more comfortable sleeping in the daytime."

An old friend of Eaton's, Father Joseph Brue, dropped in to Ft. Lauderdale for a visit in September. Susan saw it as the perfect excuse for "a night on the town." Nelson called ahead to the Tower Club atop the Landmark Bank Building and explained that she would arrive in a wheelchair and require a discreet corner table. A dozen American Beauty roses—not her favorite yellow roses, but red would do—greeted the Susan Hayward party when they arrived at the restaurant. The management had even printed up special "Miss Susan Hayward" matches for its most famous customer. Susan, Nelson and Father Brue admired the Venice-like labyrinth of canals below and, as a four-piece band played mood music, discussed the old days back in Carrollton. Toward the end of the evening, a waiter finally got up the courage to approach the star. "I know I'm not supposed to do this, Miss Hayward, but my wife would kill me if she knew you'd been here and I hadn't gotten a souvenir."

Her hands were far too shaky to sign an autograph, but

she motioned for him to come close. "There," she said, planting a kiss on his cheek. "You can tell your wife that's Susan Hayward's lipstick."

Susan received communion from Father Brue the next morning. Three days later, she was having difficulty speaking and her seizures were so frequent and so violent that she was hastily flown back to Emory for yet another brain scan. The tumor was now on its inexorable march across the right hemisphere. Within days, Nelson was told, she would lose her memory and her speech, then the swallowing reflex. She would die once that happened, for one reason—she had explicitly prohibited any "intravenous or other lifesaving crap" that would keep her alive, but merely as a vegetable. Neurosurgeon George Tindall conceded to persistent reporters that Susan Hayward was indeed "quite ill." He did not tell them the full truth—that she was in a coma and in the opinion of her doctors was not expected to live more than a day or two.

Four days later, Nelson was beside her hospital bed when, miraculously, she rallied once again. "I'm thirsty," she whispered. He gave her water and asked her what he could do. She knew what he meant. "I don't want anybody to push me over the brink," she said firmly, "and I don't want anybody to hold me back."

The memories of Eaton's death still haunted Susan, and she knew that if she was to keep putting up the fight of her life she could not go back to Fort Lauderdale. She asked Nelson to charter a private plane in Atlanta, and they took off for Los Angeles. If she was to die, it would be on her mountaintop, overlooking the city she had long ago conquered. Halfway through the flight, Susan complained that she was hungry. She was told by the pilot that there was no food on board. "So put it down," she ordered. Passenger, pilot and crew had Kentucky Fried Chicken in Midland, Texas.

Susan allowed practically no visitors once she was back at her home on Laurel Way. She had long since shut her sister Florence out of her life. "Try to visit," she told her old pal Marty Rackin, himself just getting over his own coronary problems, "and I'll never talk to you again." When Nelson brought Loretta Swit, her Miss Gooch in *Mame* and now a TV star in M*A*S*H, Susan was livid. However, her loyal brother Wally, now fully recovered from his heart attack, came by daily.

Barbara Stanwyck, that "other Brooklyn broad," repaid the kindness Susan had shown her when she had had her kidney removed. And Susan found a new friend—one she had admired practically since girlhood and who, unbeknownst to her, admired her as an actress in return. On one occasion, Wally drove up to the house to see Katharine Hepburn climbing out of her '61 Thunderbird in blue jeans. She stopped to point at his license plate: "KHH—my initials!" She bore a bouquet of flowers picked from her own garden. ("The florists around here are ripoffs.") Susan, made up and wearing her wig, brightened as Hepburn entered her room. "Hi, Susannah—it's Kate," she said in her clipped Yankee accent. "Been sticking your behind all day? Bet it hurts." The next hour or so would be devoted to talking over the old studio days, when a star was a star was a star.

January 1, 1975. Carroll Righter had been right—it was 1975 and Susan was still alive, if only barely. Still, she had beaten all odds; given two months to live, she had survived nearly three years. But by March, the end seemed imminent. Susan could speak only sporadically. She had great difficulty swallowing, and had to be turned in bed by Nelson or one of the round-the-clock nurses. For a fleeting moment, she stirred from her coma to speak to Nelson. "I'm frightened," she muttered. "Tell me about death. Will it hurt? Don't let me suffer. Don't let me die alone."

It was about this time that a power struggle of sorts developed between Timothy, now brought in to take control of his mother's affairs, and Susan's longtime nurse Carmen Perigini. Carmen had run the Hayward household for months now—she even went so far as to take Polaroid snapshots of Susan during the final days—and she was reluctant to relinquish control. The tension erupted into a furious argument in the kitchen. Bitter words were exchanged before Tim finally fired her. Nelson knew that Tim wanted him out too, but he dug in. Nelson, still suffering from a serious heart condition, had made a pact with Susan before she boarded the plane in Fort Lauderdale for her last flight home.

"Look," she had then said to him, "they *think* I've got cancer. We *know* you've had a heart attack. Make a deal? We won't talk about that crap anymore, but let's keep this special thing we've got till one of us kicks the bucket. If it's you, I'll try to be there. If it's me, you goddamn well better be or I'll come back to haunt you!" Nelson was keeping his part of the bargain.

Susan slipped into unconsciousness on March 10, but inexplicably came to four days later and telephoned her son Gregory at his veterinary practice in Neptune Beach, Florida. For over thirty months, he had been hopping planes and flying to his mother's bedside every time the doctors said she was near death. He no longer knew what to believe.

"You know I'm dying," she said softly to Greg over the phone. It was the first time she had admitted it to anyone.

What could he do, he pleaded?

"Oh, you're a veterinarian. I thought you might be able to fix up this old horse."

After a few minutes of lucid chitchat about Greg's family, Susan said good-bye. "This is my nickel, so I'm signing off now. I want you to remember something, though. Remember that I love you."

Tim was summoned from his office at Jay Bernstein's publicity firm. She told him that she had no doubts about whether he should take over her affairs. "It's the right thing," she stated. "You're my son." Then she said she loved him, whimpered and collapsed. She was given thirty-six hours to live.

Nelson waited three days longer. Susan now had survived ten days without food. The mail from concerned fans now formed a small mountain in the foyer. He had strung on a safety pin several religious medals from among dozens sent by fans and had lovingly attached the pin to Susan's pink nightgown. She had ordered him to make sure her right hand was always on the large onyx crucifix Pope John had given her fifteen years before.

At 2 P.M. on March 14, Nelson watched as Susan began to tremble with another seizure. Her temperature had soared to 106. Although totally paralyzed, she began thrashing sharply. Nelson grabbed her and held her close so she would not hurt herself. He called the nurse, who came in and put water on her lips. Incredibly, Susan turned to Nelson to speak. "How long will it take me to die?" she asked. And then, with a hint of betrayal in her voice, "But you said it wouldn't hurt." Her head wrenched sharply and her eyes turned upward. She gasped. Susan Hayward was dead. She was fifty-six.

Wally, on his way home from a day's work at the race-track, was parking his car in the garage when he heard the news on the radio. He pulled out and drove straight to the house on Laurel Way. Susan's body had already been taken away. "Pack a suitcase," Timothy told his uncle.

"We're taking Mother to Carrollton." When they boarded the midnight flight, her body was already on the plane for the trip home to Georgia.

At the mortuary in Carrollton, Wally asked to see his sister one last time. "But she isn't prepared yet," the mortician objected. Susan had asked for a closed coffin, and Wally insisted on this final glimpse. The casket lid was lifted to reveal a Susan frozen in time, her face as lovely as it had always been under a soft red wig. She wore the same dress of black sequins and lace that she had worn on Oscar night, 1973. Her hands no longer shook. At last Susan was at peace.

"There was no other case like it," marveled Dr. Siegel when it was at last over. "Nothing in the medical literature resembles it. It was amazing to live that long with this type of cancer. She was one of the great fighters. I've never seen anything else like it."

Timothy estimated that his mother had spent $350,000 to stay alive. There was plenty left. Her will made Timothy and Greg her principal heirs, leaving them to divide up $750,000 in cash—so long as they did not give a nickel to their father, Jess Barker. Susan left Wally $200,000, but Florence was specifically cut out of the will in a special codicil. Susan bequeathed to her nurse, Carmen Perigini, a white mink, a full-length sable valued at $15,000 and a 15-carat diamond ring. Ron Nelson was left memorabilia—"all my crap," as Susan referred to it. Even posthumously, Susan was up to her old tricks. In the safe deposit box where she kept $400,000 in a paper bag, Susan also had a bogus bag filled with newspapers cut up to the size of dollar bills. The bills were bound in money wrappers with a few real bills on top. Inside the bag was a note: "Where did all the dough go? I spent it, what the hell did you think?"

Under a slight drizzle in the chill of the Georgia air, Susan's body was driven the seven-mile route from the mortuary in downtown Carrollton to Our Lady of Perpetual Help, the little church Eaton had dreamed about and together they had built. A Georgia Highway Patrol honor guard escorted the cortege. Signs were posted along the roadside. "Good-bye Susan. We'll always love you," read one. Poor farmers, black and white, stood tearfully at the roadside. In the forecourt of the tiny church, Susan was laid to rest next to the one man who had made her, for too short a time, genuinely happy.

Every year on March 14, the anniversary of her death—the following memorial notice is placed in *Variety* anonymously:

A Star, Is A Star, Is A Star!

ACADEMY AWARD WINNING ACTRESS

SUSAN HAYWARD

JUNE 30, 1918—MARCH 14, 1975

The Films of Susan Hayward

1. *Hollywood Hotel* (Warner Brothers, 109 minutes) 1937
DIRECTOR: Busby Berkeley
With Susan Hayward, Dick Powell, Rosemary Lane, Louella Parsons, Frances Langford, Carole Landis, Ronald Reagan, Benny Goodman and Orchestra, Harry James, Gene Krupa, Lionel Hampton.

2. *The Amazing Dr. Clitterhouse* (Warner Brothers, 87 minutes) 1938
DIRECTOR: Anatole Litvak
With Susan Hayward, Edward G. Robinson, Claire Trevor, Humphrey Bogart, Allen Jenkins, Donald Crisp, Ward Bond and the voice of Ronald Reagan.

3. *The Sisters* (Warner Brothers, 95 minutes) 1938
DIRECTOR: Anatole Litvak
With Susan Hayward, Bette Davis, Errol Flynn, Anita Louise, Ian Hunter, Donald Crisp, Beulah Bondi, Alan Hale, Dick Foran, Jane Bryan.

4. *Comet Over Broadway* (Warner Brothers, 69 minutes) 1938

DIRECTOR: Busby Berkeley
With Susan Hayward, Kay Francis, Ian Hunter, John Litel, Donald Crisp.

5. *Campus Cinderella* (Warner Brothers, 18 minutes) 1938
DIRECTOR: Noel Smith
With Susan Hayward, Johnnie Davis, Penny Singleton, Anthony Averill, Oscar O'Shea.

6. *Girls on Probation* (Warner Brothers, 63 minutes) 1938
DIRECTOR: William McGann
With Susan Hayward, Jane Bryan, Ronald Reagan, Henry O'Neill, Elizabeth Risdon, Esther Dale, Sig Ruman.

7. *Beau Geste* (Paramount, 120 minutes) 1939
DIRECTOR: William A. Wellman
With Susan Hayward, Gary Cooper, Ray Milland, Robert Preston, Brian Donlevy, Jr., J. Carrol Naish, Broderick Crawford, Albert Dekker, James Stephenson, Donald O'Connor.

8. *Our Leading Citizen* (Paramount, 87 minutes) 1939
DIRECTOR: Alfred Santell
With Susan Hayward, Bob Burns, Joseph Allen, Jr., Elizabeth Patterson, Gene Lockhart, Kathleen Lockhart, Charles Bickford, Clarence Kolb.

9. *$1,000 a Touchdown* (Paramount, 71 minutes) 1939
DIRECTOR: James Hogan
With Susan Hayward, Martha Raye, Joe E. Brown, Eric Blore.

10. *Among the Living* (Paramount, 68 minutes) 1941
DIRECTOR: Stuart Heisler
With Susan Hayward, Albert Dekker, Harry Carey, Frances Farmer, Rod Cameron, Catherine Craig.

11. *Sis Hopkins* (Republic, 97 minutes) 1941
DIRECTOR: Joseph Santley
With Susan Hayward, Judy Canova, Charles Butterworth, Bob Crosby and Orchestra with the Bobcats, Jerry Colonna.

12. *Adam Had Four Sons* (Columbia, 80 minutes) 1941
DIRECTOR: Gregory Ratoff

With Susan Hayward, Ingrid Bergman, Warner Baxter, Richard Denning, Fay Wray, June Lockhart, Robert Shaw.

13. *Reap the Wild Wind* (Paramount, 124 minutes) 1942
DIRECTOR: Cecil B. De Mille
With Susan Hayward, Paulette Goddard, Ray Milland, John Wayne, Robert Preston, Raymond Massey, Lynne Overman, Charles Bickford, Louise Beavers, Hedda Hopper, Walter Hampden, Milburn Stone.

14. *The Forest Rangers* (Paramount, 87 minutes) 1942
DIRECTOR: George Marshall
With Susan Hayward, Fred MacMurray, Paulette Goddard, Albert Dekker, Lynne Overman, Rod Cameron.

15. *I Married a Witch* (United Artists, 82 minutes) 1942
DIRECTOR: René Clair
With Susan Hayward, Fredric March, Veronica Lake, Robert Benchley, Cecil Kellaway, Elizabeth Patterson.

16. *A Letter From Bataan* (Paramount, 15 minutes) 1942
DIRECTOR: William H. Pine
With Susan Hayward, Richard Arlen, Janet Beecher, Jimmy Lydon.

17. *Star Spangled Rhythm* (Paramount, 99 minutes) 1942
DIRECTOR: George Marshall
With Susan Hayward, Walter Abel, Eddie Anderson (Rochester), William Bendix, Gladys Blake, Eddie Bracken, Rod Cameron, MacDonald Carey, Jerry Colonna, Bing Crosby, Gary Crosby, Albert Dekker, Cecil B. De Mille, Eva Gabor, Paulette Goddard, Bob Hope, Betty Hutton, Alan Ladd, Veronica Lake, Dorothy Lamour, Fred MacMurray, Mary Martin, Ray Milland, Dick Powell, Robert Preston, Franchot Tone, Arthur Treacher.

18. *Hit Parade of 1943* (Republic, 90 minutes) 1943
DIRECTOR: Albert S. Rogell
With Susan Hayward, John Carroll, Eve Arden, Gail Patrick, Count Basie and Orchestra.

19. *Young and Willing* (United Artists, 82 minutes) 1943
DIRECTOR: Edward Griffith
With Susan Hayward, William Holden, Eddie Bracken, Barbara Britton, Robert Benchley.

20. *Jack London* (United Artists, 92 minutes) 1943
DIRECTOR: Alfred Santell
With Susan Hayward, Michael O'Shea, Virginia Mayo, Harry Davenport, Frank Craven, Ralph Morgan, Jonathan Hale.

21. *Skirmish on the Home Front* (Paramount, 13 minutes) 1944
Made for U. S. Office of War Information
With Susan Hayward, Alan Ladd, Betty Hutton, William Bendix.

22. *And Now Tomorrow* (Paramount, 84 minutes) 1944
DIRECTOR: Irving Pichel
With Susan Hayward, Alan Ladd, Loretta Young, Barry Sullivan, Beulah Bondi, Cecil Kellaway, Grant Mitchell.

23. *The Fighting Seabees* (Republic, 100 minutes) 1944
DIRECTOR: Edward Ludwig
With Susan Hayward, John Wayne, Dennis O'Keefe, William Frawley, Grant Withers.

24. *The Hairy Ape* (United Artists, 92 minutes) 1944
DIRECTOR: Alfred Santell
With Susan Hayward, William Bendix, John Loder.

25. *Deadline at Dawn* (RKO, 83 minutes) 1946
DIRECTOR: Harold Clurman
With Susan Hayward, Bill Williams, Paul Lukas, Jason Robards.

26. *Canyon Passage* (Universal, 90 minutes) 1946
DIRECTOR: Jacques Tourneur
With Susan Hayward, Dana Andrews, Brian Donlevy, Hoagy Carmichael, Ward Bond, Lloyd Bridges, Andy Devine.

27. *Smash-Up: The Story of a Woman* (Universal/International, 113 minutes) 1947

DIRECTOR: Stuart Heisler
With Susan Hayward, Eddie Albert, Lee Bowman, Marsha Hunt, Carl Esmond, Carleton Young, Charles D. Brown.

28. *They Won't Believe Me* (RKO, 95 minutes) 1947
DIRECTOR: Irving Pichel
With Susan Hayward, Robert Young, Jane Greer, Rita Johnson.

29. *The Lost Moment* (Universal/International, 89 minutes) 1947
DIRECTOR: Martin Gabel
With Susan Hayward, Robert Cummings, Agnes Moorehead, Joan Lorring, John Archer.

30. *Tap Roots* (Universal/International, 109 minutes) 1948
DIRECTOR: George Marshall
With Susan Hayward, Van Heflin, Ward Bond, Boris Karloff, Julie London, Whitfield Connor.

31. *The Saxon Charm* (Universal/International, 88 minutes) 1948
DIRECTOR: Claude Binyon
With Susan Hayward, Robert Montgomery, John Payne, Henry Morgan, Harry Von Zell, Cara Williams, Chill Wills, Audrey Totter.

32. *Tulsa* (Eagle/Lion, 88 minutes) 1949
DIRECTOR: Stuart Heisler
With Susan Hayward, Robert Preston, Pedro Armendariz, Chill Wills, Lloyd Gough, Ed Begley, Lola Albright, Iron Eyes Cody.

33. *House of Strangers* (Twentieth Century-Fox, 101 minutes) 1949
DIRECTOR: Joseph L. Mankiewicz
With Susan Hayward, Edward G. Robinson, Richard Conte, Luther Adler, Efrem Zimbalist, Jr., Debra Paget.

34. *My Foolish Heart* (Goldwyn/RKO, 98 minutes) 1949
DIRECTOR: Mark Robson

With Susan Hayward, Dana Andrews, Kent Smith, Robert Keith, Jessie Royce Landis, Lois Wheeler.

35. *I'd Climb the Highest Mountain* (Twentieth Century-Fox, 88 minutes) 1951
DIRECTOR: Henry King
With Susan Hayward, William Lundigan, Rory Calhoun, Barbara Bates, Alexander Knox, Gene Lockhart, Ruth Donnelly.

36. *Rawhide* (Twentieth Century-Fox, 86 minutes) 1951
DIRECTOR: Henry Hathaway
With Susan Hayward, Tyrone Power, Hugh Marlowe, Dean Jagger, Jack Elam, Edgar Buchanan, George Tobias.

37. *David and Bathsheba* (Twentieth Century-Fox, 153 minutes) 1951
DIRECTOR: Henry King
With Susan Hayward, Gregory Peck, Raymond Massey, Jayne Meadows, John Sutton, Francis X. Bushman, Gwen Verdon.

38. *I Can Get It for You Wholesale* (Twentieth Century-Fox, 91 minutes) 1951
DIRECTOR: Michael Gordon
With Susan Hayward, Dan Dailey, George Sanders, Sam Jaffe, Vicki Cummings, Barbara Whiting, Harry Von Zell.

39. *With a Song in My Heart* (Twentieth Century-Fox, 117 minutes) 1952
DIRECTOR: Walter Lang
With Susan Hayward, David Wayne, Rory Calhoun, Thelma Ritter, Robert Wagner, Helen Westcott and the voice of Jane Froman.

40. *The Snows of Kilimanjaro* (Twentieth Century-Fox, 114 minutes) 1952
DIRECTOR: Henry King
With Susan Hayward, Gregory Peck, Ava Gardner, Hildegarde Neff, Leo G. Carroll, Torin Thatcher, Ava Norring.

41. *The Lusty Men* (RKO, 112 minutes) 1952
DIRECTOR: Nicholas Ray

With Susan Hayward, Robert Mitchum, Arthur Kennedy, Arthur Hunnicut, Frank Faylen, Walter Coy.

42. *The President's Lady* (Twentieth Century-Fox, 96 minutes) 1953
DIRECTOR: Henry Levin
With Susan Hayward, Charlton Heston, Fay Bainter, John McIntire, Margaret Wycherly, Carl Betz, Whitfield Connor.

43. *White Witch Doctor* (Twentieth Century-Fox, 95 minutes) 1953
DIRECTOR: Henry Hathaway
With Susan Hayward, Robert Mitchum, Walter Slezak, Mashood Aiala, Michael Ansara.

44. *Demetrius and the Gladiators* (Twentieth Century-Fox, 101 minutes) 1954
DIRECTOR: Delmer Daves
With Susan Hayward, Victor Mature, Michael Rennie, Debra Paget, Anne Bancroft, Jay Robinson, Richard Egan, Ernest Borgnine.

45. *Garden of Evil* (Twentieth Century-Fox, 100 minutes) 1954
DIRECTOR: Henry Hathaway
With Susan Hayward, Gary Cooper, Richard Widmark, Hugh Marlowe, Cameron Mitchell, Rita Moreno.

46. *Untamed* (Twentieth Century-Fox, 111 minutes) 1955
DIRECTOR: Henry King
With Susan Hayward, Tyrone Power, Richard Egan, Agnes Moorehead, Rita Moreno, John Justin, Hope Emerson, Brad Dexter.

47. *Soldier of Fortune* (Twentieth Century-Fox, 96 minutes) 1955
DIRECTOR: Edward Dmytryk
With Susan Hayward, Clark Gable, Gene Barry, Michael Rennie, Anna Sten, Tom Tully.

48. *I'll Cry Tomorrow* (MGM, 117 minutes) 1955
DIRECTOR: Daniel Mann

With Susan Hayward, Richard Conte, Jo Van Fleet, Eddie Albert, Don Taylor, Virginia Gregg, Don Barry.

49. *The Conqueror* (RKO, 111 minutes) 1956
DIRECTOR: Dick Powell
With Susan Hayward, John Wayne, Agnes Moorehead, Pedro Armendariz, Thomas Gomez, John Hoyt, William Conrad, Ted De Corsia, Richard Loo, Lee Van Cleef.

50. *Top Secret Affair* (Warner Brothers, 111 minutes) 1957
DIRECTOR: H. C. Potter
With Susan Hayward, Kirk Douglas, Paul Stewart, Jim Backus, Roland Winters, John Cromwell, Charles Lane.

51. *I Want to Live* (United Artists, 120 minutes) 1958
DIRECTOR: Robert Wise
With Susan Hayward, Simon Oakland, Virginia Vincent, Theodore Bikel, Alice Backes, Wesley Lau, Jack Weston, Gavin McLeod.

52. *Woman Obsessed* (Twentieth Century-Fox, 103 minutes) 1959
DIRECTOR: Henry Hathaway
With Susan Hayward, Stephen Boyd, Theodore Bikel, Dennis Holmes, Barbara Nichols, Florence MacMichael.

53. *Thunder in the Sun* (Paramount, 81 minutes) 1959
DIRECTOR: Russell Rouse
With Susan Hayward, Jeff Chandler, Jacques Bergerac, Blanche Yurka and Eaton Chalkley's daughter June.

54. *The Marriage-Go-Round* (Twentieth Century-Fox, 98 minutes) 1960
DIRECTOR: Walter Lang
With Susan Hayward, James Mason, Julie Newmar, Robert Paige.

55. *Ada* (MGM, 109 minutes) 1961
DIRECTOR: Daniel Mann
With Susan Hayward, Dean Martin, Martin Balsam, Ralph Meeker, Wilfrid Hyde-White, Frank Maxwell.

56. *Back Street* (Universal/International, 107 minutes) 1961
DIRECTOR: David Miller
With Susan Hayward, John Gavin, Vera Miles, Virginia Grey, Charles Drake, Reginald Gardiner.

57. *I Thank a Fool* (MGM, 100 minutes) 1962
DIRECTOR: Robert Stevens
With Susan Hayward, Peter Finch, Diane Cilento, Cyril Cusack, Kieron Moore.

58. *Stolen Hours* (United Artists, 97 minutes) 1963
DIRECTOR: Daniel Petrie
With Susan Hayward, Michael Craig, Edward Judd, Diane Baker.

59. *Where Love Has Gone* (Embassy/Paramount, 114 minutes) 1964
DIRECTOR: Edward Dmytryk
With Susan Hayward, Bette Davis, Michael Connors, Joey Heatherton, Jane Greer, Anne Seymour, De Forest Kelley.

60. *The Honey Pot* (United Artists, 131 minutes) 1967
DIRECTOR: Joseph L. Mankiewicz
With Susan Hayward, Rex Harrison, Maggie Smith, Edie Adams, Cliff Robertson, Capucine.

61. *Think 20th* (Twentieth Century-Fox, 30 minutes) 1967
DIRECTOR: Richard Fleischer
With Susan Hayward, Julie Andrews, Richard Attenborough, Candice Bergen, Michael Caine, Bette Davis, Patty Duke, Rex Harrison, Charlton Heston, Steve McQueen, David Niven, Rachel Roberts, Frank Sinatra, Raquel Welch.

62. *Valley of the Dolls* (Twentieth Century-Fox, 123 minutes) 1967
DIRECTOR: Mark Robson
With Susan Hayward, Barbara Parkins, Sharon Tate, Patty Duke, Paul Burke, Lee Grant, Tony Scotti, Jacqueline Susann, Joey Bishop, George Jessel, Marvin Hamlisch.

63. *Heat of Anger* (Stonehenge Productions-Metromedia Producers for CBS Friday Night Movies, 75 minutes) 1972
DIRECTOR: Don Taylor
With Susan Hayward, James Stacy, Lee J. Cobb, Fritz Weaver.

64. *The Revengers* (Cinema Center, 110 minutes) 1972
DIRECTOR: Daniel Mann
With Susan Hayward, William Holden, Ernest Borgnine, Arthur Hunnicut.

65. *Say Goodbye, Maggie Cole* (Spelling/Goldberg Production for ABC Wednesday Movie of the Week, 75 minutes) 1972
DIRECTOR: Jud Taylor
With Susan Hayward, Darren McGavin, Beverly Garland, Michael Constantine, Jeanette Nolan, Dane Clark.